THE
Surrealist Movement
IN ENGLAND

THE
Surrealist Movement
IN ENGLAND

by *Paul C. Ray*

Cornell University Press

ITHACA AND LONDON

First published 1971 by Cornell University Press

Published in The United Kingdom by Cornell University Press Ltd., 2–4 Brook Street, London W1Y 1AA

International Standard Book Number 0-8014-0621-8
Library of Congress Catalog Card Number 70-145626

PRINTED IN THE UNITED STATES OF AMERICA
BY VAIL-BALLOU PRESS, INC.

For Inez

Preface

It has long been recognized that French surrealism influenced English writing in the 1920's and 1930's. What has not been so generally recognized is that in the late 1930's a native surrealist movement flourished in England which attracted such diverse talents as Sir Herbert Read, David Gascoyne, Hugh Sykes Davies, Ruthven Todd, among others. It is the intention of this work to present this neglected chapter of English literary history.

Although it stands outside the narrative stream of the rest of the book, the first chapter is designed to serve a double purpose: by supplying what is not readily available in English, that is, a faithful, systematic account of surrealist doctrine, it provides a standard against which the English achievement can be measured. Those familiar with Michel Carrouges's *André Breton et les données fondamentales du surréalisme* will recognize the extent of my debt to that brilliant and indispensable work, upon which I have drawn to unravel complex and often obscure points.

The main body of this study traces the growth of interest in surrealism in England, first in English-language periodicals published abroad, then in England itself. This interest led to the formation of an English surrealist group whose activities culminated in the first of the great international surrealist exhibitions, held in London in 1936, and in the publication of David Gascoyne's *Short Survey of Surrealism,* Sir Herbert Read's *Surrealism,* and several periodicals. The English group, like its French parent, suffered its dissensions and schisms; these are studied in detail. The final chapter traces the influence of surrealism on some English writers and on literary tendencies of the 1930's and 1940's, particularly on T. S. Eliot, Edith Sitwell, W. H. Auden, Dylan Thomas, George Barker, and the writers of the New Apocalypse.

I would like here to acknowledge the help of a number of people and institutions without whose assistance this work could not have been completed: Sir Herbert Read, Miss Ithell Colquhoun, Mr. Toni del Renzio, and Mr. Conroy Maddox generously took the time to answer my queries at length; Mr. Simon Watson Taylor lent me material in his possession and went out of his way to put me in touch with former members of the surrealist group in London; Sir Roland Penrose, Mr. George Melly, and Mr. Conroy Maddox patiently gave of their time in interviews to answer endless questions; Mr. Ruthven Todd, finally, in addition to lending me material, reminisced about his surrealist activities during a long Mallorcan afternoon and, with characteristic generosity, allowed me to read a draft of his yet-unpublished autobiography. The librarians at the Museum of Modern Art in New York with unfailing courtesy put the Museum library's superb surrealist collection at my disposal. A Faculty Summer Research Grant of the City University of New York made possible the completion of this study.

I am indebted to the following individuals and publishers for permission to quote copyrighted material:

Mr. Kenneth Allott, the Hogarth Press, and the Cresset Press for lines from Mr. Allott's "Fête Champêtre" and "Any

Point on the Circumference," from *The Ventriloquist's Doll*
(Hogarth Press, 1939); Random House, Inc., and Faber and
Faber Ltd for lines from "1929," "The Lesson," "Twelve
Songs I," and "Casino" reprinted by permission of Faber and
Faber Ltd from W. H. Auden's *Collected Shorter Poems,
1927–1957*, copyright 1964, and from Auden's *Look, Stranger*
(Faber and Faber, copyright 1935; published as *On This
Island* by Random House, 1937); Random House, Inc., and
Faber and Faber Ltd for lines, reprinted by permission of
Faber and Faber Ltd, from W. H. Auden's *Another Time*
(1940); Mr. R. Heber-Percy for "Surrealist Landscape (to
Salvador Dali)" by Lord Berners; J. M. Dent & Sons Ltd for
the lines from *Petron* (1935) by Hugh Sykes Davies; Harcourt, Brace & World, Inc., and Faber and Faber Ltd for
lines from "The Waste Land," "The Wind Sprang up at
Four O'Clock," "Whispers of Immortality," and "Rhapsody
on a Windy Night," from T. S. Eliot's *Collected Poems, 1909–
1962;* Mr. G. S. Fraser for his lines from "Reasonings in a
Dream," from *Home Town Elegy* (Editions Poetry London,
1944); Mr. Roy Fuller for his lines from "Poem" from *Poems*
(The Fortune Press, 1939); Oxford University Press for lines
from "No Solution," "Charity Week," "Unspoken," "Salvador
Dali," "Yves Tanguy," "The Very Image," "The Truth is
Blind," and "Purified Disgust," from David Gascoyne's *Collected Poems* (1965), edited by Robin Skelton, by permission
of the Oxford University Press; Mrs. Humphrey Jennings for
the lines from "I See London" by Humphrey Jennings, by
kind permission of Mrs. Humphrey Jennings; Mr. Norman
MacCaig for lines from "Poem II" and an untitled poem;
Oxford University Press and Faber and Faber Ltd for
lines from "Springboard," from *The Collected Poems of
Louis MacNeice*, edited by E. R. Dodds, copyright © The
Estate of Louis MacNeice, 1966, reprinted by permission of

I am grateful to the editors of the *Journal of Aesthetics and Art Criticism, Comparative Literature Studies,* and *Romance Notes* for their permission to reprint material that first appeared in their pages.

PAUL C. RAY

New York
January 1971

Contents

~~~~~~~~ Preface   vii

1 Definitions   1

2 English Beginnings   67

3 The Exhibition   134

4 English Evidence   167

5 Fringes and Influences   262

Epilogue   308

Bibliography   310

Index   328

THE
Surrealist Movement
IN ENGLAND

1 | *Definitions*

~~~~~~~~ The history of the surrealist movement and its origins has been told many times; [1] this chapter will not rehearse it once again. What will be attempted, rather, is an explication of the tenets of surrealist doctrine. Jules Monnerot, in his brilliant study, *La Poésie moderne et le sacré*, warned against trying to start from a definition of the word "surrealism" and advised instead gradually charging the term with meaning. The simplest way of following his advice is to divide this complex subject into its components, keeping in mind always the thought that this schematization

[1] Anna Balakian, *Literary Origins of Surrealism* (New York: King's Crown Press, 1947), and *Surrealism: The Road to the Absolute* (New York: Noonday Press, 1959); Clifford Browder, *André Breton: Arbiter of Surrealism* (Geneva, Librarie Droz, 1967); David Gascoyne, *A Short Survey of Surrealism* (London: Cobden-Sandersen, 1935); Herbert S. Gershman, *The Surrealist Revolution in France* (Ann Arbor, Mich.: University of Michigan Press, 1969); Georges Lemaître, *From Cubism to Surrealism in French Literature*, 2d. ed., rev. (Cambridge, Mass.: Harvard University Press, 1947); J. H. Matthews, *An Introduction to Surrealism* (University Park, Pa.: Pennsylvania State University Press, 1965); Maurice Nadeau, *The History of Surrealism*, trans. by Richard Howard (New York: Macmillan, 1965); and Marcel Raymond, *From Baudelaire to Surrealism*, trans. by G. M. (New York: Wittenborn and Schultz, 1949).

is artificial, simply a means to an end, and that surrealism, finally understood, is more than its components taken separately.

AUTOMATISM

André Breton, the founder and principal theoretician of surrealism, in his "Premier manifeste" (1924), recounts how, just before falling asleep one evening, he heard a sentence that had nothing to do with his preoccupations of the moment: "There is a man cut in two by the window." This sentence was accompanied by a weak visual image of a man bisected by a window perpendicular to the axis of his body.[2] Other sentences, equally gratuitous, followed the first. He concluded from the experience that any control he thought he exercised over his mental processes was entirely illusory. These imaged sentences struck him as being valuable poetic elements; and the subsequent attempt to produce them deliberately led him, together with Philippe Soupault, to the discovery of automatic writing and the production of the first work written automatically, *Les Champs magnétiques* (1919).

There is, of course, nothing new about the idea of automatism. Socrates in the *Phaedrus* and the *Ion* had spoken of the value for art and prophecy of what he called "madness," "inspiration," "enthusiasm"; and poets have always recognized the importance of "inspiration," without, however, being able to force it. Until the advent of surrealism, poets welcomed the promptings of inspiration only when these were coherent or immediately readable. In 1829, for

---

[2] André Breton, "Premier manifeste," *Manifestes du surréalisme* (Paris: Jean-Jacques Pauvert, 1962), pp. 34–36. Cf. a similar and more detailed account in Breton, "Entrée des médiums," *Les Pas perdus* (Paris: Gallimard, 1924), pp. 149 ff. All translations, unless otherwise indicated, are by the author.

example, Louis Aragon tells us, Alfred de Musset had written, before he saw Venice,

> Dans Venise la rouge
> Pas un cheval qui bouge

but had later changed "cheval" to "bateau." Aragon regrets the change, for "the verse is more beautiful with the horse and Venice too" because it is a "mythical Venice, more important than the Venice of Baedeker." [3] The many exceptions, the poets who did not reject the direct promptings of imagination, are of course those who occupy the places of honor in the surrealist pantheon. To Tristan Corbière, Breton says, goes the honor of being the first, in his *Amours jaunes,* to let himself be carried on a wave of words, free of all conscious control.[4]

The important discovery of surrealism is that there is a continuous discourse going on below the level of consciousness to which one needs only pay attention in order to register it; equally important is the surrealist insistence that this discourse deserves the most intense attention, even when it seems discordant or incoherent. Automatism, shortly after Breton's discovery, became the very basis of surrealism, and Breton's first definition of surrealism is really a definition of automatic writing:

SURREALISM, n.m.: Pure psychic automatism by which it is intended to express, verbally, in writing, or by any other means, the real process of thought, without any control exercised by reason, outside of all aesthetic or moral preoccupations.[5]

---

[3] Louis Aragon, *En Etrange pays dans mon pays lui-même* (Monaco: Editions du Rocher, 1945).

[4] Breton, "Tristan Corbière," *Anthologie de l'humour noir,* 3d ed. (Paris: Jean-Jacques Pauvert, 1966), p. 202. First published in 1940.

[5] "Premier manifeste," p. 40.

This, in spite of all the qualifications that Breton later attached to the practice of automatism, became, perhaps because of its succinctness, the standard definition of surrealism. That it is a fragmentary definition will be seen in the following pages. A good deal more must be said before one can accept the definition of surrealism as simply "pure psychic automatism."

In this definition, Breton makes a sharp distinction between the activity of thinking, "the real process of thought," and reason. The distinction is crucial because for the surrealists, as for the dadaists before them, and the symbolistes and romanticists before *them,* reason had demonstrated its inability to cope with the world. The chaos of the First World War and the years following seemed to Breton's generation proof enough of the bankruptcy of reason. For the dadaists, complete negation and destructiveness had seemed the only attitudes to take toward the world. For the surrealists, however, some values remained, but outside the realm of intellectual activity—on the level, rather, of intuition: something other than reason, it was clear to them, was needed to guide the destinies of man. That something Breton found in "the real process of thought," that is, in thought freed from logic and reason; in short, in the unconscious.

Breton, who had worked in a mental hospital during the war, was familiar with the theories of Freud.[6] He recognized the similarity between his experience of the man cut in half by the window and its attendant train of images on the

[6] Breton, *Entretiens, 1913–1952* (Paris: Gallimard, 1952), p. 29. The range and depth of Breton's knowledge and understanding of Freud at this time are debatable. We must remember that Breton was only eighteen years old when the war began and twenty-two when it ended. The important point, however, is not how well he understood Freud, but simply that he took from Freud what he needed.

one hand, and the delirium of the mental patient and the process of free association on the other. As Freud had noted, in free association and in dreams the repressing forces of conscious control are relaxed, allowing the contents of the unconscious to rise to the surface. Repression, Freud says,

is the process by which a mental act capable of becoming conscious . . . is made unconscious and forced back into the unconscious system. And we also call it *repression* when the unconscious mental act is not permitted to enter the adjacent preconscious system at all, but is turned back upon the threshold by the censorship.[7]

However, another process intervenes before the latent, unconscious thoughts are allowed to find their expression, a process which Freud calls the "dream-work." "The term 'dream,'" he says, "can only be applied to the *results of the dream-work*, i.e., to the *form* into which the latent thoughts have been rendered by the dream-work."[8] The function of the dream-work, then, is to translate the latent thoughts into dream-images; that is, ideas, abstractions, relations, must be rendered in visual terms. This requirement involves a greater or lesser degree of simplification:

All the verbal apparatus by means of which the more subtle thought-relations are expressed, the conjunctions and prepositions, the variations of declensions and conjugations, are lacking, because the means of portraying them are absent; just as in primitive grammarless speech only the raw material of thought can be expressed, and the abstract is merged again in the concrete from which it sprang. What is left may well seem to lack coherence. It is as much the result of the archaic regression in

[7] Sigmund Freud, *A General Introduction to Psychoanalysis*, trans. by Joan Riviere (Garden City, N.Y.: Garden City Publishing, 1943), p. 299.
[8] *Ibid.*, p. 162.

the mental apparatus as the demands of the censorship that so much use is made of the representation of certain objects and processes by means of symbols which have become strange to conscious thought.[9]

Temporal relations, for example, are always turned into spatial ones by the dream-work: "Thus, one may see in a dream a scene between people who look very small and far away. . . . The smallness and spatial remoteness here mean the same thing; it is remoteness in time that is meant, the interpretation being that it is a scene from the remote past." [10] Similarly, the translation of an abstract relation into a visual image frequently involves a return to the roots of words; for example, the idea of "possessing" an object is translated in a dream into a literal "sitting upon it (possess = potis + sedeo)." [11] Sometimes a different process takes place, when "the dream-work seeks to condense two different thoughts by selecting, after the manner of wit, an ambiguous word which can suggest both thoughts." [12] Or, composite figures may be formed of elements that do not belong together in reality but which have at least one common attribute.[13]

What Breton recognized in Freud's dream theories is the fact that Freudian psychology, as Lionel Trilling says, "makes poetry indigenous to the very constitution of the mind," that "the mind, as Freud sees it, is in the greater part of its tendency exactly a poetry-making organ." [14] It is precisely the purpose of automatic writing to find access to that

---

[9] Freud, *New Introductory Lectures on Psycho-Analysis*, trans. by W. J. H. Sprott, 2d ed. (London: Hogarth Press, 1937), p. 32.

[10] *Ibid.*, pp. 39–40.   [11] Freud, *General Introduction*, p. 156.

[12] *Ibid.*, p. 153.   [13] *Ibid.*, pp. 152–153.

[14] Lionel Trilling, "Freud and Literature," *The Liberal Imagination* (New York: Viking Press, 1950), p. 52.

region of the mind which is "a poetry-making organ." This it succeeded in doing by producing a state similar to sleep, in which unconscious thoughts pass through the censorship in order to find expression in images. In doing so, the latent thoughts undergo in automatic writing the same metamorphoses to become verbal that they do in dreaming to become visual: condensation, displacement, symbolization, dramatization, and secondary elaboration.[15]

An important distinction must, however, be made between automatic writing and dreaming: the motive power of the dream is images; that of automatic writing, words. Freud has shown that the succession of images in a dream may be caused by words, and often by puns. In the depths of the unconscious, however, there probably is no distinction between words and images, which are already translations of something more basic; only in dreams, i.e., in the product of the dream-work, attention is turned to the images; in automatic writing, to the words. True automatic writing, however, is *not* a description of dream-images or of dreams. This is a point of crucial importance in the whole theory of automatic writing and of surrealism: if automatic writing were simply an attempt to describe dreams or dream-images, or an attempt to render them verbally, then it would not be automatic, but the rendition of something previously given. It would differ from other descriptions only in subject matter, not in kind. Automatic writing stands in the same relation to the unconscious as does the dream: the dream is one method by which the contents of the unconscious find expression; automatic writing is another. Automatic writing, in fact, is a kind of dream, but a waking dream, which differs from a sleeping dream only in being

[15] Jean Cazaux, *Surréalisme et psychologie: endophasie et écriture automatique* (Paris: Librairie José Corti, 1938), p. 52.

verbal, not visual. As Breton says, "Lautréamont, Rimbaud did not enjoy *a priori* what they described, which is the same as saying that they did not describe; they restricted themselves in the dark corridors of their being to listening to indistinct speech without understanding, while they were writing, any better than we do at a first reading. . . . 'Illumination' comes later." [16]

The techniques of automatic writing are described in some detail in the "Premier manifeste": [17] the writer is to put himself in the most passive, most receptive state possible and start writing without a preconceived subject in mind, rapidly enough not to be tempted to look back on what he has written. If silence threatens because he is thinking, the writer is to stop and start again by putting down any letter, but always the same letter, bringing back the arbitrary by making that letter the initial of the next word. To avoid monotony, Breton recommends varying the speed of writing, from slow to very fast—legibility being the limit. Stenography, he thinks, would reveal much, but he does not know if it has ever been tried. [18]

But automatic writing is, for Breton, not just a simple means of opening the floodgates and letting everything pour out. In fact, he criticizes those who let their pens run on paper "without observing what was going on within them." [19] This comment does not betoken a backward step toward a reintroduction of consciousness or of aesthetic and literary considerations. The awareness for which Breton is asking

[16] Breton, "Le Message automatique," *Minotaure*, no. 3–4 (December, 1933), p. 63. Cf. Michel Carrouges, *André Breton et les données fondamentales du surréalisme* (Paris: Gallimard, 1950), pp. 160–161; Breton, "Entrée des médiums," *Les Pas perdus*, pp. 149–152.

[17] Breton, "Premier manifeste," pp. 44 ff.   [18] *Entretiens*, p. 82.

[19] "Second manifeste," *Manifestes*, pp. 189–190.

is not one that intervenes from the outside in order to control the automatic flow; it is an awareness, rather, of what automatism in itself is, an alertness to the integrity and true direction of the flow. The danger of deflection is one of the principal obstacles to the success of the experiment and is, unfortunately, inherent in the very nature of automatism. It is impossible, as Carrouges has noted, to ascertain the homogeneity of the discourse, for many strands may be intertwined. The slightest pause may indicate a new departure in another direction; or the dictation may offer two words, each leading in a different direction. When the initial flow is disrupted, true automatism is replaced by chaos. This danger is a real and persistent one, for there is more than one voice dictating, more than one source of images and words clamoring for the attention of the conscious mind. Successful avoidance of this particular danger, if it is possible, requires, as Breton says, an awareness of the internal process, an intuitive understanding of, and response to, what he has called the "magnetic fields."

The successful practice of automatic writing must overcome other obstacles as well. Because it is verbal and is practiced by writers, it is susceptible to the imposition of qualitative judgments, of critical criteria—in short, to what Breton calls "the execrable poetic rivalry." [20] Very early in the history of automatic writing, Breton had to admit that external considerations, such as conscious control and the awareness of the possibility of publication, destroyed the value of the experiment.[21] But the most serious obstacle to surmount, one which inheres in the very nature of automatic writing, is the continual irruption of purely visual, and therefore incommunicable, elements in the verbal flow. The

[20] *Point du jour* (Paris: Gallimard, 1924), p. 244.
[21] *Les Pas perdus,* p. 151.

strength to resist the seductiveness of these visual images and to overcome the desire to render them verbally requires of the poet a determination, a singleness of purpose, an asceticism that even Orpheus did not possess.[22] Even if this most difficult obstacle is overcome, a final, insurmountable one remains, one that psychoanalysis must constantly grapple with—the fact that speaking or writing a dream, whether a waking or sleeping dream, interposes the screen of translation into words, of phrase-making, between the stuff of the dream and its rendition; and the further fact that the very attempt to make the transcription fit the purity of the vision in itself alters the process and content of the dream.

Breton admitted that it is all too easy to make pastiches of automatic writing and that, in the absence of any objective criteria of origin, it is very difficult, if not impossible, to tell the real article from the fake.[23] Finally, he was forced to admit, in 1933, that "the history of automatic writing in surrealism is . . . that of a continuous misfortune." [24] He conceded, in a letter to Rolland de Renéville, that no surrealist text could be considered a perfect example of verbal automatism, that there always remained a certain degree of conscious direction, if only in the arrangement of the text on the page.[25]

In spite of these all but insuperable difficulties, Breton did not renounce automatic writing: "I expect revelation to come only from it. I have never ceased being persuaded that nothing that is said or done that does not obey this magical dictation is worth anything." [26] But instead of considering

[22] Breton, "Le Message automatique," pp. 62–63.
[23] *Point du jour*, p. 229.   [24] "Le Message automatique," p. 57.
[25] *La Nouvelle Revue Française*, July 1, 1932, p. 152.
[26] *Les Pas perdus*, p. 150.

automatism the starting point of surrealist endeavor, Breton transformed it into the ideal limit of surrealist striving.[27] Years later, in 1948, he reaffirmed his faith in the process: "Automatic writing, with everything that moves in its orbit, you cannot know how dear it remains to me." [28] And although he admitted that automatic writing had failed in its mission of liberating man from the shackles of the intellect, Breton continued to insist on its importance. The essential, he said, was that the *climate* of automatism had been felt, that man had become aware of another region which asks only to be revealed. He hoped, he said, that a means would be found to pass into that region and return into this one at will. If this were possible, all the perspectives of the world would be shaken, and "the real life" of which Rimbaud speaks would begin.[29] This "real life" would consist in part of the mind liberated from its subjection to immediate sensory perceptions which, in large measure, make it a toy of the exterior world.[30]

Breton, then, was forced to revise his definition of surrealism as "pure psychic automatism." Pure automatism remained the theoretical limit of surrealist endeavor, but it also had a more immediate practical application: "Psychic automatism . . . never constituted for surrealism an end in itself. . . . The point was to elude, to elude forever the coalition of forces that stand watch to prevent any violent irruption of the unconscious: a society which feels itself menaced from all sides like bourgeois society, thinks . . . that such irruption could be fatal." [31] Automatism became,

---

[27] "Le Message automatique," p. 61.   [28] *Entretiens,* p. 256.
[29] *Ibid.,* pp. 82–83.   [30] *Ibid.,* p. 79.
[31] Breton, *Position politique du surréalisme* (Paris: Editions du Sagittaire, 1935), p. 57.

then, a weapon against the bourgeois view of the world which imposes the restraints of logic, morality, and taste on the free expression of the unconscious.[32] Discrediting that world and its conception of reality became the first task of surrealism.

Freud's dream analysis had shown that the laws of non-contradiction and of causality as they are understood in waking life do not obtain in the dream and, therefore, in the unconscious; that the subject-object opposition can be easily broken down, since the dreaming subject can become an object in his own dream; that traditional verbal or visual associations are easily dissolved. For the surrealist, the value of the dream and, by analogy, of automatism, lay in the demonstration that the distinctions and oppositions that seem rooted in reality—between the real and the imaginary, the subject and the object, life and death even—are artificial fabrications of the rational mind, and that they can be reconciled in a realm outside the one governed by rationality.

The reconciliation of opposites became the new doctrine of surrealism, a doctrine which is, as we shall see, an extension of the basic insights afforded by automatism. In a famous passage in the "Second manifeste" (1929), Breton wrote:

Everything leads to the belief that there exists in the mind a certain point from which life and death, the real and the imaginary, the past and the future, the communicable and the incommunicable, the high and the low, are no longer seen as contradictory. It is in vain that one would look in surrealist activity for any motive other than the hope of fixing that point. It is clear, therefore, how absurd it would be to see in that activity a meaning that is either destructive or constructive: the

---

[32] Breton, *Entretiens*, p. 79.

point in question is, *a fortiori,* one where construction and destruction can no longer be brandished against one another.[33]

A new emphasis, it is clear, has entered surrealism: it is
no longer the "pure psychic automatism" that is at issue, but
a possibility that has been revealed by that automatism—
the reconciliation of dialectical opposites. The surrealists
had discovered Marx, and through Marx, Hegel. The task of
the theoretician of surrealism became now the reconciliation of Freud and Marx. This Breton attempted to do in
Les Vases communicants (1932). The title refers to Breton's
image of man's life as two linked vessels—dream and waking, conscious and unconscious—whose contents constantly
interpenetrate and affect each other. Freud's insistence that
dreams can have only a material origin laid the grounds for
the synthesis of his views with those of Marx. Freud had
shown that free association is anything but free, that its
content and direction are rigorously determined and not at
all a matter of choice, that " 'creative' fantasy can, in fact,
invent nothing new, but can only regroup elements from
different sources." [34] Dreams, Freud had demonstrated, obtain their substance from reality—they are not supernatural,
nor are they creations *in vacuo* of the brain, nor yet are they
mere fancies. They represent, rather, a kind of synthesis of
the impressions of reality and of the active unconscious
forces of the id. Dream and reality, for Freud and for Breton
after him, are closely interwoven, the dream drawing on
reality and in turn supplying reality with practical emotional syntheses. For Breton, the acute distinction between
dream and action is a purely formal one, and, by extending
the point, he says that "human life, conceived outside of

[33] P. 154.
[34] Freud, *General Introduction,* p. 153; see also pp. 98–99.

its strict limits of birth and death, is to real life no more than the dream of one night is to the day that has just passed." [35]

The dialectical interaction of dream and reality is nowhere better illustrated than in the dream within the dream. This phenomenon, according to Wilhelm Stekel, whom Breton quotes, is usually the result of a real memory which interferes with the wish-fulfillment of the dream in which it occurs and which is therefore depreciated into another dream. This process, Breton says, is "the formal negation of an event which has occurred but which must at any cost be surmounted, the result of a veritable *dialectization* of the dream-thought which, in order to reach its ends, breaks the last limits of logic. An event which has happened must be thought of as if it had not happened, *must upon the dreamer's awaking, be lost in oblivion.*" [36]

Surrealism proposes a similar dialectization, a similar negation of the supremacy of reality, and a synthesis of dream and reality on a higher plane where all contradictions will be resolved. But Breton is careful to insist that there is nothing mystical about this higher plane, that it is merely the "supreme point" to which Hegelian dialectics leads. [37] But again, in spite of the homage Breton has paid to Hegel ("Where Hegelian dialectics do not operate, there is for me no thought, no hope of truth" [38]), it is not to Hegel's idealism but to his dialectics, to his definition of knowledge as the fusion of object and subject, that he is attracted. In 1934, Breton defined and summarized the new emphasis of surrealism:

[35] *Les Vases communicants,* 2d ed. (Paris: Gallimard, 1955), p. 156.
[36] *Ibid.,* pp. 80–81.   [37] *Entretiens,* p. 151.   [38] *Ibid.,* p. 152.

We have attempted to present interior reality and exterior reality as two elements in process of unification, of finally becoming *one*. This final unification is the supreme aim of surrealism: interior reality and exterior reality being, in the present form of society, in contradiction . . . we have assigned to ourselves the task of confronting these realities with one another on every possible occasion, of refusing to allow the pre-eminence of the one over the other . . . allowing us to observe their reciprocal action and interpenetration and to give this interplay of forces all the extension necessary for the trend of these two adjoining realities to become one and the same thing.[39]

So far we have considered the action of the external world on the internal: Freud's interpretation of dreams had shown how conscious life affects the dream. Seeing reality now in the light of Hegelian dialectics, the surrealists turned their attention to the other side of the coin: the effect of the dream on the external world. In this, the surrealists were still being faithful disciples of Freud, who in *The Psychopathology of Everyday Life* had studied the evidences of the unconscious to be found in waking life and had shown how such trivial events as slips of the tongue, absent-mindedness, the experience of *déjà-vu*, superstitions, and the like, are all indications of the unconscious forcing its way beyond the censorship and impinging on the conscious, daylight world.

But the new philosophical position of the surrealists brought them into conflict with Freud's essentially therapeutic purposes. From the beginning, the surrealist intention had been to weaken, if not destroy completely, the supremacy of reason. Freud's discoveries concerning the uncon-

---

[39] Breton, *What Is Surrealism?* trans. by David Gascoyne (London: Faber and Faber, 1936), p. 49.

scious and its role were proof enough for the surrealists that reason was not the sole ruler. But Freud's purpose in uncovering the unconscious was, clearly, a therapeutic one: by bringing as much as possible of the unconscious into consciousness, he was extending the empire of the conscious, strengthening the rule of reason, and trying, as he said, to establish the reign of "ego over all." This purpose is, naturally, predicated upon a certain view of reality, of "normality," of human life. For Freud, if a man's unconscious impinges so strongly upon his conscious that the rule of ego is threatened, that man is aberrant; for Breton, on the contrary, that man is on the way to freedom from the rule of the ego, whose content is rigidly conditioned by the hated bourgeois society. For Freud, Breton said, " 'psychic reality' is a special form of existence which must not be confused with 'material reality' "; [40] for Breton, this is a restrictive, narrowly positivistic, undialectical view of reality.

Breton's Hegelianism, that is, his idea of "interior reality and exterior reality as two elements in process of unification," collided with Freud's views when he turned his attention to the mysteries of prophetic dreams and coincidences. For Freud, these mysteries are apparent only, easily explained as simple illusions or as manifestations of the individual unconscious, an unconscious not to be confused with "material reality"; they do not demonstrate any possible correspondence between the individual unconscious and outside, material reality, as they were increasingly to do for Breton. Speaking of superstitions, Freud said:

I . . . differ from a superstitious person in the following manner: I do not believe that an occurrence in which my mental life takes no part can teach me anything hidden concerning the

[40] *Les Vases communicants*, p. 23.

future shaping of reality; but I do believe that an unintentional manifestation of my own mental activity surely contains something concealed which belongs only to my mental life—that is, I believe in outer (real) chance, but not in inner (psychic) accidents. With the superstitious person, the case is reversed: he knows nothing of the motive of his chance and faulty actions; he believes in the existence of psychic contingencies; he is therefore inclined to attribute meaning to external chance, which manifests itself in actual occurrence, and to see in the accident a means of expression for something hidden outside of him. There are two differences between me and the superstitious person: first, he projects the motive to the outside, while I look for it in myself; second, he explains the accident by an event which I trace to a thought. What he considers hidden corresponds to the unconscious with me, and the compulsion not to let chance pass as chance, but to explain it as common to us both.[41]

As Jules Monnerot put it, Freud exercised a kind of doctrinal imperialism over his material, reducing dreams and psychic activity in general to biographical facts or to a limited number of uniform mechanisms which transform these facts to serve rigorously predetermined ends.[42] In other words, Freud saw the dream as revelatory of the past only, involving external reality only insofar as that reality influences the individual unconscious. Breton, on the contrary, saw the dream as revelatory of the future, involving external reality in a complex dialectical relationship.

Committed to his essentially positivist view of reality, Freud only late in his career reluctantly admitted the possibility of parapsychic phenomena; Breton on the other

[41] Freud, "The Psychopathology of Everyday Life," *The Basic Writings of Sigmund Freud,* trans. and ed. by A. A. Brill (New York: Modern Library, 1938), p. 164.

[42] Jules Monnerot, *La Poésie moderne et le sacré* (Paris: Gallimard, 1945), p. 115.

hand, ever in rebellion against narrow definitions of reality, always had the feeling of exploring a limitless, mysterious world. As early as 1928, Breton had, in *Nadja*, turned his attention to those events which suggested to him the existence of forces other than those of a narrowly conceived reality, events which, to the "daytime" consciousness, seem nothing more than coincidences:

My life . . . insofar as it is at the mercy of chance . . . as it momentarily escapes my control, introduces me into an almost forbidden world of sudden parallels, of petrifying coincidences . . . of lightning flashes that make one see, but really *see*. . . . It is a question of events which belong to the order of pure observation, but which every time possess all the appearances of a signal . . . events that convince me of my error whenever for any length of time I think that I am at the helm.[43]

The occurrence of meaningful coincidences that somehow have the effect of revelation, led the surrealists to the scrutiny of what they called *le hasard objectif*—"objective chance." These coincidences, which at first glance seem completely fortuitous but which under examination soon lose that character, became the basis of the second tenet of surrealism: "The practice of psychic automatism has in all areas considerably widened the field of the arbitrary. Now, this is the important point: this arbitrary, under examination, has tended violently to deny itself as arbitrary." [44]

OBJECTIVE CHANCE

The examination of certain troubling events, of certain overwhelming coincidences, to which *Nadja, Les Vases communicants,* and *L'Amour fou* are given over, leads

---

[43] *Nadja* (Paris: Gallimard, 1928), pp. 22–23.
[44] Breton, *Position politique*, p. 145.

directly to the question of objective chance, "that kind of chance through which is manifested, still very mysteriously for man, a necessity which escapes him, even though he feels it as necessity." [45]

The idea of the *merveilleux*, the marvelous which expresses itself through chance, was not new to surrealism; it had been one of the earliest foci of surrealist interest, and it figures large in the "Premier manifeste." By the mid-1920's, however, the concept was undergoing a serious crisis. The nature of this crisis can best be shown by retelling one of Breton's stories of the *merveilleux*. He, de Chirico, and several others were seated in a café when a little flower-vendor appeared. They were struck by the boy's appearance, and de Chirico, whose back was turned to the child and who therefore had not seen him, took out a pocket mirror to study him and asserted that the boy was a phantom. This story is presented in all seriousness by Breton as an example of the intrusion of the marvelous into daily life.[46] One cannot avoid the impression that Breton and his friends were trying to force the marvelous to produce itself, in defiance of the most elementary principles of reality and credibility. The crisis defines itself as a danger that surrealism faced then—that of wandering off into indefensible and often meaningless irreality, often of a most trivial kind. The adoption of Marxist materialism, of Hegelian dialectics, and of psychoanalytic principles served to bring a stricter discipline to the whole pursuit. With *Nadja* (1928), surrealism entered into a period in which the marvelous manifested itself more and more strongly in the external world, at the same time strengthening its bonds with its profound sources

[45] *Ibid.*, p. 146.
[46] Breton, *Le Surréalisme et la peinture*, 2d ed. (New York: Brentano's, 1945), pp. 43–44. First published in 1928.

in man. The importance of *Nadja* lies in the proofs it provides that the marvelous no longer manifests itself only within the mind of the surrealist lost in automatism in his study, or in the trivialities of such games as "the exquisite corpse," or in the chance collocation of words and phrases cut out at random from newspapers, but in the street, among other human beings. The irruption of the supra-normal into "real" life becomes objective, observable fact. As interior automatism mingles with the exterior world, the streets, Paris itself, become transformed by the atmosphere of hallucination.

In *Nadja*, from the very beginning of the story, a break occurs with the conventional limits of human experience when to Breton's question, "Who are you?" Nadja replies, "I am the wandering soul." The heroine of the book is a woman who by any clinical standards would be adjudged insane; but Breton's point is that this person, in whom the repressive forces of reason and logic have been eliminated and whose unconscious can consequently irrupt unhindered into her everyday activities, is guided by forces more fundamental, more closely attuned to the real workings of the universe than conscious, logical thought. This break with the conventional gives Breton the hope of attaining that "supreme point" where contradictions are reconciled because he has felt the passage of a life free of ordinary human limits and in touch with occult worlds.

It would be a mistake, however, to believe that Breton had abandoned his materialist bias in favor of a belief in a "world beyond," in ghosts, or in the possibility of communicating with the dead. He was, as we have seen, profoundly interested in the idea of the "subliminal message," [47] in the methods of automatic writing and speaking, interests

47 Breton, *Point du jour*, p. 241.

that he shared with spiritists. However, he violently rejected the basic premise of spiritism—that contact with other worlds, or with the souls of the dead, was possible; or even that such worlds or such souls existed. In insisting that the only voice that the medium could hear was that of his own unconscious, Breton echoes Freud's objections to superstition. Spiritism dissociates the psychological personality of the medium—he becomes merely the instrument of an external force. Surrealism, on the contrary, by seeking closer contact between the unconscious and the conscious elements of the personality, attempts to integrate that personality. This is to say that for the surrealists, the question of an external "voice" does not even arise.[48]

As the means of investigating objective chance, automatism, a term which in its broader meanings includes the dream, may express prefigurations of the individual future or telepsychic communication. But behind this extension of the meaning of automatism lies a reaffirmation, not an abandonment, of materialism. In its widest applications, automatism involves the recognition that man is not an epiphenomenon added to the universe, but a fragment of nature; and automatism, by sinking deep into man's unconscious, becomes also a means of investigating and revealing the world. The startling lesson of *Nadja* is that by losing oneself in automatism, one comes in close touch with the obscure laws of the universe which are inaccessible to the rational intellect. Nadja herself is so closely attuned to these obscure workings that she can, for example, predict the exact moment of the lighting up of a window or keep an appointment with the narrator although he, by mistake, is not at the appointed place.

Les Vases communicants (1932) is a further investigation

[48] Breton, "Le Message automatique," p. 61.

of these phenomena, although the emphasis seems to be on evidences of the intrusion of the dream into waking life. The divinatory impulse of *Nadja* is still present, but its role is smaller; Breton seems to be concentrating on phenomena rather similar to those Freud explored in the *Psychopathology of Everyday Life*, still keeping, however, within the bounds of the Marxian cosmology. The hallucinatory feeling of *Nadja* is missing from the later book: Breton is more concerned with establishing the surrealist experience on a sound materialist basis.

One of the consequences of the image contained in the title of the book, that of the two linked vessels with the constantly intermingling contents, is that the dream, or the incursion of the unconscious into the conscious, involves the immediate future. The prophetic value of automatism is further investigated in *L'Amour fou* (1937). In this book, Breton devoted a long analysis to a poem of 1923, "Tournesol," demonstrating that the poem was a detailed, although obscure, prophecy of events that occurred in 1934. The fundamental assumption of the book is that the poem, written in a state of automatism, described a train of events that was to unfold in the external world several years later. These events, at the time of writing, were merely a hope, the embodiment of an obscure desire which was later fulfilled in reality.

The literature of surrealism is full of such accounts of premonitory events. For example, Pierre Mabille, in *Minotaure* (no. 12–13), tells of witnessing a street incident in which his friend Victor Brauner, the painter, lost an eye. After the event, Mabille discovered many one-eyed creatures in Brauner's earlier paintings. There is, of course, nothing new in the idea of the premonitory dream or vision: the literature of extrasensory perception is full of them; nor is the experience restricted to those with so-called "psychic" powers: Goethe, in his conversations with Eckermann and in *Dichtung und Wahrheit* recounts several such experiences. What is new, however, is the surrealists' attempt to establish the whole point of objective chance on some sort of philosophical, if not scientific, basis.

In the course of reporting the results of their inquiry on the "encounter," Breton and Eluard presented a short historical survey of the idea of objective chance beginning with the Aristotelean notion of finality and ending with their own materialist definition, a synthesis of Engels and Freud, in which "objective chance is the form of the manifestation of exterior reality which opens a path for itself in the human unconscious." [49] Breton is careful to insist, however, that the encounter argues neither supernatural agency nor cosmic purpose. He sees it simply as the consequence of a series of events unfolding in the past and moving toward the startling and revealing manifestation of what seems like chance to the logic-bound intellect. The encounter, in order to be startling and revealing, must in some way answer some internal, perhaps unconscious need. Objective chance shows external reality as answering the mind's desires; it presupposes an affinity, a complex net of correspondences, between the universe and the individual unconscious. And since the dream or automatism is the means whereby that unconscious is investigated and revealed, that same automatism is the means whereby external reality is investigated and revealed. It has been suggested that this idea is no more preposterous than the supposition of orthodox rationalism that there exists an affinity between the universe and the rational mind.[50] Or,

[49] *Minotaure*, no. 3–4 (December, 1933), p. 102.
[50] Georges Lemaître, *From Cubism to Surrealism in French Literature*, p. 221.

as Monnerot puts it, "pure rationalism . . . is not a universal norm, but a specialized method . . . whose empire over all other domains we assert, even when this theoretical rule does not in fact apply everywhere we profess to recognize it." [51] In 1952, Breton himself insisted on this point:

Philosophically, objective chance . . . seemed to me to constitute the knotty point of what for me was the *problem of problems*. It was a question of the elucidation of the connections that exist between "natural necessity" and "human necessity," correlatively between necessity and freedom. I see no way of speaking of it in less abstract terms; this problem can be posed only thus: how is it that phenomena collide and mingle . . . which the human mind can attribute only to independent causal series; how is it that the light that results from this fusion is so vivid, although so ephemeral? Only ignorance can induce the belief that these are preoccupations of a mystical order. If one remembers that Engels himself could say, "Causality can be understood only in relation to the category of objective chance, a form of manifestation of necessity," one might as well make Engels pass for a mystic.[52]

This statement in no way contradicts Breton's objection to Freud's refusal to admit the possibility of prophetic dreams. It is not to Freud's materialism that Breton objects, but to the narrow positivism that prevented him from admitting the existence of any phenomenon that cannot be explained in terms of his psychology.

Jung, however, went further than Freud and supplied— quite independently of Breton's preoccupations, it would appear—a theoretical elaboration of Breton's idea of the interaction of external necessity with human necessity. A really staggering coincidence, says Jung, has about it a

[51] Monnerot, *La Poésie moderne et le sacré*, pp. 100–101.
[52] Breton, *Entretiens*, pp. 136–137.

strong quality of the numinous. Chance events that have some connection with each other, that is, meaningful coincidences, Jung says, quoting Wilhelm von Scholz, "are arranged as if they were the dream of a 'greater and more comprehensive consciousness, which is unknowable.'" [53] In an attempt to explain these meaningful coincidences, Jung developed the concept of "synchronicity," "a hypothetical factor equal in rank to causality as a principle of explanation." Synchronicity is not to be confused with synchronism which means simply the simultaneous occurrence of two events, whereas the former means the simultaneous occurrence of two or more causally unrelated events that have the same or similar meaning. Two factors must be present for synchronicity to occur: the coming into consciousness of an unconscious image in the form of an idea, dream, or premonition; and an objective, external situation that coincides with the psychic content. The question is: how does that unconscious image arise, and how the coincidence? Drawing upon experiments in extrasensory perception in which the factors of time and space, and hence causality, were eliminated, Jung found that a connection other than causality must exist between such events. This connection is *meaning*. Although meaning is not an objective fact but an anthropomorphic interpretation, it nevertheless "forms the indispensable criterion of synchronicity," even though what "that factor which appears to us as 'meaning' may be in itself we have no way of knowing." Whereas the principle of

[53] Carl G. Jung, "Synchronicity: An Acausal Connecting Principle," trans. by R. F. C. Hull, in C. G. Jung and W. Pauli, *The Interpretation of Nature and the Psyche* (London: Routledge, 1955), p. 22. An earlier and shorter version of this essay appeared in *Man and Time*, Eranos Yearbooks no. 3, Bollingen Series XXX (New York: Pantheon Books, 1957).

causality asserts that the connection between cause and effect is a necessary one, the principle of synchronicity "asserts that the terms of a meaningful coincidence are connected by *simultaneity* and *meaning*." Jung, of course, does not adduce anything startlingly new; he simply recognized that the classical notion of causality is not sufficient to explain the relation between certain kinds of events, and that "there is another fact in nature which expresses itself to us as meaning." He concludes by saying that "for the primitive mind synchronicity is a self-evident fact; consequently at this stage there is no such thing as chance," and here rejoins Breton, who uses the word *hasard* because it is the common one used to describe concidences, but who, by modifying it with the adjective *objectif*, means that there is no such thing as chance, only necessity.

Breton used the word "necessity" to describe the unfolding of events not only in the physical realm, but also in the mental; and an odd contradiction in Breton's thought becomes apparent. He spoke of elucidating "the connections that exist between 'natural necessity' and 'human necessity,' correlatively between necessity and freedom." If the connection between the two realms, the physical and the mental, can be shown to exist—and Breton believes that it can—then it is precisely freedom that is eliminated from the human, or mental realm. The only freedom man has gained is from positivist notions of causality, only to become subject to another kind of causality whose effects we experience, but whose operations we do not understand. It appears that Breton is less concerned with establishing absolute human freedom than with claiming for man freedom from the conventional, stultifying modes of seeing and experiencing the world, from the positivism of bourgeois perception.

What Breton wants to establish is the revolutionary point of view which demands a thorough knowledge of the laws that govern the world in order to effect a general transformation of that world.[54]

But we must return now to the further examination of the principle of *hasard objectif*. The most striking manifestation of objective chance occurs in the encounter of love; this, better than any other, illustrates the mysterious meeting of an external object with an inner desire. The hope for this kind of encounter is the motive behind all those promenades through Paris described in *Poisson soluble*, in *Nadja*, in *Les Vases communicants*, in *L'Amour fou*, in Aragon's *Le Paysan de Paris*. These wanderings require as a precondition *disponibilité*, the availability for any kind of experience. This *disponibilité* is, of course, nothing other than the state of passive receptivity needed for successful automatic writing removed from the study and brought out into the street. In fact, all the marvelous encounters that Breton describes in his several books occurred only when he was in the proper receptive state:

Still today, I await nothing but what will come from my availability, from this thirst for wandering to encounter everything, of which I am sure that it keeps me in mysterious communication with other available beings, as if we were called to meet suddenly. . . . Aside from what happens or does not happen, it is the expectation that is magnificent.[55]

---

[54] André Breton and Diego Rivera, "Pour un art révolutionnaire indépendant," in *Documents surréalistes*, vol. II of Maurice Nadeau, *Histoire du surréalisme* (Paris: Club des Editeurs, 1948), pp. 372–378. In *Entretiens*, p. 190, Breton admitted that his collaborator in this manifesto was not Rivera, but Trotsky, whom he had visited in Mexico in 1938.

[55] *L'Amour fou* (Paris: Gallimard, 1937), p. 41.

Or, as Joyce's Leopold Bloom says, "When you feel like that you often meet what you feel." [56]

These quests were often resolved in the discovery of an "object" which, in some mysterious way, answered some obscure, perhaps unknown need in the finder. In *L'Amour fou*, Breton describes the finding of a strange spoon by himself and of an equally strange mask by Alberto Giacometti while they were wandering through the Flea Market. A detailed analysis of the experiences proved to him that the principle of objective chance was involved: in the strange design of the spoon were embodied several obsessions to which he had been subject for several days; the mask provided Giacometti with the model he needed to complete a sculpture. These objects, and none other, answered their respective needs, needs they were not consciously aware of until they found them answered by the objects.

Every real encounter, then, involves a convergence of two series of events: one which results in the existence of the object and its being in the right place at the right moment, and the other in the need for just that object in the seeker and on his being in the right place at the right moment. The fulfillment of all these conditions produces the flash of revelation that is the sign of objective chance, of the reconciliation of the subjective with the objective, of the world answering the mind's desire on the plane of the surreal.

THE SURREALIST OBJECT

The surrealist program to discredit conventional reality included an attack on the object, the basic, irreducible component of that reality. The first and easiest step in this procedure is to remove the object from its habitual surround-

[56] James Joyce, *Ulysses* (New York: Modern Library, 1961), p. 369.

ings, or simply to change the angle from which it is customarily perceived. Lewis Carroll in a mild way was doing precisely that in the following: "I like very much a little mustard with a bit of beef spread evenly under it; and I like brown sugar—only it should have some apple-pudding mixed with it to keep it from being too sweet. I also like pins, only they should always have a cushion put around them to keep them warm." [57] Marcel Duchamp went several steps further than Carroll by violently wrenching real objects from their normal contexts and claiming that he was raising them to the level of works of art simply by the act of choosing them. In 1914 Duchamp signed an ordinary bottle rack made of galvanized iron. Three years later, he submitted a urinal standing on its side, signed "R. Mutt" and titled "Fountain," to the Salon des Indépendants in New York, only to have it rejected on the grounds of immorality and plagiarism. The first charge Duchamp dismissed, but to the more serious second charge, he replied that "whether Mr. Mutt with his own hands made the fountain or not has no importance. He CHOSE it. He took an ordinary article of life, placed it so that its usual significance disappeared under the new title and point of view—created a new thought for the object." [58]

The banal object deliberately and systematically torn from its realistic context and put to an unbecoming use becomes a source of radiating energy. Duchamp's signed urinal, elevated to the status of a work of art, comments eloquently on the sentimental and cosmetic role usually

[57] Quoted by Lawrence Durrell, *Key to Modern Poetry* (Norman, Okla.: University of Oklahoma Press, 1952), pp. 86–87.
[58] Quoted by Marcel Jean, *The History of Surrealist Painting*, trans. by Simon Watson Taylor (New York: Grove Press, 1960), p. 36.

assigned to art in bourgeois society. From the surrealist point of view it goes a long way toward achieving the shock to "normal" categories essential to the achievement of the "alienation of sensation" on which the surrealist revolution is predicated. For the surrealist, Duchamp's "ready-mades" serve yet another function: they point to the existence in external reality of objects that in some obscure way correspond or answer to inner desire.

Duchamp's activity, however, went beyond simply choosing and signing "ready-mades." He manufactured objects whose sole purpose was to discredit reality by confusing the viewer's perceptions. His "Why Not Sneeze" is an excellent example: it consists of a bird-cage filled with what look like sugar cubes but in reality are painstakingly shaped pieces of marble; a thermometer is stuck among the cubes, perhaps to measure the temperature of the spectator's surprise when he lifts the unexpectedly heavy cage. This object is a kind of *trompe-l'oeil*, of which Breton said, "this trick is worth almost all the tricks of art put together." [59]

The idea of deception was further extended by Duchamp with his "rotary glass plaques" and "rotoreliefs." The former consist of rectangular opaque glass plaques of graduating sizes decorated with black and white lines and spaced on a meter-long axis. In motion, these lines create an illusion of concentric circles on a flat surface, reducing a three-dimensional object to two dimensions.[60] The "rotoreliefs" do the opposite: they consist of spirals and circles drawn on phonograph records, producing optical illusions of three-dimensional objects when set in motion. These forms, in the words of Duchamp's sister, "result from a sort of deliberate confu-

[59] *Les Pas perdus*, pp. 197–198.
[60] Harriet and Sidney Janis, "Marcel Duchamp, Anti-Artist," *Horizon*, XII, no. 70 (October, 1945), 260.

sion of values and arbitrary limits with which conventional thought distinguishes between the concrete and the abstract, Art and Everyday life." [61]

Although they serve the surrealist aim of confusing conventional notions of reality, Duchamp's mechanical creations are too carefully, too deliberately constructed to qualify as true surrealist objects. These, like Breton's wooden spoon and Giacometti's mask, must bridge the gap between internal and external reality; they must be the concrete realization of some unconscious need. Clearly, the objects that best demonstrate the existing link between desire and reality are those that do not need to be made but already exist in reality, and in *Les Vases communicants* Breton expressed his preference for the found object over the consciously made one.[62] In *L'Amour fou,* he explained that "the finding of the object rigorously fulfills the same function as the dream in the sense that it frees the individual from affective, paralyzing scruples, comforts him and lets him understand that the obstacle he thought insuperable has been overcome." [63] The *objet trouvé,* then, is another manifestation of objective chance at work; it becomes, in a very real sense, an *objet retrouvé,* depending for its wealth of suggestiveness on the shock of recognition attendant upon objective chance. The infrequency of the experience and its essential passivity had led Breton in 1924 to call for the manufacture of objects seen in dreams; [64] after Dali's appearance on the scene, this became one of the important surrealist activities.

[61] Gabrielle Buffet, "Coeurs volants," *Cahiers d'Art* (June, 1936); quoted by Marcel Jean, *History of Surrealist Painting,* p. 253.

[62] Pp. 74–75.   [63] P. 46.

[64] Breton, "Introduction au discours sur le peu de réalité," *Commerce,* III (Winter, 1924), 25–27.

Before Dali joined the movement, surrealist activity had been largely passive and receptive; it consisted mainly of the search for the manifestations of objective chance. Under his impetus, it became more active and aggressive in that mental phenomena where deliberately imposed upon the physical world. One form that this new impetus took was the manufacture of objects that function symbolically, "objects which fulfill the necessity of being open to action by our own hands and moved about by our wishes." [65] The germ of the idea of the spectator's participation was contained in Duchamp's "Why Not Sneeze" which requires specific action on the spectator's part, and in Breton's observation in his "Introduction au discours sur le peu de réalité" that visitors to museums or galleries frequently show the desire to touch the objects on display. One of the earliest objects that function symbolically is Giacometti's troubling "The Hour of Traces," described by Dali as "a wooden bowl having a feminine impression . . . suspended by means of a fiddle-string over a crescent, one tip of which just touches the cavity. The spectator finds himself instinctively compelled to slide the bowl over the tip, but the fiddle-string is not long enough for him to do so more than a little." [66]

Breton regretfully noted that in objects of this kind, the latent content, usually of a sexual nature, is too deliberately concretized and imposed on the manifest content, thereby weakening the tendency to dramatization and magnification which the censorship otherwise makes use of; [67] but in spite

[65] Salvador Dali, "The Object as Revealed in Surrealist Experiment," *This Quarter*, V, no. 1 (September, 1932), 205 (translator unnamed).

[66] *Ibid.*, p. 205. A photograph of this object reproduced in Jean, *History of Surrealist Painting*, p. 226, shows that it consists of a ball, not a bowl.

[67] *Les Vases communicants*, pp. 74–75.

of Breton's reservations, Dali saw in the very deliberateness
of the procedure a means of wilfully imposing inner desire
on the external world in order "to systematize confusion and
. . . contribute to the total discrediting of the world of
reality." [68] This method is, of course, his famous "paranoia-
criticism." The starting point for Dali's idea was Breton's
and Eluard's *L'Immaculée conception*, in which the authors
proved by means of automatic writing that it is possible to
simulate mental disease, with the result that, Dali said, "we
are led to regard the world of objects, the objective world,
as the true and manifested content of a new dream." [69] Dali
refined the method of *L'Immaculée conception* by choosing
paranoia as the mental disease through which to view the
objective world because "paranoia uses the exterior world to
set off the obsessing idea, with the troubling peculiarity of
making the reality of this idea valid for others." [70] What
impressed Dali about paranoia was that its victims interpret
the outer world consistently and systematically in terms of
their own obsessions; that, in other words, they refashion
reality according to their own desires. Because they do not
act directly on reality but only reinterpret it, they can often
bring others to perceive and verify their re-creation. Breton
cites as an example of this faculty Hamlet's seeing in a cloud
first a camel, then a whale, and convincing Polonius of the
reality of what he saw. [71] Another example described by
Breton is Leonardo's instructions to his pupils to paint whatever they saw after staring a long time at the surface of an
old, cracked wall.

Dali defined paranoiac-critical activity as the "spontaneous

[68] Dali, *La Femme visible* (Paris: Editions Surréalistes, 1930),
p. 11.
[69] "The Object as Revealed," p. 202.
[70] *La Femme visible*, p. 12.   [71] *L'Amour fou*, pp. 125–126.

method of irrational knowledge based upon the interpretive-critical association of delirious phenomena," and elaborated this definition as follows:

Paranoiac-critical activity organizes and objectivizes in an exclusivist manner the limitless and unknown possibilities of the systematic associations of subjective and objective phenomena, which appear to us as irrational solicitations, exclusively in favour of the obsessive idea. By this method paranoiac-critical activity discovers new and objective "significances" in the irrational; it makes the world of delirium pass tangibly onto the plane of reality.[72]

In the final development of the idea of the surrealist object, "the object tends to bring about our fusion with it and makes us pursue the formation of a unity with it." In *Calligrammes*, Apollinaire had written poems in the shape of the object that the poem was about, or, as Dali put it, "The shapes of things . . . were seeking to take the very form of writing." But this was not going quite far enough: "The object's action is allowed to influence, but there is no attempt at acting on the object," and Dali suggested doing *Calligrammes* one better: writing on the object itself, "devouring of things by writing": "I dream of a mysterious manuscript in white ink and completely covering the strange, firm surfaces of a brand-new Rolls-Royce. Let the privilege of old be conferred on everyone: let everyone be able to read from things." [73]

This suggestion became Breton's *poème-objet*, defined as "a composition which tends to combine the resources of poetry and of plastic arts by speculating on their reciprocal

---

[72] *Conquest of the Irrational*, trans. by David Gascoyne (New York: Julien Levy, 1936), p. 17.
[73] "The Object as Revealed," pp. 204–205, 207.

powers of exaltation." [74] These object-poems are diverse objects on or beside which appeared obscure but provocative words or lines of verse, attempting, as does all surrealist activity, to juxtapose or fuse the most disparate elements of experience. In *Les Vases communicants*, Breton recorded the creation of one of these poetic objects: an empty white envelope, without address, is sealed with red wax and is decorated with a lateral handle and eyelashes on the edges. The word "silence," which accompanies the object, contains the motive power for the creation of the object.[75] Certainly the object has no utilitarian or even aesthetic value, but since it provoked an emotion in the poet, it possesses the same value as a poetic image. The nature of that emotion is obscure, but the object, in spite of its seeming gratuity, contains or expresses some profound preoccupation; like a dream-image, it has a latent content. Upon close analysis, Breton discovered that content: the object was a chamber pot distorted by the censorship.[76]

The *Enveloppe du silence* illustrates the process of constructing a poetic object, a process similar to that at work in the formation of images in the dream: disparate elements are joined into a new reality under an obscure impulsion. The true power of such objects, Breton thought, is that they are a disguise and at the same time a concretization and revelation of some unconscious obsession. For this reason, they are preferable to Dali's more deliberately wrought, symbolically functioning objects, which for all their "explosive" value, present a narrower field of investigation since they already contain their own interpretation.

[74] Breton, *Entretiens,* p. 162.
[75] In French, the word contains an untranslatable pun: cil = eyelash; anse = handle.
[76] Breton, *Les Vases communicants,* pp. 70–73.

For Breton, the successful surrealist objects owe their suggestive and evocatory power to the fact that they are solidified dream-images or that, at any rate, they are the product of the same unconscious process that governs the formation of dream-images. These, Freud has shown, are disguises for obscure, perhaps unknown, preoccupations of the unconscious. Not coincidentally, objects that have an organic sexual content are the most troubling and therefore the most successful. Speaking of the surprising, suggestive power of certain common objects, Breton cites the example of the electroscope, which with its perfectly joined leaves that draw apart when a rubbed stick is brought near them, serves to fascinate children with the study of physics.[77]

Perhaps the most famous surrealist object, one that embodies most of the requirements for success, is Méret Oppenheim's fur-lined tea set. It is essentially an *objet trouvé*, a perfectly banal piece of equipment which has been subjected to a paranoiac interpretation—the addition of the fur —which has made manifest a latent content previously so remote as to be lost. This object, Cyril Connolly has said, "is not ridiculous but alarming, for there is something more horrible than one would expect about drinking from a fur-lined cup, tea and cup having a deeply buried Freudian content which the fur brings to the surface."[78] What has happened, simply, is that the object has broken with its usual, banal associations; by being subjected to new relationships with elements normally foreign to it, it has acquired a more vital reality. This process, by discrediting conventional notions of reality, leads to the "alienation of sensation," that is, to a condition in which the new juxta-

[77] *Ibid.*, p. 75.
[78] Cyril Connolly, "Farewell to Surrealism," *World Review* (March, 1952), p. 35.

position of elements can be accepted as real. We are now in the realm of Lautréamont's fortuitous encounter of the umbrella with the sewing machine on the dissecting table. This famous image, which contains all of surrealism in a nutshell, has been analyzed in detail by Max Ernst; his account is worth quoting in full, for it describes the process involved in the creation of a surrealist image, verbal or visual:

Let a ready-made reality with a naive purpose apparently settled once for all (i.e. an umbrella) be suddenly juxtaposed to another very distant and no less ridiculous reality (i.e. a sewing-machine) in a place where both must be felt as *out of place* (i.e. upon a dissecting table), and precisely thereby it will be robbed of its naive purpose and its identity; through a relativity it will pass from its false to a novel absoluteness, at once true and poetic: umbrella and sewing-machine will make love. This very simple example seems to me to reveal the mechanism of the process. Complete transmutation followed by a pure act such as the act of love must necessarily occur every time the given facts make conditions favorable: *the pairing of two realities which apparently cannot be paired on a plane not suited to them.*[79]

This process, as Ernst noted, is identical with that of collage, which is described as follows by Breton:

It is the wonderful power to grasp two mutually distant realities without going beyond the field of our experience and to draw a spark from their juxtaposition; to bring within easy reach of our senses abstract forms capable of the same intensity and distinctness as others; and, *while depriving us of any system of reference, to put us out of place in our very recollection.*[80]

[79] Max Ernst, "Inspiration to Order," *This Quarter*, V, no. 1 (September, 1932), 80–81 (translator unnamed); reprinted in Max Ernst, *Beyond Painting* (New York: Wittenborn and Schultz, 1948).

[80] Breton, Preface to the Max Ernst Exhibition of May, 1921; quoted by Ernst, "Inspiration to Order," p. 81 (italics mine).

The italicized passages in both quotations point to the key of the whole procedure: the juxtapositions *appear* incongruous from the point of view of logic or habitual perception; from the point of view of the dream, they do not. These violent unions are not bizarre just for the sake of being bizarre; they serve first, as Breton says, to deprive us of any system of reference; second, they acquire a revelatory potency by showing us not the actual, but the possible. In the realm of the surreal, once logic has been transcended, similarity and contradiction are abolished, analogies cease to exist, everything becomes possible:

The time of Baudelairean "correspondences" . . . is past. For my part, I refuse to see in them anything but the expression of a transitional idea . . . which no longer counts for anything. Oneiric values have once and for all succeeded the others, and I demand that he who still refuses, for instance, to *see* a horse galloping on a tomato be looked upon as a cretin. A tomato is also a child's balloon, surrealism, I repeat, having suppressed the word "like." [81]

Or again:

In reality, if you know now what is meant by that, a nose is perfectly in place next to an armchair, it even takes the form of the armchair. What difference is there fundamentally between a couple of dancers and a beehive cover? The birds have never sung better than in this aquarium.[82]

These strange couplings bring us to the threshold of a consideration of the surrealist image.

THE SURREALIST IMAGE

The basic surrealist doctrine of the image is an extension of Freud's analysis of the dream-work. We have seen that

[81] Breton, *What Is Surrealism?*, p. 25.
[82] Breton, *Le Surréalisme et la peinture*, p. 76.

in the dream, the unconscious content that strives for expression acquires, through the agency of the repressing censorship, a mask that permits it to slip by that censorship. These masks, borrowed from recent daytime activity, are what constitute the visual, or manifest, element of the dream —the images. In the dream, the categories that govern daytime activity—time, space, noncontradiction, logic, etc.—are abolished, and a nose can indeed take the form of an armchair, or a sewing machine and an umbrella can be at home on a dissecting table. We have seen also that in the dream the image may depend for its particular form on a word, a succession of words, a pun, and that the succession of images may be governed by the mysterious process of association—either visual or auditory.

In the preceding section, we saw that the surrealist object is, basically, a solidified dream-image. Breton's *Enveloppe du silence* does little more than concretize visually the pun hidden in the word "silence." Only after the fact, after performing a minor psychoanalysis, did Breton discover in the image a hidden chamber pot, and in that chamber pot the motive force that led to the formation of the image. The surrealist image, whether in painting or in poetry, results from precisely the same process. Its most striking characteristic is the incongruity of disparate elements brought into a context in which they do not seem to belong. So far, the surrealist image seems no more than a harmless game, a verbal transcription of an interior landscape, in contrast to the traditional image which transcribes an external landscape. But if this were all that is involved, surrealism would hardly deserve all the attention it has received. It is important to remember at this point that Breton always insisted that surrealism is not an aesthetic movement, that its purpose is not to provide merely a new way of writing or painting; it intends nothing less than the complete transformation of

life. For a number of reasons, its proofs are best seen in the
realms of art, but this should not obscure the fact that these
are proofs, nothing more.

As we have seen, the claims of surrealism are based upon
Freud's discoveries. Poets have always proclaimed the
greater reality of the "psychic" over the material, but not
until Freud did this claim have anything but a kind of
metaphoric importance. Freud demonstrated the existence
of the unconscious and its influence on the conscious side
of life. For Freud, however, the reality of the unconscious
is, if one may speak in such unphilosophical language, inferior to the material reality of the "real" world. It is on this
ontological point that the surrealists broke with Freud, for
behind Freud's view they detected a strong bourgeois bias.
Since the surrealists denied the superior value of the material bourgeois world, they saw no reason for subordinating
the unconscious to it. In the encounters of "objective
chance" they found proof that the unconscious possesses
greater reality than Freud had been willing to grant. They
found that the unconscious and the external world exist together in a close, intricate relationship; they discovered that
the unconscious is, in fact, an instrument for the exploration
and revelation of the material world. Therefore, automatism,
the traditional method of investigating the unconscious, is
for them also a method of investigating material reality;
the dictates of the unconscious have importance not only for
the unconscious but also for material reality. It is only the
intellect committed to traditional modes of perception that
denies the validity and importance of the surrealist discoveries. The purpose of many of the surrealist enterprises
was precisely to unsettle these traditional habits of perception, to present a world ruled by chance. Once these traditional habits have been broken, the world reveals itself as

full of unlimited possibility, as suffused with the "marvelous."

The surrealist image—both verbal and visual—serves, then, a complex triple purpose. First, by juxtaposing seemingly irreconcilable elements, it disrupts psychological expectations and prevents the passive enjoyment of the world. Secondly, the surrealist image is heuristic. These unexpected, illogical juxtapositions arrived at by chance [83] are in a sense exploratory of the nature of a world in which chance rather than logic rules: the image is no longer the end product of the aesthetic imagination trying to produce beauty or trying to illustrate thought or perception, but the beginning of a new exploration of the unknown. The traditional role of the image has always been to compare the remote with the near, the unknown with the known in order to assimilate the former to the latter. The surrealist image does the opposite: it leads from the known to the unknown, from the near to the remote in order to fill the familiar with mystery.

The third function of the image is revelatory. We have seen that in the encounters of objective chance, external necessity has found a way into the unconscious, and that the external and the internal worlds are ruled by the same necessity. Since the images by which the unconscious is expressed in the dream and in automatic writing combine elements of both worlds, they become the nexus of these two worlds. Surrealist poems, like Breton's "Tournesol," or surrealist paintings, like Victor Brauner's pictures of one-eyed creatures, become prophetic of actual events in the external world. The seeming arbitrariness of so many surrealist images—even of those that deliberately employ chance—is shown, as Breton has said, not to be arbitrariness

---

[83] See, for example, Max Ernst's accounts in *Beyond Painting*.

at all, but the expression of that necessity that rules everywhere.

The surrealists, then, partly with the sanctions gained from Freud, felt justified in endowing their new juxtapositions with as much reality as is traditionally granted the external world; and under the impulsion of Breton's and Eluard's experiments in *L'Immaculée conception* and of Dali's "paranoia," they considered their creations assaults upon conventional reality. Initially, these gave proof of the omnipotence of mind and provided a remedy against the narrow pragmatism which seeks to impose the everyday world as the only reality. Later these creations became one of the elements in the endless dialectic process that goes on between matter and mind. Language is in this view the primary weapon against the old pragmatic reality:

Does not the mediocrity of our world depend essentially on our power of articulation? Poetry in its most sterile seasons has often proved it: what an orgy of starry skies, of precious stones, of dead leaves. . . . What has been said over and over . . . welds us to this vulgar universe. . . . What prevents me from scrambling the order of words, from assaulting in this manner the completely apparent existence of things? Language can and should be torn from this servitude. . . . After you, my beautiful language.[84]

The early justification for the surrealist practices in poetry came from Pierre Reverdy's definition of the image as "the bringing together of two very distant realities of which only the mind [*esprit*] has seized the similarities." [85] This defini-

---

[84] Breton, "Introduction au discours sur le peu de réalité," pp. 48–49.
[85] Pierre Reverdy, *Le Gant de crin;* quoted in *L'Art poétique,* ed. by Jacques Charpier and Pierre Seghers (Paris: Editions Pierre Seghers, 1956), p. 525. Everything in this definition hinges on the untranslatable word *esprit.* I have chosen "mind" because Breton

tion implies a large degree of conscious awareness; in the "Premier manifeste," Breton denied that the two distant realities can be consciously brought together: "It is false, according to me, to maintain that 'the mind has seized the similarities' of the realities. It has seized nothing consciously." It is beyond the power of human consciousness, says Breton, to effect the *rapprochement* of the two realities: the principle of the association of ideas forbids it; nor is it simply a matter of ellipsis, which Breton rejects as a mere rhetorical device. The two terms of the image cannot consciously be brought together: "the *rapprochement* happens or it does not." In other words, neither a surrealist image nor a dream-image can be made deliberately. Surrealist images, like hallucinatory or dream-images, are not evoked, but force themselves on the poet. Breton goes so far as to deny that Reverdy's own images show the slightest degree of premeditation.[86]

The surrealist image, then, effects a juxtaposition that is, from the point of view of logic, completely arbitrary. One must insist on the qualifying phrase "from the point of view of logic," for, as we know, there is nothing arbitrary in the functioning of the unconscious. What the two terms of the image have in common, that which effects their conjunction, exists, it would appear, only in the unconscious and can be revealed only in a process akin to that of psychoanalysis. Those images that awaken an echo in the reader's own unconscious are those that have the greatest degree of success. For example, Breton finds the power of Lautréamont's image of the umbrella and sewing machine on the dissecting table in its obvious though latent sexual content: the um-

---

objected precisely to the degree of consciousness implied in the definition, but *esprit* may well include the more unconscious aspects of mental processes.

[86] Breton, "Premier manifeste," p. 52.

brella is male, the sewing machine female, and the dissecting table a bed.[87]

It has been amply demonstrated by Freud that in the dream, the limits imposed on "things" by the waking intellect are easily dissolved, that they do not in fact exist: a coffin becomes a womb; a room, a female; a necktie, the male organ. To the waking mind, the relation between the room and the female is symbolic; to the dreamer, the connection is closer: he reacts to the room as if it were the female, the room in fact *is* the female. Since the primary object of surrealist activity has always been to bring the dream out into the open, to make the human unconscious effective in the "real" world, the fact of interchangeability is brought out of the dream and imposed upon "reality." Things lose their identity; conventional associations are exploded; the "real" world falls into ruin. As Marcel Raymond has said, "Every surrealist text presupposes a return to chaos, within which is outlined a vague super-nature; 'stunning' chemical combinations between the most dissimilar words, and new possibilities of synthesis are suddenly revealed in a flash." [88] But the chaos that the surrealists want to achieve is more than verbal, for, as Aragon said,

We saw, for example, a written image which at first appeared fortuitous, arbitrary, affect our senses and strip itself of its verbal aspect in order to put on phenomenal modalities which, fixed and external to our fantasies, we had always believed it impossible to elicit. . . . *Absolute nominalism* found in surrealism a dazzling proof, . . . *there is no thought outside of words:* all of surrealism supports this proposition.[89]

[87] Breton, *Les Vases communicants,* pp. 71–72.
[88] *From Baudelaire to Surrealism,* p. 289.
[89] Louis Aragon, "Une Vague de rêves," *Commerce,* II (Autumn, 1924), 102.

This, then, is the background against which the surrealist image must be seen, and the apparent absurdity of so many of these images granted their seriousness of purpose:

Comparing two objects as far removed from each other as possible . . . remains the highest task to which poetry can aspire. Its unique and unequaled power must strain to this end, which is to show the concrete unity of the two terms brought together and to communicate to each . . . a vigor it lacked as long as it was taken in isolation. What must be broken is the purely formal opposition between these two terms; what must be overcome is their apparent disproportion which depends only on the imperfect, childish notion we have of nature, of the externality of time and space. The stronger the element of dissimilarity seems, the more it must be overcome and denied. It is the whole import of the object that is in question. Thus, two dissimilar bodies, rubbed against one another, achieve, by means of the spark, their supreme unity in fire.[90]

This view of language and of the role of images is destructive of conventional notions of reality and of the conventional view of the function of language that such notions entail. The surrealist plea for freedom from conventional reality, from logic, taste, and morality, extends to language also: one of the steps in freeing man from the mediocrity of the universe is to dissolve the forced marriage between words and their meanings. Words, for the surrealists, exist outside of their common denotative or connotative functions. Words have a far more active life than any dictionary or etymology can guess; for, as Michael Leiris has said, associations of sounds, of ideas, even of the shapes of words, play their part.[91] In an essay characteristically entitled "Words without Wrinkles," Breton insists that words must

90 Breton, *Les Vases communicants,* pp. 148–149.
91 *La Révolution surréaliste,* III (1925), 6–7.

be studied in themselves, aside from their dead weight of etymology and meaning. By assigning colors to vowels, Rimbaud had turned the word away from its old function as sign; from that day on, Breton says, the word was born to a new concrete existence which had never been suspected. The alarm has been sounded, and it is dangerous from now on to speculate on the innocence of words. They have already acquired sonority; they are beginning to be paintbrushes; soon we shall have to consider their architectural properties. In fact, Breton adds, the expression of an idea depends as much on the appearance of words as on their meaning; there are even words that work against the idea they are supposed to express; finally, even the meanings of words are not fixed, for, Breton suggests, the figurative sense of a word acts progressively on its literal sense.[92] Breton reports that it took him six months to write a thirty-word poem because he had to weigh each word to determine its connection with innumerable others with which it came in contact in his mind as he was writing, to measure the amount of space the words allowed between each other.[93] The surrealist purpose is "to act . . . upon the matter of language itself by forcing words to reveal their secret life and to betray the mysterious dealings they maintain outside of their meanings." [94] Words seen in this manner, as discrete entities with mysterious affinities and oppositions, freed from "things" and dictionaries, "make love." [95] This, again, is in keeping with Freud's analysis which shows that in dreams words act upon each other according to a logic other than obtains in the waking world.

The precursor of surrealism in this particular area was

[92] Breton, "Les Mots sans rides," *Les Pas perdus*, pp. 168–169.
[93] Anna Balakian, *Surrealism: The Road to the Absolute*, p. 117.
[94] Breton, *Entretiens*, p. 106.   [95] Breton, *Les Pas perdus*, p. 171.

Raymond Roussel, to whom the surrealists more than once acknowledged their debt but who consistently refused to join them.[96] Roussel, more than anyone before him, had exploited the creative power of words. This creativity depends upon a kind of magic nominalism in which the word creates the thing, and a series of sentences entails the recreation of the universe, of a special world to take the place of the common one. Roussel, says Michel Leiris, had recovered one of man's most ancient mental habits: the creation of myths from words. His method was the following: first, he made puns or sentences with multiple meanings which in turn suggested the elements to be confronted with each other; second, he established a logical train which would unite these elements, no matter how incongruous; third, he formulated these relations on as realistic a plane as possible into a text composed with a maximum of strictness, without any concern for form for its own sake, obeying only grammatical and stylistic rules.[97] In this manner, Roussel constructed an entirely imaginary Africa in his *Impressions d'Afrique* (1910).

Marcel Duchamp did comparable violence to words by displacing letters or syllables, by using them for their consonances, assonances, or multiple meanings. The results of these manipulations cannot, unfortunately, be translated. Max Ernst is another who played with words in this manner in an example which, although somewhat puerile, illustrates these practices and attempts to do verbally what the collage does plastically:

[96] Breton, *Entretiens*, pp. 106–107.

[97] Raymond Roussel, *Comment j'ai écrit certains de mes livres,* quoted by Michel Leiris, *Nouvelle Revue Française*, XLVI, no. 268 (January, 1936), 113–114; see also Breton, "Raymond Roussel," *Anthologie de l'humour noir*, 3d ed., pp. 290–291.

What is a phallustrade? It is an alchemical product composed of the following elements: the autostrade, the balustrade and a certain quantity of phallus. A phallustrade is a verbal collage. One might define collage as an alchemy resulting from the unexpected meeting of two or more heterogeneous elements, those elements provoked either by a will which—from a love of clairvoyance—is directed toward systematical confusion and disorder of all the senses (Rimbaud), or by chance, or by a will favorable to chance. Chance, as Hume defined it, is *the equivalent of the ignorance in which we find ourselves in relation to the real causes of events,* a definition which is increasingly corroborated by the development of calculations regarding probabilities, and by the importance which this discipline holds in modern science and political life.[98]

What is important in these "experiments" is the motivating intention rather than the value of the result. In all these manipulations, the words have been used as things in themselves; they have been endowed with a concrete, independent existence that has nothing to do with their significatory function. Freed from their enslavement to "things," words restore to language its ancient, creative role.[99] Surrealist images, unlike conventional ones, are not illustrations, for in the surrealist context, there is nothing for images to illustrate —an image becomes simply the name of the thing it is about. Or, as Aragon said, "We were busy marrying sounds to each other in order to rebuild things, endlessly proceeding to metamorphoses, calling forth strange animals." [100]

The image, then, ceases to be the vehicle for the expression of something other than itself; it ceases to be anything but itself in an instant of time. The image becomes a new

[98] Max Ernst, *Beyond Painting,* trans. Dorothea Tanning, p. 16.
[99] Breton and Paul Eluard, *Notes sur la poésie* (Paris: Editions G.L.M., 1936), n.p.
[100] Quoted by Hubert Juin, *Aragon* (Paris: Gallimard, 1960), p. 24.

reality, different from the reality of the everyday, familiar, disused world. As Gaston Bachelard noted about Lautréamont, "His language is not the expression of a previous thought. It is the expression of psychic force which suddenly becomes language." [101] Reversing the usual order of things in which the image illustrates or clarifies or embodies a thought, Eluard succinctly says, "images think for me." [102] And since images depend for their content on the associations of the unconscious, everything becomes possible, and everything that is expressed in a true surrealist image becomes true:

> The earth is blue like an orange
> Never a mistake words do not lie [103]

The image becomes the new basic unit of reality: words cannot lie any more than objects can, for words and images have become objects:

Images are, images live, and everything becomes image. They were long mistaken for illusions because they were restricted, were made to undergo the test of reality, an insensitive and dead reality, when reality should have been made to undergo the test of its own interdependence which makes it alive, and perpetually moving.[104]

Such verbal and poetic images, Breton says, possess a force of persuasion that is rigorously proportionate to the initial shock they produce; in this manner they acquire the character of revelation.[105] But in order for images to be seen and

---

[101] *Lautréamont*, 2d ed. (Paris: Librairie José Corti, 1956), p. 97.
[102] *L'Amour la poésie* (Paris: Gallimard, 1929), p. 122.
[103] *Ibid.*, p. 18.
[104] Eluard, "Poetry's Evidence," trans. by Samuel Beckett, *This Quarter*, V, no. 1 (September, 1932), 146.
[105] *L'Amour fou*, pp. 130–131.

accepted as truly revelatory, man must be able to change his modes of thinking and perceiving. Everything in the surrealist program aims toward that end and joins Rimbaud who charged poetry with the ultimate revolutionary task: "to change life." This, clearly, has been the mission of surrealism—to free man from the shackles of reason, to remove the blinders of purely intellectual sight so that he may finally *see:*

A day will come . . . when man will come out of the labyrinth, having gropingly recovered the lost thread in the night. This thread is that of poetry such as yet only a few of us understand it, poetry which we, like Lautréamont and Rimbaud, have wanted such that it change life. This thread is the same as the one which endlessly winds itself on the spool of the occult tradition.[106]

Surrealism, through its categories of automatism and objective chance, its demand for human freedom, its need to change life and remake man, joins the occult tradition.

THE OCCULT

As early as 1930, in the "Second manifeste," Breton had called for "the profound, true occultation of surrealism." [107] He had often noted that the important poets of the nineteenth century—Hugo, Nerval, Baudelaire, Lautréamont, Rimbaud, Mallarmé—had been interested in the occult, and insofar as surrealism was the result of the same historical process as had involved them, it was inevitable that it too should come to the occult. But surrealism, Breton insisted, came to its interest in the occult not out of curiosity, but out of its own internal necessity: "It was out of its own movement, I mean brought by motives which seemed to me

---

[106] Breton, *Entretiens*, p. 278.   [107] P. 211.

then [in 1925] strictly poetic, that [surrealism] was made to blend certain fundamental esoteric theses." [108]

We have seen how the idea of the supreme point where all contradictions are reconciled grew out of the principles of automatism; how all the energies of surrealism were directed to the freeing of man from the restrictive forces of logic and reason so that the unconscious could project itself onto the external world. All these fundamental doctrines of surrealism, which have here been discussed as if they were separate, merge and point to one end: "Let us remember that the idea of surrealism leads simply to the total recovery of our psychic power by a method that is none other than the dizzying descent into ourselves, the systematic illumination of the hidden places." [109] The idea of the recuperation of lost or forgotten psychic powers, powers that would reveal the true nature of the universe and man's real place in it, is fundamental to all occult philosophy. Breton, in fact, sees in the task that Rimbaud assigned to poetry, that of changing life, one that is identical to the "Great Work" of alchemy.[110] The essential purpose of alchemy— that is, alchemy understood in its serious purpose of transmuting man, not in its vulgar attempts to transmute base metals—as of all occult practices, is to repair the consequences of the Fall and reintroduce man into the Garden of Eden, into a state in which he could perceive the reality beneath the flux of appearances, in which he lived so close to the real nature of things that he knew their names, in short, a state in which he had perfect knowledge and understanding. The particular task of occultism is to enable certain initiates to anticipate the hour of recuperation of man's

[108] *Entretiens*, p. 270.
[109] Breton, "Second manifeste," pp. 167–168.
[110] Breton, *Entretiens*, pp. 270–271.

lost powers, and in this is quite close to the fundamental purpose of surrealism which is, simply, to make man *see*.

The idea of the supreme point where all contradictions are reconciled, the cornerstone of surrealist thought, is central to all occult doctrine, although it appears there in different guises. For Christian Rosencreutz, the center of the Cross is the point of synthesis of all opposites; in Muslim esotericism, it is the "divine station"; in Eastern mysticism, it is the "unmoving center" that is the place of perfect equilibrium symbolized by the hub of the "cosmic wheel." The origin of the idea of the supreme point has been in fact traced to the *Zohar,* one of the fundamental texts of Cabbalism, and has been found in the doctrines of John Dee, Guillot de Givry, Khunrath, Paracelsus.[111] In the Paracelsian idea of the micro- and macrocosm, Breton sees a restatement of his own principles of the interconnections between the inner and the outer worlds—since man is a "small world," knowledge of himself brings knowledge of the large world, of nature.

Surrealists have often testified to the generative power of the image, that is, the power of the image to involve the poet more deeply in the poetic state.[112] The practice of automatism, of which poetry is one product, assumes then a function analogous to the rituals of occultism: automatism —if we understand the term in its widest meanings—leads man into the mysteries of the cosmos, and by revealing to him the links between his own unconscious and the universe, begins his metamorphosis. Automatism becomes much more than the simple exploration and expression of the individual unconscious; it becomes the means whereby objective chance reveals itself to man:

111 Michel Carrouges, *André Breton et les données,* pp. 24 ff.
112 See, for example, Breton's account of the image of the man bisected by the window in "Premier manifeste," pp. 34 ff.

The rock of Sisyphus? The surrealists disagree with Camus in that they believe that some day it will split, abolishing as if by magic, both the mountain and the torture; they tend to think that there may be a propitious way of rolling it. They do not hold as incurable the "break" observed by Camus between the world and the human spirit. They are very far from admitting that nature is hostile to man, but believe that man, who originally possessed certain keys which kept him in close communion with nature, has lost them and since then, more and more feverishly, persists in trying others *that do not fit.*

Scientific knowledge of nature can have value only on the condition that the *contact* with nature through poetic and, I venture to say, mythic means, can be reestablished.[113]

In 1945, Breton published *Arcane 17*, a book largely devoted to the occult. The title refers to the Tarot card known as "The Star," symbol of hope and resurrection. The book recounts Breton's despair during the dark war years, then progresses toward the renewal of hope as the war neared its end and Breton met a young woman who became for him the embodiment of "The Star." He saw once again in this concatenation of events the working of objective chance, another example of the external world answering the mind's desire. In this encounter with love, fairly late in life, Breton saw a reaffirmation of the need to surrender the disastrous masculine values to the irrational feminine in order for man to find his true place in nature and achieve his salvation: "The great malediction is lifted; it is in human love that the power to regenerate the world rests." [114]

Woman as the vehicle for the regenerative power appears in surrealist mythology as Mélusine, who, half winged-woman and half serpent, is another symbol of the reconciliation of contraries: her serpentine aspect links her with the

---

[113] Breton, *Entretiens*, p. 248.

[114] Breton, *Arcane 17* (New York: Brentano's, 1945), p. 78.

animal and telluric forces of nature and therefore with the unconscious; as a woman she partakes of the human world; and through her flight she communicates with superior worlds. As the synthesis of the three worlds, Mélusine has long been a symbol in the occult tradition: Eliphas Lévy, the great nineteenth-century magus, referred to her as "the siren revelatory of harmonies," "the analogical alliance of contraries." [115]

Another such symbol of synthesis appears in *Arcane 17* in another quotation from Eliphas Lévy, "Osiris is a black god," of which Breton says, "obscure words and more radiant than jet! It is they which, at the limit of human questioning, seem to me the richest, the most charged with meaning." [116] The image of a black god from the Eleusinian mysteries supplied Breton with an exciting synthesis: to the traditional idea of god is added black, the color of the infernal powers. A black god is the synthesis of the divine and the demoniac, of the opposition between good and evil.

Although obscure in detail and application, the point of occultism is clear: it leads man to believe that his mind has the power to know the secrets of the cosmos, to seize and control the world he inhabits. The aims of science are the same; only its methods differ. Science proceeds by rational, occultism by irrational means; but in both instances, man relies upon himself for his salvation. Underlying occultism —and perhaps scientific endeavor as well—is the myth of lost harmony and the belief than man by supernatural means can win divine powers for himself and restore the harmony between himself and the cosmos.[117] In its attempts

[115] Quoted by Carrouges, *André Breton et les données*, p. 253.

[116] *Arcane 17*, p. 154.

[117] Cf. Albert Béguin, "Poetry and Occultism," *Yale French Studies*, II, no. 2, 12–25.

to determine the supreme point of reconciliation, surrealism is rather close in purpose, if not in method, to the goals of occult endeavor.

One important point of difference, however, needs to be stressed: the occult, at least in some of its branches, notably Cabbalism, is a species of religious mysticism in that it attempts to restore man to close relation with God; it becomes heretical in some of its forms, but the question of man's relation to God is always at issue. Surrealism, although in this particular aspect seems to approach mysticism, is careful to assert always its essential materialist bases. The surrealist interest in the occult is an extension of its doctrine of "objective chance," which, we have seen, maintains its positive roots in a materialist view of things. The flash of objective chance, of the surreal, occurs when that material world is seen to be linked to the human unconscious by some unknown net of correspondences. Occultism, for the surrealists, is one of the means of investigating these correspondences; it serves primarily as further evidence for the existence of that net.

One last category remains to be examined in this survey of surrealist doctrine—that of humor, in which all the others merge.

HUMOR

The origin of the surrealist notion of humor, or "objective humor," is once again Hegel, who, in the *Philosophy of Fine Art*, defined humor as the synthesis of the dialectical opposition between man's inner world and the objective world:

Romantic art had as its fundamental principle the concentration on itself of the soul which, finding that the objective world does not fully satisfy its intimate nature, remains indifferent to it. This opposition developed in the period of romantic art to the point that we have seen the attention fixed either on the contingent aspects of the external world or on the whims of the personality. But if this attention goes so far that the soul becomes absorbed in the contemplation of an external object and at the same time humor, while still retaining its subjective and reflective character, lets itself be captivated by the object and its real form, we get in this intimate penetration a *humor* which is in some manner *objective*.[118]

Humor in this definition is part of the attitude that the "soul" takes toward an external world that does not satisfy its needs; and in the romantic view, it assumes a double role, both as weapon against the world and as shield from it. This double function was stressed by Jacques Vaché, the mysterious patron saint of surrealism, who defined humor, or, as he called it, *umour*, as "a sense of the theatrical and joyless uselessness of everything." [119] Humor arises from a destructive, annihilating view of the *uselessness* of the world; but by providing distance and perhaps laughter, it also shields from the despair that must result from such a view. This completely negative and passive view of the world was, of course, that of dada; in time it became insufficient for the surrealists. It was Freud who, once again, provided the basis for the surrealists' theory of humor, and their efforts were again directed to reconciling Freud and Hegel.

Freud had, early in his career, seen that the origin of wit lay in the conflict between the unconscious and "reality"; that, in order to express itself, the unconscious content

[118] Friedrich Hegel, *The Philosophy of Fine Art*, trans. by F. P. B. Osmaston (London: G. Bell & Sons, 1920), Vol. II, pp. 397–398. Quoted in *Anthologie de l'humour noir*, 3d ed., p. 13.
[119] Quoted in *Anthologie de l'humour noir*, 3d ed., p. 380.

must get past the censorship by a process similar to that of the dream-work: by displacing the thought from the essential to the trivial idea; by the use of illogical trains of thought; by indirect presentation by means of allusions, analogies, and puns. Wit, for the individual, serves the same function as the dream: it permits the expression of what would otherwise be kept suppressed by the censorship. But wit has one important advantage over the dream: the latter is "a perfectly asocial psychic product" which must guard against being understood; wit, on the other hand, "is the most social of all those psychic functions whose aim is to gain pleasure," and must be accessible to intelligence.[120]

Humor, in Freud's scheme, serves the principles of economy: it saves the expenditure of the psychic energy that would be needed to repress what is expressed by the witticism, and is, therefore, the result of the pleasure principle at work. Since, as Freud said, wit is more public than the dream, it functions in a manner analogous to Dali's "paranoia-criticism": it sees incongruities in the outside world and makes others share in that vision. By provoking laughter, it conquers the discrepancy of which Hegel speaks between the "soul" and the objective world and imposes the supremacy of the pleasure principle over the reality principle; it represents a victory of mind over the world. Breton, in a detailed explanation of humor in Freudian terms, points to its synthesizing power over the opposing tendencies of id, ego, and super-ego.[121] In a remarkable historical analysis of literary and artistic tendencies in the nineteenth and twentieth centuries, Breton, following the suggestion in Hegel's definition of objective humor, noted an oscillation between

---

[120] Freud, "Wit and Its Relation to the Unconscious," *Basic Writings,* pp. 760–761.
[121] *Anthologie de l'humour noir,* pp. 362–363.

the two poles of imitation of the outside world on the one hand, and humor on the other. Imitation of outward accidental aspects of nature took several forms during the centuries under review: realism, naturalism, impressionism, cubism, futurism. Humor, he pointed out, becomes particularly conspicuous in times of trouble and testifies "to the artist's imperious need of dominating the accidental when it tends to impose itself objectively: first the symbolism of Lautréamont and Rimbaud synchronous with the war of 1870; pre-dadaism (Roussel, Duchamp, Cravan), and dadaism (Vaché, Tzara) concurrent with the war of 1914." [122]

The surrealist view of humor, then, is a fairly complex synthesis of the Hegelian and the Freudian. In the Hegelian view, humor enters into synthesis with the imitation of nature in its accidental forms and results in "objective humor"—that is, a kind of humor that has relevance in the material world and serves as a link between that world and what Hegel calls the "soul." In the Freudian view, humor serves the principle of economy of psychic energy—it is the result of an encounter between the individual unconscious and the external world, representing a victory of the former over the latter while still being the product of the dialectical interaction between the two realms. Humor, in the surrealist synthesis, combines the Hegelian point of the "objectivity" of humor with the Freudian point of the defensive activity of the unconscious when confronted with unpropitious external conditions. There is, then, in the surrealist view of humor, as in the Freudian, something liberating: it achieves pleasure through the activity of the mind—the ego affirms its victory over external reality by refusing to let itself be overwhelmed by that reality, by even finding means to pleasure in it.

[122] Breton, "Surrealism Yesterday, To-Day, and To-Morrow," trans. by E. W. Titus, *This Quarter*, V, no. 1 (September, 1932), 42.

The supreme example of humor that conquers the world is Alfred Jarry's *Ubu Roi*, which Breton subjected to an analysis in Freudian terms in order to determine the source of its liberating power:

The *id* arrogates to itself, under the name of Ubu, the right to correct, to punish which belongs in fact only to the *super-ego*. . . . The *id,* promoted to supreme power, proceeds immediately to the elimination of all noble sentiments . . . of the feeling of guilt . . . and of the feeling of social dependence. . . . The aggressiveness of the hypermoral *super-ego* toward the *ego* is thus transferred to the totally amoral *id* and gives complete license to its destructive tendencies. Humor, as a process which permits the pushing aside of the distressing elements of reality, is here exercised only at the expense of others. . . .

Such, according to us, is the profound significance of the character of Ubu.[123]

This kind of destructive—and at the same time protective—humor was called *black humor* by the surrealists; but the distinction between black humor and objective humor is, at best, a tenuous one: they tend to merge into one another. Breton admitted that black humor cannot be defined comprehensively, that it cannot be made explicit in order to serve didactic ends. In any case, it excludes skeptical irony, the innocent joke and, above all, sentimentality. It is not Rabelais's laughter, nor yet Voltaire's, but rather Swift's. The essential difference between these last two, Breton noted, is that Voltaire sees all things through his reason, never his feelings, that he has taken refuge in skepticism, and is in the grip of a perpetual mocking laughter; while Swift, glacial and impassive, takes things in an inverse manner, is forever indignant, and provokes laughter which he does not share.[124] He occupies first place in the surrealist

[123] Breton, *Anthologie de l'humour noir,* p. 273.
[124] *Ibid.,* pp. 19–20.

pantheon of black humorists as the real initiator of the "ferocious and dismal jest."

Another favorite of the surrealists is Lewis Carroll, whose *Hunting of the Snark* was translated in 1928 by Louis Aragon and in whose "nonsense" Breton found another example of the reconciliation of opposites:

Lewis Carroll's "nonsense" draws its importance from the fact that it constitutes for him the vital resolution of a profound contradiction between, on the one hand, the acceptance of faith and the exercise of reason; on the other, between an acute poetic consciousness and rigorous professional duties. The characteristic of this subjective solution is that it also takes an objective form which is precisely of a poetic order: the mind [*esprit*], face to face with all kinds of difficulties, finds an ideal outlet in *the absurd*.[125]

Humor is, then, another victory of man over the external world. By laughing at the world, man destroys its power over his own subjectivity; if he can go one step further and laugh at his own despair, he can destroy the power of his own emotions—he succeeds then in completely alienating himself from the world and from his ordinary self. If he can laugh at himself, it is because he treats himself as if he were someone else. By this process, he abandons to the world that part of himself that is irretrievably engaged and retreats into his alter ego where he enjoys absolute detachment and freedom.[126] Or, to put it in Freudian terms, black humor is the extreme means by which the ego surmounts the traumas of the external world and demonstrates that for the great distresses of the ego, the remedy can come only from the id.[127] In this respect, objective humor serves a function

[125] *Ibid.*, pp. 140–141.
[126] Carrouges, *André Breton et les données*, pp. 113–114.
[127] Breton, *Entretiens*, p. 231.

analogous to that of automatism; it removes the emotional pressure on man of the external world and permits the conscious to feel the magnetic impulses of the unconscious. In other words, it discredits the immediacy of the external world and creates a kind of vacuum in which the forces of the unconscious may make themselves felt. Like automatism, it prepares the ground for the occurrence of objective chance. In its power to liberate man from bondage to the external, to raise him from despair to omnipotence, black humor is, in Breton's view, a modern analogue to magic or alchemy in that it initiates man into modes of feeling and being which point toward his eventual liberation from logic and reason, and to the freedom that must result from that liberation. Black humor is an essential step in the mental alchemy needed to reach the supreme point of the surreal. Or, in Breton's typical oracular language, "the black sphinx of objective humor cannot fail to meet on the dusty road, the road of the future, the white sphinx of objective chance, and all ulterior human creation will be the fruit of their embrace." [128]

CONCLUSION

The foregoing presentation of surrealist doctrine under various headings tends unavoidably toward an artificial schematization and fragmentation of what is a remarkably unitary, not to say organic, and, in many ways, revolutionary point of view; but everything points to the one purpose: to repossess for man those parts of the universe that he has lost. But in order to achieve this profoundly humanistic goal, man must first overcome the schism within himself that artificially separates him from the deepest sources of his

[128] Breton, *Anthologie de l'humour noir*, p. 13.

own being. This schism is the result of prejudice that accords greater value to rationality, to the products of the ego, to daylight reality than to the other side of the coin—to the unconscious, to the dream, to desire. Freud, who has, if not uncovered the unconscious, at least attempted to establish its existence and reality on "scientific" bases, had in the eyes of the surrealists betrayed the value of his discovery by straining his efforts toward bringing "the content of our psychic inner world" under the rule of logic, toward making man accept the superior value and reality of the outside world. The surrealists, using Freud's own discoveries, in a manner of speaking turned him upside down: now that the existence of the unconscious is established, it must be granted equal status—an equal degree of reality—with the conscious. What seemed at first in the surrealist program a perverse aberration from "normal" modes of perception and cognition—that is, the insistence that the unconscious, revealed in automatism, possesses equal value and reality with the conscious—soon, under the impetus of the doctrine of "objective chance," found that the unconscious is as clearly involved with the objective world as the conscious, that the unconscious in fact can be prophetic of events in the outer world.

Up to this point, surrealism seemed like little more than an extreme form of the romantic preference for the inner psychic world over the hard, unresponsive, external world. The principle of "objective chance" is an explosive rebuttal of the accusation leveled against the surrealists that they had sacrificed the outer world to the inner. They could now claim that, instead of repudiating the outer world, they were, on the contrary, more deeply involved with it than any rationalist could be. The charge of solipsistic individualism crumbles before the proofs that the surrealists adduced for the existence of the subtle net of correspondences that links the individual unconscious to the objective world. That world, in fact, in unexpected and inexplicable ways, responds to the unconscious, to man's desires. The surrealists succeeded, in Bachelard's striking phrase, in "translating desires into metamorphoses." [129]

Once the principle was grasped by the surrealists, they considerably modified their emphases: they ceased to claim exclusive rights for the unconscious and to desire the obliteration of the rational. The mind immerses in the unconscious, but, as we have seen in the discussions of automatism, a large degree of lucidity is preserved in order to guide the process of automatism and understand what it reveals—for it is only through understanding that the links that bind the unconscious and the outside world are revealed. The title of Dali's *Conquest of the Irrational* is deliberately ambiguous: the irrational is both conqueror and conquered.

With this shift in emphasis came a gradual redefinition of the surreal. At first it seemed little more than the Freudian unconscious, a child's paradise in which everything is possible, in which all juxtapositions seem revelatory of a new reality. But, it must be admitted, this new reality is a highly individual and subjective one. What syntheses are achieved here are merely those of the startling image, usually put together by chance, as in the game of "exquisite corpse" or in the writing of poems with words cut out of newspapers and tossed into a hat. These often produce startling and amusing conjunctions, but beyond providing a new means of breaking the rules of rationality—a salutary but still subjective exercise—their "value" as fragments of reality is practically nil. It is one thing to claim objective validity for these children of automatism or chance; it is

[129] Bachelard, *Lautréamont*, pp. 126–127.

another to prove it. They possess reality, but they do not correspond to anything in the objective world.

But when an unconscious desire is suddenly fulfilled, when an object seen in a dream is found in the Flea Market, when the impossible coincidence occurs, or when a poem written in a state of automatism proves revelatory of real events, then the products of the unconscious assume a different degree of validity. The unconscious irrupts into the waking world and somehow makes that world respond to it —or, rather, reveals an affinity between it and the world. Surrealism, whether verbal or visual, introduces us into a world of the marvelous which is at first subjective and personal but which very soon becomes "intersubjective," "transpersonal." [130] These discoveries—that the mind in a state of automatism and the objective world correspond—rather than leading to a redefinition of surrealism in the direction of the transcendental, reaffirmed instead, as Breton says, the "desire to deepen the foundations of the real, to bring about an ever clearer and at the same time ever more passionate consciousness of the world perceived by the senses." [131]

The attempt to bring about a "more passionate consciousness" led surrealism to the edge of the occult and to the recognition that the "transmutation of man" that is the basis of all hermeticism is closely analogous to the surrealist plan to "transform man." The purpose of this transformation is to reintroduce him into the paradise he lost when he allowed his disintegration to occur and gave his allegiance to only one part of himself. The alchemist's dream of recovering the philosopher's stone became the same as the surrealist's dream of reaching the supreme point of total reintegration

[130] These words are Monnerot's, *La Poésie moderne et le sacré*, p. 135.

[131] *What Is Surrealism?*, p. 128.

of man with himself and with his universe—the final synthesis which would constitute the resolution of all human contradictions.

Until very recently, the surrealist program for the transformation of human life has been largely ignored in favor of its productions in the literary and plastic arts. I say "until very recently" because certain revolutionary manifestations in contemporary thought—those embodied in Norman O. Brown's *Life against Death* and Herbert Marcuse's *Eros and Civilization,* for example, or in the current drug cults, in revolutionary moral and sexual attitudes—all bear startling similarities with the surrealist program. Surrealism is not an artistic or literary movement, Breton insisted with constant iteration. It is, as Cyril Connolly rightly said, "a new interpretation of life"; [132] it is an attempt at arriving at a new declaration of the rights of man, Aragon said. As far as literature is concerned, surrealism is an extension of romanticism, but it exceeds the usual limits of literature because it wishes much less to produce literature than to bring man into a fantastic world of marvels, to organize the analysis and conquest of that world. This desire, says Carrouges, explains Breton's interest in both the procedures of psychoanalysis and in the esoteric and metapsychic perspectives opened by the practice of automatism. [133]

The tools of surrealism are poetry and painting, but these must be understood for what they are: their purpose is extra-artistic—they are meant to make man *see.* As William Carlos Williams perceptively said: "By retaining a firmness of extraordinary word juxtapositions while dealing wholly with a world with which the usual mind is unfamiliar a counter-foil to the vague and excessively stupid juxtapositions com-

132 Cyril Connolly, "Farewell to Surrealism," p. 30.
133 Carrouges, *André Breton et les données,* p. 143.

monly known as 'reality' is created. The effect is to revive the senses and force them to re-see, re-hear, re-taste, re-smell, and generally re-value all that it was believed had been seen, heard, smelled, and generally valued." [134]

As philosophy, that is, as a guide to action, surrealism has undoubtedly so far failed—there are few signs that its passage has been noted or its message heeded, except by a few, but the nobility of its humanism is undeniable. For a time, the gates of the marvelous seemed about to be opened, life seemed fuller of possibilities—every moment seemed full of meaning, of possible revelation; every encounter, even the most trivial, could be the beginning of a new insight, a new contact with the unknown, perhaps even a new life.

[134] Introduction to Charles Henri Ford, *The Garden of Disorder and Other Poems* (London: Europa Press, 1938), p. 9.

2 | English Beginnings

～～～～～ The progress of surrealism across the Channel to England was gradual. One must assume that there were always people in England who kept abreast of new artistic and literary developments on the Continent, but one cannot speak of an English surrealist movement until evidences of it appeared in English publications. This did not happen until the early thirties. Before that time, occasional notices of dadaist and then surrealist activity appeared in publications that were concerned with cultural exchanges among America, England, and France. Of these, *transition* was, of course, the most important, but there were others.

Among the first to take note of the new movement was the *Little Review*, which, after moving to New York from Paris in 1917, retained Ezra Pound as its foreign editor and under his direction devoted much attention to new trends in both English and French letters. Among its frequent contributors were T. S. Eliot, W. B. Yeats, and, of course, James Joyce.

In the July–August, 1920, issue, John Rodker quoted and tried to explain some dada verses in an article that initiated the *Little Review*'s interest in the new movement. The next issue but one (January–March, 1921), printed some untranslated verse by Louis Aragon and Philippe Soupault, together with a two-page spread entitled "Dada soulève tout." In Autumn, 1921, Francis Picabia joined the editorial board of the magazine, and until 1926, every important member of the dada-surrealist group appeared in its pages: Picabia himself, Tzara, Ribemont-Dessaignes, Man Ray, Breton, Eluard, Aragon, Baron, Soupault, Péret, Reverdy, Crevel, Mesens, Rigaut, Leiris, Limbour. It even printed "A Rotten Corpse," a translation of the famous surrealist attack on Anatole France, in the Autumn–Winter, 1924, issue.

Interestingly enough, no explanation or theoretical justification of dada-surrealism ever appeared in the *Little Review,* with the insignificant exception of Rodker's initial piece. The same assumption that its readers knew what the movement was all about was shared by Ford Madox Ford's *Transatlantic Review,* which began its life in Paris in January, 1924. For its first few numbers, Ford had engaged two leading surrealists, Philippe Soupault and René Crevel, to report on literary activity in Paris. But curiously, Soupault, who had collaborated with Breton on the first surrealist texts, *Les Champs magnétiques* (1919), and coedited several of the surrealist periodicals, made no mention of surrealist activity in his "Letter from Paris" in the first, second, and fifth numbers of the *Transatlantic Review* (January, February, and May, 1924). This is doubly puzzling when one remembers that 1924 was the year of the official birth of surrealism, the date of its first manifesto. The only possible explanation is that, even for a collaborator in the inception of the new movement, it was at the time an event of interest only to a small coterie. The April, 1924, number of the *Review,* however, printed several poems by Jacques Baron, later a member of the surrealist group. These poems are not surrealist—more than anything else they bear the stamp of Apollinaire. In the same number, René Crevel, reporting on new books from Paris, mentioned dada and books by Louis Aragon, Philippe Soupault, and Tristan Tzara. The article contained no word about surrealism and no explanation of dada, but only a passing remark that dada's campaign against "all dogmatism" had had its effect. The same number contained several fragments from Tristan Tzara's *Monsieur Aa l'anti-philosophe*. Ernest Hemingway, reporting to America for the *Review*, wrote in the May, 1924, issue, "Dada is dead although Tzara still cuddles its emaciated little corpse to his breast and croons a Roumanian folksong written by Princess Bibesco, while he tries to get the dead little lips to take sustenance from his monocle."

René Crevel, again reporting on new books, took sharp issue in the August, 1924, number with some aspects of surrealist activity. After announcing the death of dada, "since, as Tristan Tzara has said, *the lack of system is still a system*," he took Aragon and Breton severely to task for being literary. Breton, he said, "proclaims . . . *Let go of your wife, let go of your friends, let go of everything!* but lets go of nothing . . . [and] I think that he is making fun of me . . . [that] he is not really taking himself seriously and speaks not as a *man*, but as a *man of letters*." Both in Aragon's *Libertinage* and in Breton's *Les Pas perdus*, "one feels the desire for some monstrous torment rather than the torment itself, which leads to the feeling of a certain lack of purity." And then, most damning of all, "for not having gone down into the street where, after all, more surprises await us than in the most beautiful pages of Lautréamont, in the verses of Reverdy and Germain Nouveau, Louis Aragon and André Breton fall into literature." What is significant about this statement, aside from its inherent interest, is that Crevel and, presumably, Ford himself counted on considerable literary sophistication on the part of the Anglo-American readers of the *Transatlantic Review* and assumed that they understood what Crevel was talking about.

Except for seven poems by Tristan Tzara in the last number (January, 1925), these few comments represent all of the *Review*'s reportage of dada and surrealist matters. Although it is difficult to ascertain how well known the *Review* was in England, it is probably safe to assume that, in view of the eminence of its editor and its distinguished list of contributors, it was widely read. In addition to publishing the first excerpts from Joyce's *Work in Progress* in the April, 1924, issue, it printed a part of Gertrude Stein's *The Making of Americans*, verse by Ezra Pound, E. E. Cummings, William Carlos Williams; fiction by Dorothy Richardson, Ernest Hemingway, John Dos Passos; and criticism by Ford Madox Ford.

In England proper, F. S. Flint, reviewing French periodicals for T. S. Eliot's *Criterion*, took occasional although consistently hostile notice of surrealist activity across the Channel. In the July and December, 1925, numbers, he dismissed surrealism in harsh, contemptuous, and essentially ignorant terms. This, from the man who had always been extremely sympathetic to modern French literature, and who had done so much a decade earlier to familiarize the British public with the newest French poetry, represents a curious hostility, or at least an unwillingness to find out what the new movement was about.

The first English-language magazine to welcome surrealist doctrine was *transition*, which began publication in Paris in April, 1927. The fact that sections of James Joyce's *Work in Progress* appeared fairly regularly in *transition* assured the magazine a large number of English readers.

The second number of *transition* (May, 1927) published

the first English translations, by Eugene Jolas, of Paul Eluard: several prose passages from *Les Dessous d'une vie* and several poems from *Capitale de la douleur*. In the same issue, Robert Sage used the occasion of a review of Louis Aragon's *Le Paysan de Paris* to present the fundamental tenets of surrealism. Quoting with approval Aragon's statement that "nothing can assure me of reality. Nothing, neither the exactness of logic nor the strength of a sensation, can assure me that I do not base it on the delirium of interpretation," Sage used it as a springboard for an attack on the limitations of realistic writing, which prohibit the free play of the imagination: "The dream and thought tangents of an imaginative person organized upon paper or canvas do not vulgarly 'mean' anything, yet they are no less real than a brick house. Their reality supersedes that of the realists for it merges the internal and the external and floats creation above copy."

The next number of *transition* (June, 1927), in addition to some nonsense poems by the dadaist Kurt Schwitters ("Blue is the color of thy yellow hair/Red is the whirl of thy green wheels") and translations of works by Georges Ribemont-Dessaignes, contained an editorial which echoes some surrealist principles:

We believe in the ideology of revolt against all diluted and synthetic poetry, against all artistic efforts that fail to subvert the existing concepts of beauty. . . . We prefer the skyscraper spirituality, the immense lyricism and madness of illogic.

We are no longer interested in the photography of events . . . let [the poet] not forget that only the dream is essential.

By re-establishing the simplicity of the word, we may find again its old magnificence. Gertrude Stein, James Joyce, Hart Crane, Louis Aragon, André Breton, Léon-Paul Fargue . . . are showing us the way. . . . Are not the workings of the instincts and the mysteries of the shadows more beautiful than the sterile world of beauty we have known? [1]

The August, 1927, issue contained André Breton's important *Introduction au discours sur le peu de réalité* in a translation by Eugene Jolas. In this essay, Breton had laid the foundations for the surrealists' rejection of external reality, basing his argument on a refusal to accept the trustworthiness of sense-perceptions. It is in this essay, also, that Breton called for the fabrication of objects seen in dreams.

In the same issue, Elliot Paul, the coeditor of the magazine, welcomed the symptoms of the breakdown of conventional logic and of the conventional uses of language: "If logic is to crash for such trivial reasons as innovations in grammar, spelling and syntax or because a few fresh flowers are placed upon its balconies, I say, 'Let it crash.'"

The campaign waged by *transition* against conventional literature and conventional modes of perception, a campaign which, clearly, owes much to the surrealist program, brought down on the heads of its editors the wrath of Wyndham Lewis. In January, 1927, Lewis had started *The Enemy*, a periodical which, as its name indicates, was resolutely opposed to much that was current in the arts. Lewis's great enemy was the idea of time, flux, change: "As a *realist* . . . what is the strongest impression you receive from the external world, or nature? Certainly stability, I, as a realist, should say: decidedly not one of change." [2] The philosophy of flux, Lewis said, provided an excuse to escape from the real and concrete moment into an artificial mental state, to

[1] Eugene Jolas and Elliot Paul, "Suggestions for a New Magic," *transition*, no. 3 (June, 1927), pp. 178–179.

[2] Wyndham Lewis, *Time and Western Man* (Boston: Beacon Press, 1957), p. 205; first published in 1927.

avoid individuality, to embrace the infantile and the primitive.[3]

The whole modern age is marked, he said, by its "progressive prescission of all that is individual, its rage to extinguish the independent life of persons."[4] His own position is best summarized by a later statement: "In contrast to the jelly-fish that floats in the centre of the subterranean stream of the 'dark' unconscious, I much prefer, for my part, the shield of the tortoise, or the rigid stylistic articulations of the grasshopper."[5] For Lewis, the danger of the "time-philosophy" and its artistic expression is that they destroy the stability that he, as a realist, saw in nature:

The actual merging of the dream-condition and the waking-condition (of *the external* and *the internal*) must result in a logical emulsion of the forms and perspective of life as we know them. Translated into art-expression, it will approximate most closely to the art of the child. That is, of course, what has already everywhere occurred with the theorists of that persuasion. The *infantile* is the link between the Super-realists and Miss Stein.[6]

Since reality, especially the reality of art, Lewis insists, is already a merging of the external and the internal, super-reality would result in a "radical shifting of the normal real towards the *unconscious* pole. If thoroughly effective it would result, even, in a submergence of the normal, conscious real into the unconscious."[7]

The second number of *The Enemy* (September, 1927) contained a long and typically intemperate attack on *tran-*

[3] *Ibid.*, p. 36 and *passim.*

[4] "Editorial," *The Enemy*, no. 1 (January, 1927), p. x.

[5] *Men without Art* (London: Cassell, 1934), p. 120.

[6] *The Diabolical Principle and the Dithyrambic Spectator* (London: Chatto & Windus, 1931), p. 65.

[7] *Ibid.*, p. 67.

sition for providing a forum in English for the surrealists, "the intellectual wing . . . of the communist party in Paris," for publishing James Joyce and Gertrude Stein; for, in general, being on the side of the unconscious.

In their reply to Lewis, the editors of *transition* reaffirmed their principles ("We believe that only the dream matters"[8]) and clarified their differences with orthodox surrealism:

Our conception of literature . . . is not the formalized one of the Surrealists. We believe with them that the artist's imagination should be placed above everything else in importance, but we do not hold with them that writing should be exclusively of the interior. . . . We believe in a new romanticism . . . which achieves magic by combining the interior and the exterior, the subjective and the objective, the imaginary and the apparently real.[9]

Written in 1927, three years before Breton's "Second manifeste," this statement is a striking anticipation of the manifesto's central doctrine of the supreme point in which all antitheses are resolved. The crucial difference between the *transition* credo and the doctrine elaborated in the manifesto, however, is that the former is concerned exclusively with art and literature.

In June, 1929, *transition* issued its famous "Proclamation," which announced the "Revolution of the Word." Some of its points bear a close resemblance to certain fundamental tenets of surrealism:

The imagination in search of a fabulous world is autonomous and unconfined.

[8] Eugene Jolas, Elliot Paul, and Robert Sage, "First Aid to the Enemy," *transition*, no. 9 (December, 1927), p. 168.
[9] *Ibid.*, p. 175.

Pure poetry is a lyrical absolute that seeks an a priori reality within ourselves alone.

The literary creator has the right to disintegrate the primal matter of words imposed . . . by dictionaries.

The writer expresses. He does not communicate.

Eugene Jolas supplied a theoretical justification for the Proclamation:

[The poet] feels it to be his function to create the unity of an organism which is composed of elements by nature hostile to each other. Through the autonomy of his visionary operations, he proceeds to the synthesis which alone can satisfy him. He brings together realities far removed from each other, that seem without any organic relationships, that are even tending to mutual destruction. But his imagination demolishes the tyranny of the world by eliminating its customary analogies and substituting new ones.

In order to give spontaneous and radical expression to this impulse, the poet becomes a composer of the word.

The similarity of this to surrealist doctrine is so evident that it requires no elaboration.

Wyndham Lewis, in the meantime, had responded to *transition*'s reply to his initial attack. In June, 1929, Eugene Jolas, in turn, answered in an essay entitled "The Innocuous Enemy," which is important for defining the areas of agreement and disagreement between Jolas and the surrealists. The basic difference was Jolas's rejection of the surrealists' political commitment. Next in importance is a philosophical difference: "While [the surrealists] were determined to completely deny the physical world, basing themselves on a Hegelian interpretation, I continued to believe in the possibility of metamorphosing the real. I envisaged a dualism, I believed that the external world should be made the basis from which to proceed into the supernatural and the magical." Other objections to the surrealists were "that, after applying Freudian and Dadaist discoveries, they did not transcend them," [10] that they "refused to consider the problem of the word in the struggle of a new reality," [11] and that they were willing to limit their revolutionary activity within the confines of the traditional style.

Although he recognized the signal service that surrealism had performed in the rebellion against convention, Jolas finally rejected surrealist doctrine for restrictively assigning value to the products of the unconscious only, for failing "to see that there is a difference between the symbols of the dream and those of art," [12] thereby missing the point of the surrealists' claim that they were not interested in "art."

In June, 1930, *transition* reprinted, from the Cambridge magazine *Experiment,* "Dreams," a short article by the young English painter Julian Trevelyan, later a contributor to the International Surrealist Exhibition in London. The essay demonstrates that the surrealist campaign did not go unnoticed in England; for, although it shows a naive, romantic disregard for Freud, it extols the dream as a fruitful source of creative inspiration:

In the state of dreaming . . . the mind loses that self-consciousness which in its waking hours it can never quite banish, and begins to move silently through a timeless, spaceless world, where neither Destiny nor Chance have stepped . . . [where]

[10] Jolas, "Notes on Reality," *transition,* no. 18 (November, 1929), p. 19.
[11] Jolas, "Literature and the New Man," *transition,* no. 19–20 (June, 1930), p. 14.
[12] Jolas, "The King's English is Dying—Long Live the American Language," *ibid.,* p. 144.

the tension which relates mind to matter in the waking hours disappears. . . . Aesthetic pleasure justifies itself in the fantasies of a dream-world. . . . Let us gladly shout TO DREAM IS TO CREATE.

After its June, 1930, number, *transition* suspended publication for almost two years. When it reappeared, in March, 1932, as *Transition,* Eugene Jolas had developed the philosophy he called "Vertigralism," best summarized in the following items from the manifesto, signed by Jolas, Hans Arp, Samuel Beckett, and others, entitled "Poetry Is Vertical":

The reality of depth can be conquered by a voluntary mediumistic conjuration, by a stupor which proceeds from the irrational to a world beyond a world.

The transcendental "I" with its multiple stratifications reaching back millions of years is related to the entire history of mankind, past and present, and is brought to the surface with the hallucinatory irruption of images in the dream, the daydream, the mystic-gnostic trance, and even the psychiatric condition.

Poetry builds a nexus between the "I" and the "you" by leading the emotions of the sunken telluric depths upward toward the illumination of a collective reality and a totalistic universe.

Vertigralism accepted some of the irrationalism of surrealism, but it rejected automatism as an end in itself and, of course, the Marxist commitment. Leaning heavily on Jung's idea of the collective unconscious, Jolas proclaimed that through the "night mind," that is, through the states of hypnotic trance, of dreaming or half-waking, contact with the "world-soul" is achieved. The revelation of this contact becomes the proper function of art.

The "Revolution of the Word," according to Jolas, owes

its genesis to Rimbaud, the futurists, the early dadaists, Gertrude Stein, Léon-Paul Fargue; "it owes nothing to Surrealism." [13] The insufficiency of the surrealists, Jolas insisted, lay in their inability "to see that the expression of the unconscious demanded new means. It was not enough to whirl the unaccustomed realities of the dream-state together. It was essential . . . to express the nocturnal world with a nocturnal language. It was essential to find a means of creating the a-logical grammar which alone can mirror the new dimension." [14]

In the following sample of the new revolutionary language and grammar, Jolas recounted a dream:

The sun of the organ withdraws into a name. The jowlers creakling in the rolapane lip risarills. All the dranamidosas wait for the nigthblessed wonders. This is the manitoulade of the lalopeer. Is the brilune in the ralstamine? There is a trembleglance that flashsends verbs. The transcendence of the singthroats strikes the substantives. All things are mine. A villalope grilltosses drastalures.[15]

The superficial resemblance of this to the language of Joyce's *Finnegans Wake* is obvious—but whereas Joyce's artificial words awaken an almost endless resonance because of their fullness of content, Jolas's seem to be either puerile combinations of real words (flashsends, singthroats) or of nonsense syllables (dranamidosas, lalopeer, ralstamine). It is equally obvious that this linguistic revolution owes nothing to surrealism except the right to be irrational. But again

[13] Jolas, "What Is the Revoluton of Language," *Transition,* no. 22 (February, 1933), p. 125.

[14] Jolas, "From a Letter," *ibid.,* p. 113.

[15] Jolas, "From a Dream Book," *Transition,* no. 25 (Fall, 1936), p. 165.

a distinction must be made: the surrealist irrationality is the irrationality of the dream, which, we know, has a logic and significance of its own; what is one to make of "This is the manitoulade of the lalopeer"?

The fundamental difference between the surrealists and the editors of *Transition* hinges on two points. The surrealists seemed to Jolas to depend too much upon the unconscious, at the expense of other manifestations of reality. The necessary concomitant of this attitude is an ever-increasing monotony—as any reader of surrealist texts can testify. This criticism was to be directed against surrealism by surrealists themselves, notably Nicolas Calas and André Masson. Jolas anticipated later surrealist doctrine in his attempt to combine the interior and exterior worlds of man's experience, without, however, submitting to the Hegelian and Marxist justification for this synthesis. Jolas went further than the surrealists in his adoption of Jungian doctrine and his emphasis on the supernatural, which, we have seen, the surrealists reject vehemently. *Transition,* Jolas wrote, seeks to "destroy the dualism between the individual and the universe, idea and reality, spirit and nature, God and the world." [16]

Whatever direction *Transition* may have taken in its later years, its service to surrealism was a very real one. It was the first magazine to bring surrealism to an Anglo-American public. As Stuart Gilbert has explained,[17] the surrealists were a fiercely exclusive group and did not, at the time, publish outside their own review, *La Révolution Surréaliste,*

[16] Jolas, *"Transition:* An Epilogue," *American Mercury,* XXIII, no. 189 (June, 1931), 190.

[17] "Five Years of *Transition," Transition,* no. 22 (February, 1933), p. 141.

and its successor, *Le Surréalisme au Service de la Révolution*. It was Eugene Jolas's friendship with the surrealists that enabled him to publish translations of their texts.

Another and perhaps more important exception to surrealist exclusivity occurred in September, 1932. Edward W. Titus, the editor of *This Quarter*, another American magazine published in Paris, concerned with the inaccessibility of the work of the surrealists to English and American readers, devoted a whole number of the magazine to a presentation of surrealist theory and texts in translation. Editorship of this special number was turned over to André Breton, and the only restrictions imposed upon him were that he "eschew politics and such other topics that might not be in honeyed accord with Anglo-American censorship usages." [18] The result is one of the best treatments of surrealism to be found anywhere.

Breton himself contributed a long essay, "Surrealism Yesterday, To-Day, and To-Morrow," a concise presentation of surrealist doctrine, in which he acknowledged the debt of surrealism to several English precursors: Swift, "who is found complete in Jarry and Vaché"; the Horace Walpole of *The Castle of Otranto;* Mrs. Radcliffe, "whom Lautréamont calls the 'crazy spectre' "; Monk Lewis, who had contributed " 'the indispensable revolutionary impulses' which had begun to agitate the Europe of that time"; Charles Maturin, who "is described by Lautréamont as *'le compère des ténèbres' ";* Edward Young, "unquestionably the most authentic forerunner of the surrealist style, whose secret Lautréamont was the first to appropriate: 'O nights of Young! You have given me many a headache!' "; and, finally, J. M. Synge, whose *Playboy of the Western World*

[18] Edward W. Titus, "Editorially: By Way of Introducing This Surrealist Number," *This Quarter*, V, no. 1 (September, 1932), 6.

"alone links us with him—a play whose poetical and moral career is still far from being terminated." [19]

Breton traced the development of surrealism from its automatic beginnings through the second manifesto with its emphasis on the occult and on the synthesis of man's external and internal worlds: "One may express the essential characteristic of surrealism by saying that 'it seeks to calculate the quotient of the unconscious by the conscious.'" Breton concluded by stressing the commitment of surrealism to the world: "In the same measure as we continue to hold surrealist expression to be definitely committed to the automatism I have stressed, we shall also—and this must be clear by now—cling to our critical attitude with regard to the various intellectual and moral problems of contemporary interest."

In addition to this essay by Breton, several other important accounts of surrealist theory were included: Dali's "The Stinking Ass" (an explanation of Dali's double images and paranoiac activity), translated by J. Bronowski, editor of the Cambridge magazine *Experiment;* Dali's important essay, "The Object as Revealed in Surrealist Experiment," [20] René Crevel's "The Period of Sleeping Fits," an account of early surrealist experiments in hypnosis and automatism; Paul Eluard's "Poetry's Evidence," translated by Samuel Beckett —an early version of an essay that later appeared in England; and Max Ernst's "Inspiration to Order," one of the basic texts of surrealist painting—an explanation of frottage, collage, and automatism in painting. Also included, in addition to the theoretical material, was a small anthology of surrealist works in translation: works of Benjamin Péret, Breton, Eluard, and Tzara, translated by Beckett; Marcel

[19] Trans. by E. W. Titus, *ibid.,* 9–10.
[20] See Chapter 1, pp. 32–34.

Duchamp's notes for his painting "The Bride Stripped Bare by Her Bachelors, Even," translated by J. Bronowski; and the complete scenario of the Dali-Buñuel film "An Andalusian Dog" ("Un Chien Andalou").

In England itself, notices of surrealist activity—mainly in painting—appeared sporadically during the early 1930's in such periodicals as the *Spectator*, the *New Statesman and Nation*, and the *Criterion*.

Early in the career of surrealism, Montgomery Belgion, a regular contributor to T. S. Eliot's *Criterion*, devoted an essay to a detailed criticism of the assumptions of surrealist theory.[21] Responding to the surrealist's claim that the "real operation of thought" is revealed by automatism, Belgion argued that this revelation can be effected only on the spectator or reader, that the artist cannot tell whether there is or is not revelation, only the spectator can, and that the surrealists have neglected to bring forward the spectator's testimony. The surrealist claim of revealing the operation of thought free of rational control is, Belgion insists, based on a misconception: "What we always do is, first to think, and then, only afterwards, to see if our thought is rational. Logic does not show us how to think; it merely tells us if what we have thought is valid." Further, the fact that the surrealist at work is unaware of the control of reason over his thought does not mean that reason is inactive; it means that he may be unconscious of its activity: "Whenever we think, there appears to be a tendency to think rationally or logically as far as we are able, and this tendency is not affected by our being conscious or unconscious of it." In arguing that using dreams in writing does not require "psychic automatism,"

21 "Meaning in Art," *The Criterion*, IX, no. 35 (January, 1930), 201–216.

Belgion adduces the example of "Kubla Khan," which was "conceived in a dream. But it was not written when its author was in a state of psychic automatism."

It is not entirely clear what the point of this argument is; if it is that we are never completely free of the restraining forces of reason, then the surrealist would surely agree; but this fact does not negate the value of the attempt to free oneself from these restraining forces. Similarly, the example of Coleridge's "Kubla Khan" proves nothing except that Coleridge was not a surrealist poet and that "Kubla Khan" is not a surrealist poem. "Kubla Khan" was frequently used by English critics as a stick to beat the surrealists with, always with the same lack of relevance. Belgion's criticism, however, differs from that of many others in that he was willing to discuss the subject seriously; but like so many opponents of surrealism, he spends his arrows on an illusory target: what he presents as surrealism has little resemblance to the doctrine.

The tone of many of the notices of surrealism, which were, in the main, reviews of exhibitions, was one of amused curiosity, gentle condescension, honest English puzzlement, or, sometimes, downright anger.

Peter Quennell, who surely knew better, started a short article in the *New Statesman and Nation* by saying: "The horrid question—'What is it all about? Perhaps there is something in it after all; something that I am too dense to capture?' haunts our imagination when we think of Surrealism." [22] In order to reassure his readers that there was little new in surrealism, Quennell pointed to pre-surrealists —Nerval, Carroll, Mrs. Radcliffe, Young, Coleridge, Blake— and added, "Unconscious associations, phrases and rhythms

[22] "Surrealism and Revolution," *New Statesman and Nation*, VI, no. 131 (n.s.) (August 26, 1933), 237–238.

that derive their value from the forgotten past, and which reach the paper as unaccountably as 'spirit messages,' are part of the fabric of most poems." He complained that much surrealist art was intended to "shock, alarm, annoy and distress"; that Dali was preoccupied with "sadistic extravagances"; but he concluded, oddly, by saying that "one's own nightmares [are] usually more picturesque." In other words, there is nothing new in surrealism, but it is extravagant, sadistic, alarming, and, besides, our nightmares are better. Striking a more serious note, however, he saw in the tendency of surrealism to exploit violence for its own sake a symptom "of a larger movement of which the spread has begun to be felt all over the world."

Alexander Watt, the art critic of the *New Statesman and Nation,* was less condescending and a good deal angrier. In a review of the Dali exhibition at the Zwemmer Gallery in 1934, he attempted to discredit surrealist doctrine by the simple device of making one tenet of the doctrine stand for the whole. He noted that Dali's paintings had received both severe and laudatory criticism and attributed this to the surrealists being Marxists. Watt treated the subject of his review in much the same manner: "The art of Salvador Dali is not art . . . it is psycho-sexual exposition; it is literature. . . . And who is interested in the fantastic manifestation of a strange individual's sexual repressions?" Refusing to grant any merit to Dali's work, he added, "I am . . . stung to infer that the bright colour schemes in Dali's paintings may be due to heightened blood pressure." [23]

The same Dali exhibition elicited similar comments from the reviewer for *Apollo,* the well-known art magazine. Dali's works, he said, "are aesthetically as delightful as they are morally or ethically repulsive. . . . The wheel has come

[23] "Salvador Dali," *New Statesman and Nation,* VIII, no. 184 (n.s.) (September 1, 1934), 264.

full circle again, and . . . in these *surréaliste* works abstract design has gone by the board, and we are once more in the thick of literary subject interest. But what subjects!" [24]

Anthony Blunt of the *Spectator,* in reviewing the exhibition of post-cubist art held at the Mayor Gallery in the spring of 1933, at least treated surrealist painting seriously and tried to show its position as the successor to cubism.[25]

Michael Roberts, in the *Criterion,* struck a note which was to become the refrain of English commentary on surrealism—that surrealism is little more than the reaffirmation of the ideas of the romantic age concerning the imagination; that there is little that is fundamentally new in surrealism; that all poets, in a sense, are surrealists. Roberts quoted from E. S. Dallas's *The Gay Science* (1866): "There is a mental existence within us . . . which is not less energetic than the conscious flow, an absent mind which haunts us like a ghost. . . . To lay bare the automatic or unconscious action of the mind is indeed to unfold a tale which outvies the romances of giants and ginns, wizards in their palaces." Roberts added: "When we consider the poetry of Young, Coleridge and Shelley, and their successors, the Symbolists and the Surrealists, we recognize the force of that contention [of E. S. Dallas], especially if we remember that the poet's imagination at the moment of uncontrolled phantasy-building, or inspiration, is primarily verbal." [26]

These comments and reviews are fairly typical of the general attitude toward surrealism in England during the early 1930's. It was not until 1935 that knowledge of surrealism in any serious or systematic way began to penetrate into England. But even then, people who should have known

[24] H[erbert] F[urst], *Apollo,* XX, no. 120 (December, 1934), 348.
[25] "Post-Cubism," *The Spectator,* CL, no. 5,470 (April 28, 1933), 603–604.
[26] Michael Roberts, *The Criterion,* XIII, no. 52 (April, 1934), 506.

better showed a curious lack of understanding of surrealism. W. H. Auden, for example, said, "Even the most surrealistic writing of Mr. James Joyce's latest prose shows every sign of being non-automatic or extremely carefully worked over," [27] and contradicted himself within the small compass of one sentence, for if the writing is extremely worked over, then it is not surrealistic, and the adjective does not apply to Joyce's *Work in Progress*. What Joyce was doing was nothing less than *consciously* creating the unconscious of his hero, E. C. Earwicker. The manifestation of that unconscious, the world-encompassing dream of Earwicker, is the substance of the book; and only if one forgot that Joyce had written it, if one thought that this was the real dream of a real person, could one say that this was anything approaching surrealism.

The year 1935 may be said to mark the turning-point in the career of English surrealism. During that year appeared the first English manifesto of surrealism, issued by David Gascoyne; [28] Hugh Sykes Davies's *Petron*; Gascoyne's *A Short Survey of Surrealism*; followed, in early 1936, by Gascoyne's translation of Breton's *Qu'est-ce que le surréalisme?*

As the first formal statement of surrealist principles in England, Gascoyne's manifesto deserves some attention. He starts by boldly asserting that surrealism is not an exotic contribution to the English tradition which that tradition is free to accept or reject: it is an international system of ideas determined by the particular circumstances of the times. He

[27] "Psychology and Art," in *The Arts To-Day*, ed. by Geoffrey Grigson (London: John Lane, The Bodley Head, 1935), p. 34.

[28] An announcement of the issuance of the manifesto was made in *Cahiers d'Art*, X (1935), 112. The same issue published a fragment of it in French on p. 106. To my knowledge, the manifesto was never published in its entirety, nor did it ever appear in England.

also boldly asserts the independence of English surrealism from all foreign critical standards, whether dictated by individuals or by the Writers' International.

Surrealism, Gascoyne claims, provides the solution to the writer's problem. That problem, simply stated, is the choice between, on the one hand, the leftist attitude in which the writer's sole concern is proletarian literature or propaganda, and, on the other hand, a nonpolitical attitude in which the writer is concerned only with self-expression. Surrealism points to a third way which leads out of the snares of the other two. The ambition of surrealism, he says, is to abolish all formal distinction between dream and reality, between subjectivity and objectivity. The means to achieve this resolution of opposites is automatism in its various forms. Gascoyne concludes with a declaration of principles:

1. Complete agreement with the principles of surrealism as set forth by Breton.
2. Complete adherence to the historical materialism of Marx, Engels, and Lenin.
3. Surrealism opens vast fields of action in England in poetry, the arts, philosophy.
4. Complete and unrelenting opposition to fascism, war, imperialism, nationalism, humanism, liberalism, idealism, anarchic individualism, art for art's sake, religious fideism, and generally to any doctrine that would tend to justify the survival of capitalism.

This manifesto appeared only in truncated form and only in the French magazine *Cahiers d'Art;* it attracted no attention whatever in England: publications which took note of surrealist activities, such as *New Verse,* made no mention of it, although *Cahiers d'Art* was widely known in England. Furthermore, it is impossible to determine at this late date whether Gascoyne spoke for anyone but himself.

Hugh Sykes Davies, while still a student at Cambridge in 1930, had coedited (under the name Hugh Sykes) the magazine *Experiment*. The other editors were William Empson, J. Bronowski, Humphrey Jennings, and William Francis Hare.[29] While not a surrealist magazine, *Experiment* was interested in new trends in the arts; it printed Julian Trevelyan's article "Dreams," [30] which ended with the unequivocal statement "TO DREAM IS TO CREATE," and a poem by Hugh Sykes [Davies], entitled "Mvth," about the destruction of the Tower of Babel:

> BABEL BASALT
> roars mortared blocks
> out-boulders
> 1000 slave hacked
>
>   . . . . .
>
> BLACK BABEL
> spills eyes
> screaming
> down smooth cliffs

and, fitting typography to action:

> Jove saw and smote.
> iron seared, heart lung and entrails cleft
> while fire burst blacker black
> black BA   B   EL
>   B EL
>   b   EL
>
>   ba b
>   el [31]

[29] J. Bronowski, "Recollections of Humphrey Jennings," *Twentieth Century*, CLXV, no. 983 (January, 1959), 45–46.

[30] See above, pp. 76–77.

[31] Hugh Sykes [Davies], "Myth," *Experiment*, no. 5 (n.d. [1930]), pp. 20–21.

Though not a pure surrealist poem, "Myth" makes clear that its author was familiar with the principles of violent juxtaposition ("spills eyes/screaming/down smooth cliffs"). Davies, a classics student at Cambridge, wrote for the *Criterion* and *New Verse* on classical subjects, and did some reviewing for the former. In 1934, the *Criterion* published a short section of his novel *Petron,* which was to become one of the showpieces of English surrealism upon its publication the following year.[32]

The novel is prefaced with the statement that it was written "for those who have read Poe. . . . For those who are prevented by circumstances from seeing as often as they would wish the *Silly Symphonies* of Mr. Disney. . . . For those who are troubled by sleeplessness, and especially for those who, even when they are asleep, still live an unwelcome life, rising from their sleep unrested, the sweat of nightly terrors still on their brows. . . . For those against whom their neighbours plot." The preface ends with the hope that the readers of the novel "will read it with the utmost simplicity, not seeking a meaning where there is no meaning, more than contented with the appearance of sense."[33] The author might have added that the book was written for those who had read *Pilgrim's Progress,* for *Petron* is the tale of an interior hero buffeted by nightmares, wandering in a surreal landscape.

Part I, section 2, begins with a little verse gloss:

> Petron with a merry heart
> passing down the lanes
> Makes merry with the signposts;
> a hedger him restrains.

[32] H. S. Davies, "Banditti: From the Biography of Petron," *The Criterion,* XIII, no. 53 (July, 1934), 577–580.

[33] H. S. Davies, *Petron* (London: J. M. Dent & Sons, 1935), pp. vii–viii.

Along the lanes down which Petron passes are signs that read "Beware," "Through me men go into a dreadful place," and the like. To prevent Petron from destroying these signs, the hedger cuts each finger of his own hand into a smaller hand, subdivides each new finger into a still smaller hand and so on "until he was possessed of many thousand hands and tens of thousands of fingers." When this fails to stop Petron, the hedger passes a string through his own head, from one ear to the other, pulls a loop through his nostrils and swallows the loop. Petron, finally terrified, flees howling, never to have a merry heart again. He steps unwittingly on a toadstool from which an idiot rises who has a lower jaw so long that it drags on the ground. The idiot pursues Petron until his jaw becomes wedged between two rocks. Attempting to free himself, the idiot distends his mouth "until it seems to overspread the whole horizon." To his great relief, Petron sees that "the idiot's mouth is nothing more than the sunset, his throat the gathering night, and the sounds that issue from it are those of roosting birds, newly-risen nightingales, and owls perched on the tips of his teeth." Petron continues his wanderings, stumbling through landscapes by Salvador Dali: "Imagine, dear friend, outlined against that notable and profound blueness of summer evenings, a vast expanse of netting, in the meshes of which are hanging arms, hands, legs, and feet, but recently torn from the bodies upon which they grew, still alive, and twitching a little, so that the expanse of netting quivers in the calm air" or, "on all sides and as far as the eye can reach the ground is thickly covered with Human Hands, growing from the wrist in the furrowed sand. The fingers are loosely closed, and the thumbs crooked, for it is close on evening-time. Soon, as the sun sets, the fingers contract further, gripping the thumbs within their clasp, and so they remain through the torrid night."

The author has warned the reader to be content with a semblance of sense. The more successful sections of *Petron* hover on the edge of a meaning which, like that of a dream, lies just beyond the reach of thought. In the "Banditti" episode, for example (part I, section 4), which most closely approaches surrealist method, the author reproduces the substance of a dream: Petron, pursued by a forest of marching trees, is about to seek refuge in the ruins of a castle when he is warned by a dying man dripping blood and rattling broken bones to avoid the ruins because a gang of bandits is lurking there. Forced by the advancing trees into the castle despite the warning, Petron joins two bandits cooking their supper. As other members of the gang appear one by one, they fall upon Petron, stabbing and kicking. He manages to escape through a gap in the ruins, blood dripping and bones broken, just in time to warn another Petron who ignores the warning to avoid the castle.

Less successful sections of the novel are less nightmarish and more deliberately contrived. The whole of part II, for example, is a Freudian horror with Kafkaesque overtones told in a style that parodies the popular writers of the last century:

Alas! how had she failed to divine his mood—she who should have been so skilled in the weather of his soul? O revelation pitiably inopportune! His brows knit together, his gaze lowers, speech is prisoned in his throat as his veins swell with wrath, but at last it overwhelms him, and uttering brutal cries he seizes a branch from the nearest tree and plunges it deep into her body—into that unoffending flesh that should have been so dear to him.

The effect of this mixture of horror and stilted style is similar to that of the more gruesome Gothic novels, but with an important difference. In the more successful of these novels, the effect is often due to the unconscious Freudian content of the horrors perpetrated; in this section of *Petron* the horrors are devised deliberately for their Freudian meaning and the effect is an artificial, purely literary one. The difference between a true Gothic novel and *Petron* is analogous to that between a found object and a consciously made one, and Breton's distinction between them applies here with equal relevance: in the former, the latent content remains unconscious; in the latter it is all too conscious, it already contains its own interpretation. I am not sure that the author's parodistic intentions save this section of the book from this criticism: a poor joke remains a poor joke, no matter what the intention.

The book, however, was well received. Rayner Heppenstall, reviewing for the *Criterion* (January, 1936), called it "good popular poetry, near enough to folk-poetry, though a don's work." Heppenstall, quoting from the publisher's blurb, "It is an approach to life directly poetic, the philosophy or argument being always transformed into image and symbol," commented that this was "superbly inept." He suggests, rather, that "it is the withdrawal from life, by a method directly anti-poetic, into phenomena not yet capable of rationalization as image and symbol, much less as philosophy or argument." This, of course, is the method of the surrealist, whose images, the verbal equivalents of phenomena, are recognized as symbols only after the fact, after analysis. The question remains, however, whether Heppenstall's perceptive comment applies to *Petron:* can one be deliberately pre-rational?

Herbert Read, perhaps over enthusiastically, said that the book "would have been greeted in France as [a] brilliant example of [the] new type of literature [in which sleep and waking meet on equal terms]. This is the essential condition of that surreality which, though never a stranger to our literature, has now entered upon a deliberate and effective course." Read used the occasion of this review in the *New English Weekly* (November 14, 1935) to make a few general statements about surrealism which, although without much intrinsic importance, pointed to the direction which Read's own interest in the movement was to follow. First, he indicated the dual nature of surrealism—its political and its literary aspects. He praised the surrealists for being communists with a difference: they refuse to accept any dictation from Moscow and they dare criticize Marx. Finding the literary aspect of surrealism more important than the political, Read pointed to the fact that "under another name, or no name at all, it is already indigenous. . . . Webster, Peele, Donne, Young, Blake, Beddoes, Poe, Swinburne (besides the whole of Monk Lewis, Maturin school of fiction) might all be regarded as precursors of Surréalisme. In short Surréalisme or superrealism is but another name for the recourse to the unconscious which has been one of the distinctive features of English literature."

Read's review elicited an ill-tempered letter to the editor of the *New English Weekly* (November 28, 1935). The correspondent, Leslie H. Daiken, announced that, as a result of the split in the Paris group between Aragon and Breton, surrealism had seen its day:

Genuine Anarchism responded to the sanity of Aragon, who held out for the irreconcilability of purism with social awareness, while those of the clinical school (diehards among the surréalistes) agitated, with Breton, for "intellectual revolution" on a subjective (i.e., antisocial) plane. The diehards have since been overcome by megalomania, madness, and the forces of reaction. . . . The Soluble Fish is dissolved!

Read replied emphatically in the same issue of the *Weekly* that he saw no sign whatever that the movement was "played out"; that, on the contrary, at the International Congress of Writers in Paris in June, 1935, the surrealists alone had presented "a point of view tolerable to the artist *and* the communist"; that he had "an increasing respect" for the attainments of surrealism. But, he added, "I am not announcing my conversion to Surréalisme—but I do intend to watch its progress without prejudice."

David Gascoyne objected in *New Verse* (December, 1935) to Herbert Read's calling *Petron* surrealist on the grounds that Davies's method of writing was not sufficiently spontaneous, that his style was too deliberately contrived: "One cannot help wondering whether Petron is . . . a projection of genuine passions and inner conflicts, or whether he is merely an ingeniously manipulated puppet, made to dance to a fantastic tune that Mr. Davies once overheard in a library." Nonetheless, he found *Petron* a "curious and often exciting book, worth reading more than once."

Gascoyne's *A Short Survey of Surrealism* appeared in November, 1935, marking the official launching of the movement in England. Surrealist activity had spread from Paris to Brussels, Belgrade, Prague, the Canary Islands, Copenhagen; now it was to be the turn of London. Gascoyne announced the visit of Breton and Eluard to London in the spring of 1936 and the opening of the International Surrealist Exhibition in London to coincide with that visit. The *Short Survey*, then, may be considered a preparatory move toward the exhibition; and, since Gascoyne thanks Breton, Eluard, and Hugnet for their assistance in the preparation of the book, one may assume that it received some sort of official sanction.

Up to this time, the surrealist number of *This Quarter*

(September, 1932) had been the only coherent presentation of surrealism in English. However, since it was only after 1932 that interest in surrealism developed in England, a new and more comprehensive account was needed. That this need was real is attested to by the fact that the first printing of the *Short Survey* was exhausted very rapidly and a second appeared in February, 1936.

Although the book is a remarkable achievement for a nineteen-year-old, it is a disappointment. The *Short Survey*, largely a history of the movement, contains a brief account of the precursors: de Sade, Nerval, Baudelaire, Rimbaud, Lautréamont, Mallarmé; an account of dada that concentrates on the antics of that movement; and a description of surrealist activity since the inception of the movement, concerned mainly with the internecine feuds and with listing the contents of the various surrealist periodicals. But one who did not know what surrealism was about certainly would not learn it from this book. The chief impression that the *Short Survey* leaves is that surrealism is mainly a wild romp, a new way of having fun, and that adherence to its tenets provides a writer with sanction to do away with the need for work or for any kind of discipline. There seems to be no awareness on Gascoyne's part that the liberation offered by surrealism is one that requires an almost ascetic discipline. Breton had called for "liberty"; Gascoyne seems to have understood him to mean "license."

What is valuable about the book, aside from calling attention to surrealism, is that it contains translations of long excerpts from the two manifestoes and a small anthology of surrealist texts: verse and prose by Breton, René Char, Eluard, Hugnet, and Péret.

The *Short Survey*, then, must be regarded as deficient in what was most needed—a coherent presentation of surrealist doctrine. However, in 1936 appeared David Gascoyne's translation of Breton's *Qu'est-ce que le surréalisme,* which filled the gaps in the *Short Survey.* As companion volumes, *What Is Surrealism?* and the *Short Survey* present a well-rounded account of both the history and the doctrine.

The *Short Survey* did serve an important function in the propagation of surrealism: reviews of it were often the occasion of extended commentary on the movement as a whole. For example, the *Criterion* coupled its review of the *Short Survey* with one of Breton's *Position politique du surréalisme,* thereby giving a fairly comprehensive presentation of basic surrealist tenets and their relation to the political situation of surrealism.[34] Even the *Times Literary Supplement* (January 4, 1936) gave a fairly sympathetic account of the movement and the book, but complained that Gascoyne had failed to show any awareness of the "weakness and triviality of much of the surrealist position." The *London Mercury* (January, 1936), regretting that the book was not "steadier, slower, and more exact," wondered whether Gascoyne possessed the equipment necessary for a serious explanation of surrealism, or whether he was "merely . . . enjoying the sensation of being superior, mysterious, and ever so bold." The *Left Review* (January, 1936) thought the book good on the whole, but found in it only sympathy for the proletariat, not identification with it. Since all the opinions of the *Left Review* were dictated by the Party line, the reviewer could not resist injecting the usual clichés: "surrealist art—in spite of undoubted talent and genius, remains the complete expression of bourgeois decadence, appreciated and patronised chiefly by a very limited and sophisticated group of bourgeois intellectuals." Other notices were more

[34] Brian Coffey, *The Criterion,* XV, no. 60 (April, 1936), 506–511.

succinct: "rubbishy but amusing"; [35] "Did you ever read anything in your life in a more pompous baby-talk than [Gascoyne's] book on surrealism? And who has said boo to it?" [36]

The author of the last comment, Geoffrey Grigson, was the editor of *New Verse,* perhaps the most important "little magazine" published in England during the 1930's. Objecting only to poetry written out of rhetorical emotion rather than direct observation, or poetry that forgot the particular for the general, Grigson showed a remarkable catholicity of taste. Since its earliest numbers, *New Verse* had printed a good deal of what may be considered surrealist or near-surrealist verse, in addition to reviews of surrealist books.

In "Surrealism for the English," one of the earliest essays devoted to literary surrealism (*New Verse,* December, 1933), Charles Madge called attention to what there was in the English literary tradition that would lend support to an *English* surrealism. French poetic tradition, he said, is different from the English, and the aims of surrealism would be better served if English writers proceeded from their own tradition. Madge supplied some of the material in the English tradition that would support his idea of a native surrealism, material that comes primarily from Edward Young, but also from Coleridge and Alexander Bain. The result of such a blending with the English tradition may, superficially, have little resemblance to the French product, Madge says, but it would possess a validity that no imitation could.

A few months later, sensing perhaps the dangers implicit in his initial appeal, Madge quoted with approval Georges

[35] Michael F. Cullis, "Recent Verse," *New English Weekly,* IX, no. 14 (July 16, 1936), 276.

[36] Geoffrey Grigson, "A Letter from England," *Poetry* (Chicago), XLIX, no. 2 (November, 1936), 101.

Hugnet's admonition that "surrealism is not a literary school . . . it is a laboratory of studies, of experimentation that rejects all velleity for individuality," and added, "this should be a warning to readers who are too apt to find only what they expect to find. It is all the more needed since one cannot treat surrealist poetry separately from the other activities of the surrealist laboratory" (*New Verse*, August, 1934). This statement negates in large part his earlier appeal for a surrealism rooted in the English *literary* tradition; the warning was not heeded, with the result that surrealism in England never became more than a literary style.

Surrealist verse first appeared in *New Verse* in translations by David Gascoyne. The earliest was a translation of the dadaist Georges Ribemont-Dessaignes's "Sliding Trombone," a poem typical of that author's humorous method:

> I have a little windmill on my head
> Which draws up water to my mouth and eyes
> When I am hungry or moved to tears
> I have a little horn full of the odour of
>   absinth in my ears

In the same issue appeared Alberto Giacometti's "Poem in Seven Spaces," also translated by David Gascoyne, a typographical arrangement of squares and words. The disjointedness of the images is typical of the surrealist method:

> 2 golden claws   a drop of blood
> white spiral of wind upon two great breasts
> 3 galloping black horses
> the legs of chairs break with a dry crack
> all objects have gone far away and the sound of a
>   woman's steps and the echo of her laugh fade out
>   of hearing [37]

[37] *New Verse*, no. 6 (December, 1933), p. 8. No attempt has been made to reproduce the typographical arrangement.

In subsequent numbers of *New Verse* there appeared translations by Gascoyne of poems by Eluard and Hans Arp. Work by English poets that showed the influence of surrealism began to appear in *New Verse* and elsewhere. For example, by David Gascoyne:

> Women are often spectral
> They often walk down the street like banjos
> Their eyes are often no more than mere scraps of paper [38]

or Kenneth Allott:

> Let the tide lap your feet
> the moon hangs upside down in the caves of sleep
> the cool horizon is ringed with hanging eyes,
> and white with your immoderate thirst for love
> your smoky wishes pour into the grave.[39]

or Philip O'Connor:

> blue bugs in liquid silk
> talk with correlation particularly like
> two women in white bandages
>
> a birdcage swings from the spleen of ceiling frowning
>   her soul in large wastes
> and a purple sound purrs in basket-house
> putting rubies on with red arms [40]

Roger Roughton, who was to become quite important to the movement, published several poems in the *Criterion*. They show a feature characteristic of much of the better English surrealist verse—violence of imagery in a carefully controlled form:

[38] From "Marrow," *New Verse*, no. 15 (June, 1935), p. 5.
[39] From "Any Point on the Circumference," *New Verse*, no. 24 (February–March, 1937), p. 6.
[40] From "Blue Bugs in Liquid Silk," *New Verse*, no. 25 (May, 1937), p. 12.

A woman is crossing
And crushing the eyes,
And trees from the marshes
Will follow the cries,

Till grass like a swelling
Will rise on the hand
That feels for the marrow
And only knows sand. . . .[41]

Some years later, in 1942, there appeared a little satiric poem, "Surrealist Landscape (To Salvador Dali)," by Lord Berners, which is amusing enough to quote in full:

On the pale yellow sands
Where the Unicorn stands
And the Eggs are preparing for Tea
Sing Thirty
Sing Forty
Sing Three

On the pale yellow sands
There's a pair of Clasped Hands
And an Eyeball entangled with string
(Sing Forty
Sing Fifty
Sing Three.)
And a Plate of Raw Meat
And a Thing that's hardly a Thing

On the pale yellow sands
    There stands
        A Commode
That has nothing to do with the case.

[41] "The Skin of the Stone," *The Criterion*, XV, no. 60 (April, 1936), 456.

Sing Eighty
Sing Ninety
Sing Three

On the pale yellow sands
There's a Dorian Mode
And a Temple all covered with Lace
And a Gothic Erection of Urgent Demands
On the Patience of you and of Me.[42]

This satiric catalogue has a point: it *could* be a painting by Salvador Dali; and this bit of verse, although not to be taken seriously, is an excellent example of the major fault of much of what passed for surrealist verse. Most of it was little more than description of the fantastic visions of the surrealist painters, differing from conventional verse only in the nature of what is described. Indeed, English surrealist verse rarely, if ever, approaches anything like the real visionary power of Breton's poetry, or even genuine automatism.

Philip O'Connor's is an instructive and perhaps typical case. In his autobiography, *Memoirs of a Public Baby*, he admits that the surrealist vogue in London gave him the justification he wanted for the uncontrolled, sloppy poems he was writing: "I spent no longer than the time required to write them out twice, sometimes once—about half an hour on each. . . . They were undoubtedly mountebankery." [43]

Surrealist activity reached a crescendo in 1936, and *New Verse* devoted a good deal of space to it in spite of its editor's coolness to the movement. The issue of April–May, 1936, contained a lengthy (for *New Verse*) essay by Hugh Sykes

[42] *Horizon,* VI, no. 31 (July, 1942), 5–6.
[43] *Memoirs of a Public Baby* (New York: British Book Center, 1958), pp. 170–171.

Davies entitled "Sympathies with Surrealism" which tried to put surrealism on a solid theoretical foundation (something that its English practitioners sorely needed, if Philip O'Connor was in any way typical), or at least attempted to separate those seriously interested in surrealism from the dabblers.

Two years before, Davies had tried to provide a theoretical basis for new tendencies in poetry in an essay entitled "Homer and Vico" (*New Verse*, April, 1934). This earlier essay is interesting in that it provides an explanation for Davies's interest in surrealism; Davies, it will be remembered, had been a classics student at Cambridge and only later changed his interest to English literature.[44]

Vico, Davies says, opposed the Cartesianism and its concomitant Seicentist, Marinist poetry prevalent in his time. The Cartesian view of human nature allowed importance to only one mode of human activity—the intellectual. Opposed to this narrow conception, Vico set forth the multi-faculty psychology which originated with Aristotle, was elaborated by the Scholastics, and given its final form by Renaissance philosophers—Vives and Campanella in particular. In this view, the human mind is divided into three faculties: sensation, imagination, and intellection. The relation between these faculties is a purely temporal one, not a hierarchical one: sensory perception comes first; then imagination imposes some kind of order on the chaotic material supplied by the senses; and finally the intellect makes its own organization of this material. The importance of this psychology is that it avoids the question of the relative value of each faculty: sensation and imagination are not inferior to intellection, they are merely prior.

44 J. Bronowski, "Recollections of Humphrey Jennings," *Twentieth Century*, CLXV, no. 983 (January, 1959), 45.

The consequence of this view for poetics is to grant a greater value to the primitive aspects of language than Cartesianism was willing to do and to recognize that myth is not merely decorative, but an imaginative organization of sense data. Seen through this tripartite psychology, Homer's poetry acquires new validity as the imaginative organization of his experience.

Davies saw a contemporary situation in poetry analogous to that in Vico's time: poetic theory in the late 1920's and early 1930's centered largely upon the admiration of the metaphysical, with terms like "metaphor" and "conceit" the principal catchwords of such a theory. The consequences of this admiration were an increasing complexity of tropic texture and a growing obscurity: "Sooner or later—the sooner the better—this tendency must be modified by a broader notion of poetry, insisting on the equal, if not the superior, importance of the 'myth,' the uncontracted imaginative construction, compared with the contracted metaphor or conceit. In France, surrealism seems to be doing this, but may fail to be felt here." But even if there is no specific movement in England, Davies concludes, there can still be a protest against the too narrow tastes of the modern Seicentism: "a rich tropic texture must depend on a rich mythological attitude, and without it it is a particularly depressing kind of poetic fake."

The essay is a call for the recognition of other than intellectual values in poetry, for giving "imagination" its due. In the later essay, "Sympathies with Surrealism," Davies attempted to put the whole problem of imagination on a firm basis by relating it to the findings of psychoanalysis, an attempt analogous to the surrealists' and, as we shall see, to Herbert Read's.

There are, Davies says, two ways of becoming a sympathizer with surrealism. The first is "the way of the simple souls" who respond to official surrealist art and are influenced by it: in the plastic arts this means using "certain specific shapes"; in poetry, adopting certain recognizable tricks of imagery and structure: "some young poets have attempted to transfer into English words the material of surrealist visual art." What all these "simple souls" have in common is a commitment to "imagination," "inspiration," or "intuition," and to the view that art is produced by some part of the human personality that is not controlled by the intellect. But unless they understand what the hypothesis of the unconscious entails, what they mean is probably not very different from the romantic idea of "imagination." These artists, whatever the merit of their work, "remain simple souls of the traditional type, working by 'instinct'. . . . And it must be admitted that if they are surrealists, in the full sense of that word, then surrealism is nothing new, and may be regarded as a development of late Romanticism."

The second way of becoming a sympathizer with surrealism is more firmly based. Every artist who wants a theoretical justification for his activity will ask himself why he persists in it since it brings him no economic or physical satisfaction. Psychoanalysis is the one theory that has come close to supplying a satisfactory answer. In a footnote Davies adds that Marxism and dialectical materialism provide another starting point, but no artist beginning with this view could arrive at surrealism; he would remain within communist limits and be hostile to surrealism. Only a view based on the psychoanalytic theory of art can lead to surrealism, although dialectical materialism can lend assistance.

"What," asks Davies, "is the relation between the group who have worked with this theoretical basis, and scattered individuals who have used the same basis? How different are their conclusions? How similar is their work? These seem to me to be the real questions about surrealist sympathizers." Unfortunately, Davies does not answer these questions. Instead, he supplies some notes on orthodox psychoanalytic views on art as a basis for discussion between surrealists and their scattered sympathizers.

Any scientific theory of art must be based on the hypothesis of causation, that is, that every phenomenon has a material cause and is in no way an act of God. This rules out any idea of "inspiration" or "aesthetic intuition," since such an idea would mean that the artist creates something out of nothing; the act of creation, therefore, could not be explained in terms of its causes.

The biological explanation—the "play theory"—based on the analogy with animals which seem to engage in play activity, that is, activity not directly related to reproduction or the obtainment of food, does not satisfactorily explain the creative activity of the artist. The "playing" of the animal, for example, involves muscular activity which may in some way be pleasurable or useful; whereas the artist's muscular activity is negligible.

The only theory that offers anything approaching a satisfactory explanation is the psychoanalytic. This theory has revolutionized the biological view of man: man's organic being is only one part of the total human individual—his conscious mind; the real environment of biological man is a double one: the outer world and the inner world of instinctive, unconscious forces.

Because of the conditions attached to it, the satisfaction of human instincts is an extremely difficult matter. Fortunately, it makes no difference to the instincts whether they are satisfied in actuality or only in fantasy: dreams, therefore, are one means of satisfaction. Psychoanalysis has shown the parallels between dreams, ancient myths and rituals on the one hand, and civilized art on the other. Art, consequently, is another way of satisfying instincts; and, as Davies notes, hysteria is still another which has analogies with the way of art. The only real difference between these two is that the hysteric uses his own body, and the plastic artist the outside world as the material with which to satisfy the instincts. The world created by the poet and the painter may, in fact, approximate the world created by the insane. Is there a real difference between the two? The answer of the surrealists is "None": the burden of many of their writings, of *Nadja* and *L'Immaculée conception* in particular, is the proof that the dividing line between sane and insane does not exist.

But Davies does not go into this. He breaks off at this point, on the threshold of surrealism, and ends, rather inconclusively, by saying that "it seems probable that the surrealists and their sympathizers should be able to find a considerable body of common doctrine of a very useful and important kind in psychoanalytic theory of art. It will, however, consist mainly of parallels drawn between various expressions of the unconscious instinctual forces."

This essay, although deliberately inconclusive, is valuable for two reasons: first, it makes a sharp and important distinction between the "simple souls" and those who have a theoretical basis for their sympathies with surrealism; second, it articulates the very basic theoretical point of surrealism and provides an explanation for the nature of its products. It will be noted that Davies's sympathies are not based on any revolutionary bias, political or aesthetic. The negative, destructive emphases of dada and surrealism seem of no account in England. Those surrealists in England who were also communists managed to keep the two spheres separate; their communist commitments seemed incidental to their interest in surrealism. Most English sympathizers with surrealism, it will become clear, belonged to Davies's first group, the "simple souls"; only a few, like Herbert Read and, of course, Davies himself, belonged to the second. But even Davies's commitment to surrealism must be qualified: with the exception of *Petron*, three essays on the subject, and two poems, he produced nothing of a surrealist nature.

The next issue of *New Verse* (June–July, 1936) contained an article entitled "Honest Doubt" by "J. B." The author was later identified as W. H. Auden, who adopted John Bull's initials for the occasion. With typical acuteness, Auden asked some searching and disturbing questions on the aesthetic and political principles of surrealism.[45]

His questions regarding surrealist aesthetics focus on the issue of automatism: if surrealist writing is not "always and absolutely automatic," at what point does it cease being surrealist? "Has all repressed material an equal esthetic value? . . . Are all subjects of equal importance?" Noting that what seems to him the best kind of surrealist writing, that of Lewis Carroll, Edward Lear, and Rimbaud in *Les Illuminations,* "is the work of highly repressed individuals in a society with strong taboos," Auden concludes that surrealism can flourish only when people know nothing about their unconscious or about psychoanalysis, and when society exercises very strong political or sexual censorship: "the moment you are allowed either by yourself or society to say exactly what you like, the lack of pressure leaves you material without form."

Under the political heading, Auden asks what value the repressed unconscious can have for the revolutionary sur-

---

[45] Auden is identified as the author in Monroe K. Spears, *The Poetry of W. H. Auden: The Disenchanted Island* (New York: Oxford University Press, 1963), p. 76.

realist since the unconscious "obviously contains material which has been worked over by the conscious mind," the mind which has been conditioned by the bourgeois world and which is therefore artistically worthless. Further, "what is the peculiarly revolutionary value in the automatic presentation of . . . repressed material?" If that value is a socially moral one, i.e., holding up the mirror to the bourgeois face, is it not the duty of the artist faithfully to copy that face? If that value is a personally moral one, i.e., autoanalytic, is not automatism then only the preliminary task of the revolutionary writer?

Auden's final question is a simple one: if the surrealist rejects absolutely the use of reason and of the conscious faculties, how does he square his position with communism and psychoanalysis which are rational systems that believe in the necessity for conscious recognition of unconscious forces so that they may be understood and guided? "There is a rough and ready parallelism between the Conscious and the Unconscious, and the Masses and the Communist Party."

These questions go to the heart of the matter; an orthodox surrealist, however, would have had little trouble answering them. Answers from an English surrealist would have shed a good deal of light on the nature of the movement in England and its differences from its French counterpart. *New Verse* promised "authoritative answers" in the next issue, but the next number contained only an apology for the fact that the answers could not at present be provided because of illness. They never appeared.

Herbert Read emerged in the mid-1930's as the chief theoretician of surrealism in England. A full exploration of his critical and aesthetic position lies beyond the scope of this study; only those aspects of it that are relevant to his acceptance and subsequent abandonment of surrealism will be examined.

At the heart of Read's aesthetic is the notion of a fundamental opposition between reason and emotion, and the idea that art is made out of the conflict between, and reconciliation of, these two elements. This dualism appears in Read's criticism as reason and romanticism, romanticism and classicism, lyrical and metaphysical poetry, organic and abstract form. Read's idea of the creative process is a simple one: the poet is inspired, then strives to give form to his inspiration. All of Read's criticism may be seen as an attempt to define this process, to understand the nature of inspiration and of the forces that give it form.

Psychoanalysis provided Read with a vocabulary particularly well suited to describing the creative process:

The work of art . . . has its correspondences with each region of the mind. It derives its energy, its irrationality and its mysterious power from the id, which is to be regarded as the source of what we have called "inspiration." It is given formal synthesis and unity by the ego; and finally it may be assimilated to those ideologies or spiritual aspirations which are the peculiar creation of the super-ego.[46]

The emphasis here is on the controlling forces of reason, or the ego. In 1928, three years after this initial formulation,

[46] Read was among the first to make use of psychoanalysis: his essay "Psycho-analysis and the Critic" was published in *The Criterion* (January, 1925); revised and retitled "Psycho-analysis and Criticism," it was included in *Reason and Romanticism* (London: Faber and Gwyer, 1926); revised again under the more ambitious title, "The Nature of Criticism," it appeared in *Collected Essays in Literary Criticism* (London: Faber and Faber, 1938). This last volume was reprinted as *The Nature of Literature* (New York: Grove Press, n.d. [1958]). All references are to this last volume. The quotation above appears on p. 137.

Read restated it in less technical language, while making the emphasis on reason even stronger:

This is no less than the problem of art or no art—of whether the writer is to control his means of expression . . . or whether he is merely to abandon himself to the stream of feeling—to incantations, evocations, vague reveries, and false mysticism. In one case arduous effort, continuous self-criticism, and a definite ideal; in the other case, at the best, an inspired vague delirium, at the worst, the actual decomposition of intelligence.[47]

Another essential criterion for the work of art, a necessary concomitant of his position for which he also found confirmation in psychoanalysis, is social validity. Read borrowed Jung's distinction between passive and active fantasy, the former being a morbid state of no relevance to his theory, the latter owing its existence "to the propensity of the unconscious attitude for taking up the indications or fragments of relatively light-toned unconscious associations, and developing them into complete plasticity by association with parallel elements." [48] Read concluded that "the poetic function is nothing else than this active phantasy in its more-than-individual aspect," and that the poet is the one who can create fantasies "of universal appeal." Art, then, has the function of resolving into a unity the unconscious content and the demands of reality, not only for the artist himself, but also for those who participate in his work. And, of course, the more abnormal the artist, the more limited will be "the common social value of the symbol he produces."

The whole problem of value, then, can be solved by psychoanalysis: the artistic value of the work depends on the social validity of the symbol, and that validity can be

---

[47] Read, *Phases of English Poetry*, rev. ed. (London: Faber and Faber, 1950), p. 124; first published in 1928.

[48] C. G. Jung, *Psychological Types* (London, 1923), p. 574; quoted by Read, *The Nature of Literature*, p. 129.

determined by the psychoanalytic method: "Psycho-analysis finds in art a system of symbols, representing a hidden reality, and by analysis it can testify to the purposive genuineness of the symbols; it can also testify to the faithfulness, the richness, and the range of the mind behind the symbol." [49]

Read's position at this time may be said to incline toward the classical rather than the romantic—to use the terms loosely—and, clearly, a radical reversal was needed before he could adopt surrealism. The changes in Read's aesthetic have been subjected to a searching analysis by H. W. Häusermann [50] and need only be outlined here. According to Häusermann, what seems to have occurred is that Read discovered Whitehead and his theory of intuition. In 1929, in an essay on Descartes, Read defined intuition as

the sudden perception of pattern in life: the sudden realization of the fact that an organic event, of which we are a part, is in its turn the part of a greater unity, of a unity limited in time and space, formal and harmonious . . . it is, under the aspect of expression, the process of poetry. In this way poetry involves everything: it is the sense of integral unity without which, not only no poetry, but no philosophy—even no religion—is possible. [51]

Read's new position had consequences for his theory of the creative process and for his theory of form. In his earlier formulation, the faculty that gave form to the work of art —the ego—was, if not a fully conscious one, certainly under the control of reason. By 1931, however, any idea of conscious effort and of the demands of the super-ego has been

---

[49] Read, *The Nature of Literature*, pp. 140–141.

[50] "The Development of Herbert Read," in *Herbert Read: An Introduction to His Work by Various Hands*, ed. by Henry Treece (London: Faber and Faber, 1944), pp. 52–80.

[51] Read, "Descartes," *The Nature of Literature*, p. 195.

abandoned: "Form, though it can be analyzed into intellectual terms like measure, balance, rhythm and harmony, is really intuitive in origin; it is not in the actual practice of artists an intellectual product. It is rather emotion directed and defined, and when we describe art as the 'will to form' we are not imagining an exclusively intellectual activity, but rather an exclusively instinctive one." [52]

The consequences of the new theory were fully worked out by Read in *Form in Modern Poetry* (1932), which makes up the first four sections of the *Collected Essays in Literary Criticism* (in the U.S., *The Nature of Literature*). It appears undated in that volume before the earlier essay "The Nature of Criticism," to the confusion of the unwary reader.[53]

Read's new thesis is, briefly, as follows: There are two forms of art, the organic and the abstract, to which correspond two periods in the history of art, the romantic and the classical, and, in turn, two aspects of human psychology, personality and character. Classical art is demoted to a secondary position: "The transition from the organic type to the abstract always coincides with the transition from a period of stress and energy to a period of satiety and solidity"; [54] the organic, on the other hand, is the form of the best art because "it is the form imposed on poetry by the laws of its own origination, without consideration for the given forms of traditional poetry. It is the most original and most vital principle of poetic creation." [55]

To this distinction between organic and abstract form, a

[52] Read, *The Meaning of Art*, rev. ed. (Harmondsworth, Middlesex: Penguin Books, 1949), p. 21; first published in 1931.

[53] References to this essay are to "Form" and page numbers are from *The Nature of Literature*.

[54] "Form," p. 19.   [55] *Ibid.*, p. 20.

distinction that is absolute, Read parallels the distinction between personality and character, which he also makes absolute. In doing so, Read rather freely uses Freud's concepts of the ego and super-ego: in Freud these terms do not denote discrete entities in the psychic topography; in Read they are made to do so.

The personality Read identifies with the ego which "is identical with the conscious flow of our thoughts, the impressions we receive, the sensations we experience"; but the ego is also the force repressive of the unknown instincts and passions, never completely under control, that are given the name of "id." [56] The earlier sharp distinction which saw the substance of the work of art as the product of the unconscious, and the "will to form" as the product of ego and super-ego, has vanished. This is how Read envisions the operation of the personality:

I think, in the consistent phraseology I have tried to adopt, we might say that in . . . [the] mood of creative activity, the author stands face to face with his own personality. He stands fully conscious of the wavering confines of his conscious mind, an expanding and contracting, a fluctuating horizon where the light of awareness meets the darkness of oblivion; and in keeping aware of that area of light and at the same time watching the horizon for a suggestion of more light, the poet induces that new light into his consciousness. . . . Such lights come, of course, from the latent memory of verbal images in what Freud calls the preconscious state of mind; or from the still obscurer state of the unconscious.[57]

The important point to note is that in the earlier accounts of the creative process, Read saw the will to form and order as categorically opposed to the chaos of the unconscious; now he calls it the organic coherence of the personality.

[56] *Ibid.*, pp. 25–26. [57] *Ibid.*, p. 38.

The character, on the other hand, Read defines as "an impersonal ideal which the individual selects and to which he sacrifices all other claims, especially those of the sentiments or emotions." [58]

The relationship between the two kinds of form and their corresponding aspects in the human psychological makeup is a simple temporal one: just as in the history of art a period of organic form is followed by a period of abstract form, so the human psyche is first dominated by an inner principle of form, and then gives its obedience to external law. This may be good art history, but it is poor psychology. Freud has made it amply clear, in *The Ego and the Id* and elsewhere, that the relation between the ego and the super-ego is not a temporal one, that one does not replace the other. Freud described the super-ego as the representative of what is "highest" in the human mind; Read arbitrarily limits its function to that of dictating moralistic imperatives. Aesthetic ideals, like any other, would in Freud's scheme emanate from the super-ego; in Read's they have their birth elsewhere, presumably in the personality, i.e., the ego. This is a curious interpretation of Freud's schematization of the psyche; but it is this rather arbitary splitting of the functions of the various parts of the human psyche that enabled Read to embrace surrealism.

Rehearsing once again Freud's theory of art in *Art and Society* (1936), Read expressed dissatisfaction with Freud's failure to explain the "particular kind of sensibility which enables the artist to convert his fantasies into a material form, which form incites us to participate in his mode of creation." [59] He found a hint of explanation for this failure

[58] *Ibid.*, pp. 29–30.
[59] Read, *Art and Society*, 2d rev. ed. (London: Faber and Faber, 1945), p. 94; first published in 1936.

in Freud's casual statement that his arrangement of the psychic personality must be regarded as provisional, that certain individuals may be able to rearrange the functions of the various spheres into which he divided the psyche: "It can easily be imagined," said Freud, "that certain practices of mystics may succeed in upsetting the normal relations between the different regions of the mind, so that, for example, the perceptual system becomes able to grasp relations in the deeper layers of the ego and in the id which would otherwise be inaccessible to it." [60]

This suggestion led Read to elaborate an image of the regions of the mind as three superimposed geological strata:

We can imagine . . . a phenomenon comparable to a "fault" in geology, as a result of which in one part of the mind the layers become discontinuous, and exposed to each other at unusual levels. That is to say, the sensational awareness of the ego is brought into direct contact with the id, and from that "seething cauldron" snatches some archetypal form, some instinctive association of words, images or sounds, which constitute the basis of the work of art.[61]

But Read had not abandoned his earlier belief in the social value of art. The artist, in his moments of inspiration, reaches the deepest levels of the mind, and "at that level we suppose the mind to be collective in its representations, and it is because the artist can give visible shape to the invisible fantasms that he has the power to move us deeply." The earlier emphasis on the "social validity of the symbol" has been shifted to the depths of the unconscious where, by definition, it seems, the symbol has social validity because it

[60] Freud, *New Introductory Lectures*, p. 106; quoted in Read, *Art and Society*, p. 94.

[61] *Art and Society*, p. 94.

is collective. But the artist does not present the naked fantasms of the id, for "the artist must exercise a certain skill
lest the bare truth repel us. He therefore invests his creation
with superficial charms; wholeness or perfection, a due pro-
portion or harmony, and clarity; and these are the work of
his conscious mind, his ego." In times when the artist has
been made to be an exponent of moral, religious, or economic ideas or ideals, art has suffered, and unnecessarily so,
for "ideas, and all the rational superstructure of the mind,
can be conveyed by the instruments of thought or science;
but those deeper intuitions of the mind, which are neither
rational nor economic, but which nevertheless exercise a
changeless and eternal influence on successive generations
of men—these are accessible only to the mystic and the
artist, and only the artist can give them objective representation." [62]

Read has himself summarized his position at this date:

The essential nature of art will be found . . . in the artist's
capacity to create a synthetic and self-consistent world, which is
neither the world of practical needs and desires, nor the world
of dreams and fantasy, but a world compounded of these contradictions: a convincing representation of the totality of experience: a mode, therefore, of envisaging the individual's perception of some aspect of universal truth.[63]

The similarity of this position to that of the surrealists is
obvious. Read quoted with approval Breton's statement that
the surrealists "have attempted to present interior reality
and exterior reality as two elements in process of unification,
of finally becoming *one*. This final unification is the supreme
aim of surrealism: interior reality and exterior reality being

[62] *Ibid.*, p. 95.   [63] *Ibid.*, p. 2.

in the present form of society, in contradiction." [64] He concluded:

Perhaps for the first time in history the artist has become conscious of the springs of his inspiration, is in conscious control
of such inspiration, and able to direct it to the specific course
of art, which is the deepening of our sense of the total reality
of existence. . . . Hitherto the artist has been at the mercy of
those conventions of naturalism, moralism and idealism which
prevent and restrict the free operation of the unconscious forces
of life, *on which alone the vitality of art depends.*[65]

The view of art as the dialectical synthesis of the opposing
forces of imagination and reality was now Read's central
theory, clearly an outgrowth of his earlier distinction between organic and abstract form. In a capitalist society,
Read noted, the free dialectical process is interfered with
by economic consideration, and the result is a debased art.
In a communist society, where the profit motive has been
eliminated, art should be allowed to evolve organically, but
in the Soviet Union, "the most fatal of procedures has been
adopted: the imposition of an intellectually predetermined
conception of what art should be in a socialist community." [66]

This criticism of socialist art was the subject of Read's
contribution to a surrealist supplement in the *Left Review.*
Surrealism, Read said, is the only movement in modern art
that has an aesthetic embracing every manifestation of the
creative impulse, that breaks with every convention of bourgeois academic art, and that at the same time is a true

[64] Breton, *What Is Surrealism?*, p. 49; quoted in Read, *Art and
Society*, p. 122.
[65] *Art and Society*, p. 123.
[66] *Ibid.*, p. 129.

application of the principles of dialectical materialism. It opposes alike the bourgeois conceptions of art and the official Soviet doctrine of socialist realism, and is therefore in this matter "more marxist than the Marxians." [67] Repeating his argument from *Art and Society*, Read asked why the socialists, having thrown off all capitalist ideology, still demand that their artists be "human cameras"; the surrealists, on the other hand, have broken with the past. Art, Read repeated, is the synthesis of imagination and reality. Realism, the doctrine of Soviet art, is a static thesis—it merely reproduces—and therefore is not dialectical. Imagination, the antithesis, is "the internal activity of the mind when uncontrolled by immediate sensational awareness and when free from various moral conventions." Art, then, "projects the imaginative faculty outside the mind, seeking in the world of reality objective equivalents of its fantasies. It is an exteriorisation and a materialisation of the imagery of the mind. . . . This synthesis is the surreality of art. *Reality transformed by the imagination*—that is the definition of art and the aim of Surrealism."

The following issue of the *Left Review* printed a rejoinder to Read by T. A. Jackson, the Marxist theoretician. Jackson drew a parallel between Read's view of surrealism as the true expression of dialectical materialism and that of the early opponents of Marxism, those who wanted to eliminate all "flirting with the ideology of capitalism," who demanded that the state be abolished at once and replaced by new social conditions. This, says Jackson, is the Bakunin heresy, not true dialectics: "Neither the uncritical rejection of the Past nor the uncritical acceptance—that is the dis-

[67] Read, "Surrealism—the Dialectic of Art," *Left Review*, II, no. 10 (July, 1936), ii.

tinguishing quality of *dialectical* materialism. It is dialectical because it both destroys the Past (as to its obsolete husk) and preserves it (as to its *real* achievement)." [68]

Herbert Read had, until this time, consistently avoided the word "surrealism," preferring "superrealism" and had even used the pages of the *Times Literary Supplement* to "enter a plea for 'superrealism' in spite of the fact that Mr. Gascoyne has given 'surrealism' the dignity of his title-page." He based his argument on previous instances in which the French prefix "sur" had been rendered by the English "super": *surnaturel:* supernatural; *surhumain:* super-human; *surhomme:* superman; and on the analogy of these correspondences, insisted that " 'superrealism' is surely the commonsense equivalent of *surréalisme*. It has the advantage of immediately explaining itself." [69] This last sentence is significant of Herbert Read's approach to the whole subject: surrealism, for him, was little more than a reassertion of what he called the "romantic principle," of the right of the artist to discard what interfered with the fullest, freest expression of his "personality," thereby completely ignoring the surrealist point of "impersonality." In this respect, Read belongs in Hugh Sykes Davies's category of "simple souls" —those for whom surrealism means little else than giving free rein to their "imagination," without any concern for the rigorous system elaborated by Breton. This is not to say, of course, that Read's attitude was a naïve one, or that he was in need of Davies's lesson in elementary psychoanalytic doctrine. One may say, rather, that Read saw no need for

---

[68] T. A. Jackson, "Marxism: Pragmatism: Surrealism—A Comment for Herbert Read," *Left Review*, II, no. 11 (August, 1936), 366.

[69] Read, Letter to the Editor, London *Times Literary Supplement* (January 11, 1936), p. 3.

the strict surrealist doctrine with its scientific trappings of research and experimentation—the very aspect of the doctrine that Charles Madge had stressed.

Read's role in the surrealist movement at this time is ambiguous: his sympathies were clearly with the surrealists; he attended meetings of a surrealist group in Hampstead; [70] he was a member of the committee that organized the International Surrealist Exhibition and spoke at that exhibition; and as late as 1940 was a member of the official London group of surrealists; yet, during part of this time, it must be remembered, he frequently wrote art criticism for *The Listener,* the magazine of the B.B.C., and edited the *Burlington Magazine,* a highly conservative art magazine that weathered the thirties without once, except in a brief review of a book, mentioning surrealism. The problem reduces itself, one might say, to one of definition, and a ready analogy comes to mind: Herbert Read was a surrealist to the same extent that a non-practising Catholic is a Catholic; or, as he himself put it in a striking phrase, he played Pascal to the surrealists' Jesuitry.[71]

Read's preference for the word "superrealism" is of a piece, then, with his acceptance of the spirit but not the letter of surrealism. He admitted that his efforts to have "superrealism" adopted had been defeated by "that obscure instinct which determines word-formation in the life of a language. . . . The very clarity of the term 'superrealism' was against it; the public wanted a strange and not too intelligible word for a strange and not too intelligible thing." [72] He refused, however, to abandon the word altogether, re-

---

[70] Philip O'Connor, *Memoirs of a Public Baby,* p. 173.

[71] Letter to the author, April 24, 1966.

[72] "Introduction," *Surrealism,* ed. by Herbert Read (London: Faber and Faber, 1936), p. 21.

serving it for "the tentative and historical manifestations of what has now become a conscious and deliberate artistic principle," [73] and applying "surrealism" to that conscious artistic principle, the movement itself. *New Verse* noted the event with the announcement that "Mr. H. R. has at length retired from the pedantic pill-box of SUPER-REAL-ISM" (August–September, 1936).

Read's most comprehensive statement on surrealism is contained in the "Introduction" he wrote for *Surrealism*, the volume he edited to accompany the surrealist exhibition, which contains essays by Breton, Eluard, Georges Hugnet, and Hugh Sykes Davies, in addition to a generous sampling of photographs of surrealist paintings and objects. That Read considered—and until his death still considered—this statement to be of some importance is attested to by the fact that he allowed it to be reprinted several times under the title "Surrealism and the Romantic Principle." [74] In *The Philosophy of Modern Art,* Read prefaced the essay with a curiously ambiguous note: he allowed the essay to be reprinted, he says, "because I feel that it would be dishonest to disguise the fact that I am sometimes led away (I do not say led astray) by my sympathies. Those sympathies proceed from my 'cult of sincerity' as a poet; and no doubt this is not the only occasion . . . when the critic abdicates and the poet takes over." [75] This partial recantation indicates a curious ambivalence on Read's part: the poet in him approves,

---

[73] *Ibid.,* p. 22.

[74] Mark Schorer, Josephine Miles *et al.*, eds., *Criticism: The Foundation of Modern Literary Judgment* (New York: Harcourt, Brace, 1948); Read, *The Philosophy of Modern Art* (London: Faber and Faber, 1952; New York, 1959); Lawrence Sargeant Hall, ed., *A Grammar of Literary Criticism* (New York: Macmillan, 1965).

[75] Read, *The Philosophy of Modern Art* (London: Faber and Faber, 1952), p. 105.

the critic disapproves, and the old dualism between reason and emotion seems to be back in the saddle.

In *Art and Society,* Read had said that it would be possible to show "how closely the romantic theory of poetry, as elaborated by a great critic like Coleridge, or even by an honest Victorian like A. C. Bradley, corresponds to the theory of Surrealism" (p. 124), and in a footnote in later editions of that work stated that he himself had made the attempt in his introduction to *Surrealism.*

This essay, since it represents what may perhaps be called the "official" English position, is worth some close attention. Read begins by warning that since surrealism was "the spontaneous generation of an international and fraternal *organism,*" it would be "contrary to the nature of the movement to present, as some have suggested, a specifically English edition of Surrealism." [76] There is, nonetheless, a specifically English contribution to be made: "The evidences on which we base the claims of Surrealism are scattered through the centuries . . . and nowhere are these evidences so plentiful as in England." His purpose, then, will be to present this English evidence and relate it to the theory of surrealism.

Recalling his distinction between "superrealism" and "surrealism," Read proposes to identify superrealism, "those tentative and historical manifestations" which he finds scattered so richly throughout the English centuries, with "some of the essential characteristics of romanticism." The great claim that Read makes for surrealism is that it has settled the quarrel between romanticism and classicism—not by establishing a synthesis, as he had once hoped was possible

[76] Read, "Introduction," *Surrealism.* Since this essay has been reprinted so often, I have not given page references for my quotations from it in the following discussion.

—but simply by liquidating classicism, "by showing its complete irrelevance, its *anaesthetic* effect, its contradiction of the creative impulse." After warning of the dangers and complexities attendant upon all discussions of romanticism and classicism, Read plunges into what he considers the heart of the matter and succinctly, if narrowly, defines classicism:

Classicism . . . represents for us now, and has always represented, the forces of repression. Classicism is the intellectual counterpart of political tyranny. It was so in the ancient world and in the medieval empires; it was renewed to express the dictatorships of the Renaissance and has ever since been the official creed of capitalism. Wherever the blood of martyrs stains the ground, there you will find a doric column or perhaps a statue of Minerva.

Romanticism, of course, is the opposite: it is the "principle of life, of creation, of liberation." More simply still, romanticism is identified with the artist and classicism with society. And since psychoanalysis has shown the existence of the unconscious and proved that it is personal in only a very limited sense, that it is, in fact, collective, the demonstration of the irrelevance of classicism becomes an easy matter. The truths of classicism are simply "the temporal prejudices of an epoch," whereas "the universal truths of romanticism are coeval with the evolving consciousness of mankind." Poets and artists have always repudiated the rigid bonds of classical theory, but it is only now that the surrealists, with the aid of Marx and Freud, have been able to put the reaffirmation of the romantic principle on a scientific basis.

Leaving Marx aside, one may ask why, on the basis of Freud alone, one could not put a reaffirmation of the classical principle on the same scientific basis. If one accepts Freud's theory of the unconscious as scientific fact, then one must also, I think, accept the other components of the psychic personality—the ego and the super-ego—as fact; certainly Freud's whole therapeutic endeavor was to attempt a reconciliation or balance between the elements of the psychic personality. If the dictates of the super-ego must be granted the same validity as those of the id, then classicism, which presumably is one of them, can be established on as firm a scientific foundation as romanticism. It would appear that Read is committing the same error here as in his earlier *Form in Modern Poetry*, i.e., dividing the total psychic personality into discrete and watertight compartments. He is free to prefer the romantic to the classical, but not to invoke scientific sanction from Freud for his preference.

Read's simple division between the romantic and the classical impulses, or, in broader terms, between freedom and repression, permits him to lay the blame for wars on "the frustration which is prolonged and reinforced by adult codes of morality." Pacificism, on the other hand, is, or may be, the fruit of hedonism, of a life led in complete freedom from oppression and repression. This idea, of course, is not original with Read; it is a logical conclusion from Freud's theories, and was the subject of a popular book of the period, Edward Glover's *War, Sadism, and Pacifism* (1933), to which Read refers. The idea is an attractive one, but, aside from the rather shallow reading of Freud and oversimplified Rousseauism that it evinces, it does not explain how man is to rid himself of all the ideologies that repress him if these ideologies are the product and content of the super-ego and if the super-ego is as much a part of his psychic make-up as his unconscious. Read comes close to recognizing the paradox at the root of his position when he asserts that "the capitalist and the socialist no less than the militarist and the pacifist are moved by obscure instincts" and that we are ashamed of the elementary desire of the capitalist and militarist "in the degree of our sensibility and altruism." Aside from the question-begging in this context of the word "sensibility," is it not one of the elements of the "adult codes of morality"? And is not altruism one of these also? Having come this close to recognizing and stating the problem, Read draws back by asserting that the men who possess the proper degree of altruism and sensibility are not the priests, but the poets. And the particular distinction of the surrealists among poets is that they have put their protest on a sound nonidealistic, scientific basis.

That basis, of course, is nothing other than the application of Hegel's dialectics to the realm of art, but Hegel "turned upside down," Hegel stripped of the "mystical form of [his] dialectic." The dialectical process takes place in the opposition between the world of objective fact and the world of subjective fantasy, with the work of art as the synthesis. Such a view of art would lead, Read claims, to a total revaluation of the critical principles by which art is judged, and to a reassessment of those artists who are praised because of our present conventional standards—Dryden, Pope, Michelangelo, Poussin among them. Read suggests some examples of the areas of English literature that need such a revaluation:

1. "A fuller acknowledgment of the supreme poetic quality of our ballads and anonymous literature." Ballads, says Read, are the "most fundamental and authentic of all poetry," they are "partly collective . . . and to some degree automatic, and illustrate the intrinsic nature of surrealist poetry."

2. "Driving home the inescapable significance of Shake-

speare," a significance that consists largely of recognizing Shakespeare's irrationality. The first step in the revaluation of Shakespeare along these lines has been taken by John Dover Wilson, who, in his *What Happens in Hamlet,* holds that the incoherence of Hamlet—both character and play —cannot be explained, that *Hamlet* is, in fact, irrational and that its value lies in its irrationality.

3. "The exact relations between metaphysic and poetry." To this subject Read himself had turned his attention in "Metaphysical Poetry" (1923), an essay which had attempted to explain how metaphysical or philosophical content could be made into poetry, to explain what, in fact, the phrase "felt thought" means. But the task is not complete: "What is still necessary is some explanation of why thoughts or ideas should evoke, not merely a metaphysical imagery, but a sensuous identification with visual images: thought transmuted into dream. . . . It is only necessary to prove that even in its most intellectual forms poetry acquires its poetic quality by a process which brings it into line with the irrational sources of lyrical and romantic poetry." One may perhaps wonder why poor Dryden and Pope could not be rehabilitated by some analogous process. Accepting for the moment Read's categories, one may ask why, if it can be demonstrated that thought can be felt, it cannot be demonstrated that ideals—even abstract, classical ideals—can be felt.

4. "Lifting the moral ban." The proper revaluation of Blake, Shelley, Byron, Swinburne would "reveal the conventionality of all systems of morality." These poets are "so positive in their immorality, that morality becomes negative by comparison. . . . They prove that the most deeply rooted taboos, such as incest, can be thwarted by the individual will, and the courage they manifest in such defiance is so

absolute that a figure like Byron becomes the unconfessed hero of humanity." Although by no means a superrealist poet, Byron is, by these standards, a superrealist personality, the closest thing in England to the Marquis de Sade. Swinburne, says Read, "was bullied into conformity and bad verse and his fate is one more unforgivable crime committed in the name of the bourgeois God."

In his concluding plea for lifting the moral ban, Read becomes involved in a point that demonstrates very clearly the perils of ignoring the broader and more fundamental aspects of surrealist doctrine, of separating poetry, as Read has done, from the other products of the surrealist laboratory. "The dilemma which faces all moralists," he says, "is that the repression of instincts is apt to breed a worse disease than their free expression; incidentally it entails a feeble art." This statement leads Read into a brief discussion of the theory that art is a sublimation of suppressed instincts, and into a further statement which, it seems, invalidates much of what he has been saying. Although he denies that art is in all respects a sublimation, for sublimation "involves a conformity to collective ideals which completely submerges the individuality of the artist," art is, nonetheless, closely linked with the repressed instincts. "Actually it is a question of consciousness": that is, if we are aware of our instincts and consciously repress them, then the results will be nothing but intellectual reactions; but if we are not aware of our instincts and we allow them to be expressed in a disguised form, then we may produce interesting results. The Prophetic Books of Blake, the nonsense of Edward Lear and Carroll are products of this kind, and it is their unconscious content that gives them their significance: "From our point of view, Lear is a better poet than Tennyson; Lewis Carroll has affinities with Shakespeare." Even if we ignore the circularity of the whole argument—if art is the result of the repression of the instincts, and Read is asking that we unrepress them, where will art come from?—we are back at Auden's unanswered question in "Honest Doubt": whether it is not true that surrealism can flourish only in societies that have very strict taboos and in periods when people are ignorant of their unconscious and of psychoanalysis. If it is a question of consciousness, as Read says, then the very fact that surrealism has been put on a scientific basis destroys any claim it may have to producing art of any consequence. This may explain the fact that in the pantheon of surrealism, the really great artists are those who flourished before the advent of psychoanalysis. The surrealists themselves have avoided this pitfall by refusing to dissociate art from the rest of their doctrine, by insisting that surrealism is not a literary or artistic movement; the fact that their proofs are produced in the realm of art is only incidental to their wider purpose. Since their primary aim is not art, but the liberation of man, they have no need to hedge their discussion of art in the way that Read does.

In the field of fiction, Read suggests that, as a result of a revaluation along the lines he proposes, Monk Lewis, Maturin, and Mrs. Radcliffe should occupy a much higher position than they do relative to Scott, Dickens, and Hardy. Fiction, or prose narrative, awaits a complete transformation, and Read saw quite clearly that "in so far as it is to justify itself as art [i.e., "romantic" art], it must be transformed into poetry." This is a correct evaluation; Breton had, early in his career, dismissed the novel as an art form; in order to be art, the novel must become poetry.

In painting, a similar reassessment is needed; the preRaphaelites, in particular, are in need of such a revaluation.

Salvador Dali had earlier recognized some of the affinities between them and the surrealists, but what Read is calling for is an *English* revaluation of their accomplishments. They, like the surrealists, had a comprehensive philosophy which embraced painting, poetry, philosophy, and politics; they opposed the views of their contemporaries and rebelled against the artistic naturalism of their time: "They were not afraid to experiment with their sensations; they acknowledged the primacy of the imagination." But what they lacked was a scientific method, a dialectic, real energy. They were incapable of a revolution; they were, in a word, sentimentalists. Instead of developing romanticism from where Coleridge had left it, they developed nostalgia. One has only to compare Morris to Marx to understand the scale of their failure; their followers "degenerated into soulful weavers, mock-medieval craftsmen, bookbinders, and harpists."

English art had to wait for the influence of Picasso to show any sign of revitalization. Between the pre-Raphaelites and that influence, Read says, English art has nothing to show. There have been some potentially great artists— Wyndham Lewis is an example—but they were too eccentric, too lacking in "social coherence." English art needed the impetus of the surrealists, of Max Ernst in particular, to learn that the "physique of art" had its proper place as "an instrument subordinate to the sovereign power of the imagination." The artist is not "to be judged by the manner in which he uses the medium but by the success with which he conveys the sensations or ideas" that he set out to express. This view, according to Read, explains why certain "found objects" are cherished by the surrealists; what matters is not that the object be made, but that it express something felt by the artist or the finder of the object. "Art in its widest sense is an extension of the personality: a host of artificial limbs."

Read, drawing the parallel between the "found object" and the images of the dream, makes an interesting and valuable observation. The surrealists had always insisted that the dream possesses as great a degree of reality (if one may use such language) as the external world; they had also insisted on the existence of a point where the opposition between dream and external reality would be reconciled. But Read notes that their productions, both verbal and plastic, seemed more often than not to be concerned with one member of the antithesis—the dream—than with its synthesis with external reality. That synthesis was often left to what we would call chance. Several examples have already been mentioned: Breton's poem "Tournesol" which, according to him, proved prophetic of actual events years after its composition; Brauner's prophetic one-eyed creatures; and many experiences described in several places by Breton. Now Read suggests that the dream has not only the same degree of reality as the objective world, but may well constitute the very synthesis of the two realms: most dreams contain "the casual residues of the day's anxieties; but we find also the day-world transformed, and occasionally this new reality presents itself as a poetic unity." This is a subject to which he returned in a later essay, "Myth, Dream, and Poem," which will be discussed below.

To illustrate the similarity between poem-formation and dream-formation, that is, to demonstrate the unconscious origin of inspiration, Read describes his own experience of writing a poem based on a dream and concludes that, indeed, much of the activity of writing was similar to the activity of dreaming, that the processes at work in the

dream—regression, displacement, secondary elaboration—
were also at work in the writing. Read was certainly aware
of the degree of conscious control involved in the production of the poem; all that seems authentic dream is the
situation itself, certainly not the imagery or the language
used to describe it:

> This must be a foreign land, I say,
> and gaze about with eager eyes.

Read speaks of automatism in relation to this poem—the
unsought-for rhymes asserting themselves, the effect of the
rhythm of the moving train on which the poem was written
—but he never makes the crucial distinction between a true
automatic product and the description of a dream. The
latter, we have seen, is nothing more than the description
of something previously given, and differs in no way from
any other kind of descriptive verse except in the nature of
what is described. The former, on the other hand, is the
experience itself, not a description of it. This distinction
is one that Read was to make later in "Myth, Dream, and
Poem"; but here, in an essay on surrealism, there is no
indication that he was at all aware of this all-important difference.

The essay concludes with a brief defense—in answer to
attacks by J. B. Priestley—of the purity of the surrealists'
motives, a denial that they are, as Priestley had said, "effemi-
nate or epicene young men, lisping and undulating" or
young women "without manners, balance, dignity—greedy
and slobbering sensation-seekers," or that they represent a
new barbarism, a new decadence. On the contrary—the
surrealist stands for truth and freedom, a position that demands the destruction of current morality and values. Read
ends on a personal note, announcing his attachment to sur-

realism as the contemporary expression of the romantic principle, and his allegiance "to that dictatorship which claims
to end all forms of tyranny and promises, however indefi-
nitely, the complete liberation of man: the dictatorship of the
proletariat."

That Read's acceptance of surrealism grew out of his
earlier positions is clear; but Read, never standing still very
long, has willingly admitted the contradictions of his subsequent positions. He has almost made a virtue of them. His
commitment to surrealism lasted only a short time; perhaps
"commitment" is the wrong word, and "support" more accurate. For Read, surrealism never meant the "all or nothing"
involvement which Breton demanded from his followers;
Read, let us remember, remained the editor of the *Burlington Magazine* until 1939. Even his allegiance to the communist cause was not to last long: in 1938 he abandoned
communism in favor of his own brand of anarchism, which
did not prevent him from accepting a title from the Crown.
It is with these qualifications in mind that Read's declaration for surrealism—or any other "ism"—must be understood.

The essay we have been examining, and the volume in
which it is contained, appeared in November, 1936. References are made in it by Read and Breton to the International
Surrealist Exhibition held in London in June–July, 1936. In
spite of the lapse of a few months, Read's essay may safely
be regarded as the statement of his position at the time of
the exhibition, and this is the reason for having considered
it somewhat out of its place in the chronology of the movement. The other contributions to the volume, especially
Breton's important essay "Limits Not Frontiers of Surrealism," and Hugh Sykes Davies's essay will be examined
after an account of the exhibition.

Other events of importance were occurring during 1936. In late February, Dali had addressed the Anglo-French club of Oxford or Cambridge University, [77] explaining in a "fascinating address" that "surrealism was 'the penetration through the real world towards the world of the irrational,'" and that "the object of the surrealist painter should be to paint *concretely* the real thoughts, uncontrolled by reason or judgment." In the summer, David Gascoyne's volume of poems, *Man's Life Is This Meat*, appeared, as did a surrealist number of a new magazine, *Contemporary Poetry and Prose*. An examination of these had perhaps better be postponed since it is only in the context of the exhibition that their importance can be realized.

[77] *Fords and Bridges*, I, no. 2 (March, 1936), 27. This magazine, a joint product of both Universities, in a monthly section by "The Bystander," reported events without always making clear at which university they had occurred.

3 | The Exhibition

~~~~~~~~ The English surrealist movement owes its birth to the fortuitous encounter of Roland Penrose and David Gascoyne on a Paris street in 1935. Each had recently returned to England after living in Paris and each was in the French capital again on an errand—Gascoyne to do research for his *Short Survey*, Penrose on other business. Bewailing the state of the arts in Britain, they decided there and then to form a surrealist group upon their return to London.[1] Before the end of the year, a group had been organized and was meeting regularly in Hampstead; its activities, in addition to the usual surrealist readings and games, led to the organization of the first of the large international surrealist exhibitions, to be held in London in the summer of 1936. Its plans were sufficiently advanced for Gascoyne to announce the exhibition tentatively in the closing pages of the *Short Survey*, published in November, 1935.

The moving spirit behind the exhibition was Roland Penrose, painter, poet, art collector, friend of André Breton, Max Ernst, and Paul Eluard, a man whose wealth and enthusiasm did much to promote the movement in England. He was assisted by a committee consisting of Herbert Read,

[1] Interview with Sir Roland Penrose, London, April 2, 1964.

Hugh Sykes Davies, David Gascoyne, Humphrey Jennings, Rupert Lee, Diana Brinton Lee, Henry Moore, Paul Nash, and E. L. T. Mesens. The French organizing committee consisted of André Breton, Paul Eluard, Georges Hugnet, and Man Ray.[2]

Organized by so large a committee and consisting as it did of over four hundred items, the exhibition was somewhat chaotic in its preparation.[3] Ruthven Todd, who was at the last minute recruited as assistant secretary to the committee and general factotum, recounts that the exhibition had been hung, the items numbered, and the catalogue printed when André Breton arrived from Paris; he declared the exhibition a disaster and ordered it rehung. The catalogue as printed, therefore, has no relation to the actual order of items in the exhibition. Further difficulties added to the last-minute chaos when on June 10, two days before the opening, a packing case consigned from Copenhagen and containing paintings by Wilhelm Freddie and Leonor Fini was seized by customs and threatened with destruction because of its objectionable contents. After a meeting with Rupert Lee, who acted as chairman of the committee, the customs officials reprieved six of the eight paintings on the condition that the two worst offenders be immediately shipped back to Copenhagen. These two, entitled "The Fallen in the World War" and "Worship Exhibitionism," depicted, respectively, naked, mutilated bodies stalking about the battlefields of France, and a group of naked young

---

[2] *Catalogue* of the International Surrealist Exhibition, p. 11; *International Surrealist Bulletin No. 4*, "Issued by the Surrealist Group in England, September, 1936" (London: A. Zwemmer for the International Surrealist Exhibition, 1936), pp. 1–2.

[3] I am indebted for much of the information about the exhibition to Mr. Ruthven Todd.

men dancing in the twilight.[4] The incident, of course, was not without effect in interesting the general public in the exhibition.

The exhibitors included every prominent Paris surrealist; a number of Belgian, Scandinavian, Spanish, and Czech painters; and some artists whose connection with surrealism is, at best, tenuous, like Brancusi, Paul Klee, Alexander Calder, and Henry Moore. Among the English, Paul Nash, who had long been interested in natural objects, was "surrealist-in-chief." [5] The roster of English painters included the names of Eileen Agar, Edward Burra, Cecil Collins, Mervyn Evans, David Gascoyne, Charles Howard, S. W. Hayter, Humphrey Jennings, Roland Penrose, Julian Trevelyan.[6] In addition, children's drawings, objects of Oceanian, African, and American primitive orgin, an object made by a madman, a great many *objets trouvés*, interpreted natural objects, and made objects were shown. Among the last were Méret Oppenheim's fur-lined tea set and Salvador Dali's "Aphrodisiac Dinner-Jacket." [7] Dali was only scantily

[4] *The Times* (London), June 11, 1936, p. 14; *Daily Mirror*, June 11, 1936, p. 15; *Daily Sketch*, June 11, 1936, p. 5.

[5] Marcel Jean, *The History of Surrealist Painting*, trans. by Simon Watson Taylor (New York: Grove Press, 1960), p. 270.

[6] Robert Melville, author of an important study of de Chirico and an early supporter of surrealism, opposed the inclusion of some of the English painters as not properly surrealist and whose presence, therefore, tended to water down the idea. Interview at the Marlborough-New London Gallery, London, March 12, 1964.

[7] This object is a dinner jacket to which are attached dozens of liqueur glasses filled with green crème de menthe. Ruthven Todd, whose job it was to keep these glasses full, recounts that since the summer of 1936 was exceptionally hot, the crème de menthe evaporated quickly, leaving the glasses sticky, smeared, and stained; he solved his problem by drinking the liqueur and filling the glasses with green ink.

represented, but there was a concurrent Dali show in London at the Lefèvre Gallery.

The show at the New Burlington Galleries had been well publicized in advance, and on opening day, traffic was held up in Bond Street and Piccadilly by the crush of crowds. According to the *Star*, "lovers of Lewis Carroll, Hieronymus Bosch and William Blake, and Suburbanites, filled the rooms. . . . Lady Wimborne and Lady Juliet Duff were there. Osbert Sitwell, Sacha and Mrs. Sacha Sitwell looked as if they understood everything. Baroness d'Erlanger and Constant Lambert were in the throng." But, the paper went on, most visitors regarded the whole thing as a joke and one was heard to say, "I am going to have a brandy and soda and get a little fresh air in the National Gallery." [8]

The exhibition was accompanied by the usual antics attendant upon surrealist performances. It was officially opened by Breton, clad all in green and smoking a green pipe, a gift from Ruthven Todd. He was accompanied by his wife whose long hair was also green. One of the sensations of the opening was the Surrealist Phantom, a living object embodying one of Dali's current obsessions: a young woman, Sheila Legge, wandered through the rooms, dressed in a white satin gown, her head and face enclosed in a veil of roses; she wore long black gloves and carried a model human leg filled and covered with roses in one hand and a raw pork chop in the other.[9] The pork chop eventually had to be abandoned because of the heat. The newspapers

[8] Quoted in Julian Symons, *The 'Thirties: A Dream Revolved* (London: Cresset Press, 1960), p. 91.

[9] Several of Dali's paintings of the period illustrate the same theme: "The Man with the Head of Blue Hortensias," and "Three Young Surrealist Women Holding the Debris of an Orchestra in Their Arms," among others. See Jean, *History of Surrealist Painting*, p. 271.

printed many photographs of this charming apparition; one of them, reproduced in Marcel Jean's *History of Surrealist Painting*, shows her in Trafalgar Square, her arms covered with pigeons. Dylan Thomas walked through the rooms on opening day, offering boiled string in tea cups and politely asking, "Weak or strong?" while a lecture was going on constantly interrupted by the ringing of a loud electric bell.[10] A few days later, on June 19, Herbert Read delivered a lecture on "Art and the Unconscious" while standing uneasily on a spring sofa.[11]

On July 1, Salvador Dali also spoke, wearing a diving suit decorated with plasticine hands and a radiator cap on the top of the helmet, a jewelled dagger in his belt, and holding a pair of Borzoi hounds on leads. He was accompanied by his English manager, Edward James, who carried a brilliantly decorated billiard cue to use as a pointer on the illustrations for the lecture. The helmet of the diving suit, an old-fashioned affair, was so heavy that unless it was very tightly secured, it could fall off and easily snap the wearer's neck. Ruthven Todd, whose job it was to help Dali into the suit, screwed the wing nuts on the helmet as tightly as he could. In addition to the day being an extremely hot one, the poorly ventilated gallery was crammed to capacity. After manfully trying for a while to deliver his lecture inaudibly from inside the diving helmet, Dali could stand no more and asked Mr. James to remove the helmet. Unable

---

[10] Dylan Thomas, *Letters to Vernon Watkins,* ed. with an introduction by Vernon Watkins (New York: New Directions, 1957), p. 14. Although the story is repeated by Constantine FitzGibbon, *The Life of Dylan Thomas* (Boston: Little, Brown, 1965), p. 190, Ruthven Todd denies it.

[11] The lecture has never been reprinted, but Sir Herbert Read, in a letter to the author (June 10, 1964), says that it is substantially the same as the chapter entitled "Art and the Unconscious" in *Art and Society,* 2d rev. ed. (London: Faber and Faber, 1945).

to loosen the wing nuts by hand, Mr. James tried to use the billiard cue as a lever to work them loose while Dali, with the Borzois' leashes tangled in his legs, tried to maintain his balance under the weight of the helmet, the assaults of the cue, and the all but immovable leaded boots. Ruthven Todd finally managed to remove the helmet and untangle the dogs. Dali continued his lecture, still encased in the rubber suit. Audibility had improved, but Dali's French was so heavily accented as to be practically unintelligible. He finished his lecture, one observer commented, "in what must have been a deplorable state of unresolved contradiction between the conscious and the unconscious" [12] or, as Todd put it, in a condition of "combined paranoia and claustrophobia."

After the lecture, Dali had to be helped out of the rubber diving suit. Ordinarily, a diver wears heavy, very absorbent woollen underwear, but because of the heat, Dali had remained in his trousers and shirt. They were insufficiently absorbent and left him sloshing knee-deep in his own sweat. His clothes, of course, were ruined, and while he limply rested in an armchair, his wife, Gala, rushed to a nearby store and returned with a huge armful of clothes from which Dali restored his usual elegance. Todd, called to task by Mr. James and Mrs. Dali for having fastened the helmet so tightly, was forced to demonstrate the dangers of an improperly secured diving helmet on himself in order to still their complaints. He emerged from the demonstration with a bruised neck, but he was rewarded by Mrs. Dali with a kiss for having saved her husband's life.

William Walton, the composer, returned from lunch one

[12] Richard March, "The Swallow's Egg: Notes on Contemporary Art," *Scrutiny*, V, no. 3 (December, 1936), 252; see also W. Y. Tindall, *Forces in Modern British Literature* (New York: Vintage Books, 1956), p. 236.

day with a kipper which he attached to the hook protruding from Miró's "Object 228." Miró was delighted with the addition, but it had to be removed before the end of the day because of the smell. Miró was with great difficulty dissuaded from saving the fish as part of the object. T. W. Earp, the art critic of the *Daily Telegraph,* insisted that the object benefited from the addition.[13] A painting signed D. S. Windle, showing a woman with a real cigarette stuck in her mouth and a small artificial bird glued to her forehead with a piece of sponge, was smuggled into the gallery by an academic painter and hung on the wall for a while with the approval of the exhibition committee which regarded the whole thing as a surrealist act.[14]

There were events of a more serious nature also: on June 16, Breton spoke on "Limits Not Frontiers of Surrealism"; [15] Paul Eluard on "L'Evidence poétique" on June 24; [16] and Hugh Sykes Davies on "Biology and Surrealism" on June 26.[17] On the 26th a meeting was held at the gallery for the reading of poetry: Eluard read in French from his own works and those of Lautréamont, Baudelaire, Rimbaud, Cros, Jarry, Breton, Mesens, Péret, and Picasso; translations in English together with some English surrealist verse were read by David Gascoyne, Humphrey Jennings, and George Reavey. Since both Breton's and Eluard's talks were re-

[13] T. W. Earp, "Surrealism in Art," *Daily Telegraph,* June 12, 1936, p. 19.

[14] Symons, *The 'Thirties,* p. 92; Conroy Maddox in an interview with the author in London, March 16, 1964.

[15] Reprinted in Herbert Read, ed., *Surrealism* (London: Faber and Faber, 1936), and, in a different translation, in Justin O'Brien, ed., *From the NRF* (New York: Meridian Books, 1959).

[16] Reprinted in H. Read, ed., *Surrealism* and in *Cahiers d'Art,* Vol. XI, no. 6–7.

[17] Only excerpts of this lecture are reprinted in the *International Surrealist Bulletin No. 4.*

printed in Herbert Read's *Surrealism,* an account of these will be given in the next chapter where that volume is discussed. Davies's lecture will be considered later in this chapter.

All these events, together with the publicity afforded by the extensive coverage in the press and by Movietone News, brought in the public. More than twenty thousand people visited the exhibition, the largest number ever to attend an art show in London up to that time. According to one account, the exhibition kept "old men from Lord's cricket ground, young men from Henley, and Mayfair damsels from garden parties." [18] Dali's one-man show at the Lefèvre Gallery was having a similar success: two hundred pounds' worth of sales were made at a private showing, a sum large enough at the time to be worth reporting in the press.[19]

The catalogue of the exhibition, a handsome little volume with a cover by Max Ernst (but which has no relation to the order in which the exhibits were finally hung), contains a preface by André Breton and an introduction by Herbert Read which in little sum up the profound differences between the French parent and the English child. Speaking of the bankruptcy of "realistic" art and its final defeat by photography, Breton says, in what amounts to a superb summary of the whole surrealist endeavor, that

The only domain that the artist could exploit became that of purely mental representation, in so far as it extends beyond that of real perception, without therefore becoming one with the domain of hallucination. But here it should be recognised that the two domains are by no means clearly separated, and that all

[18] Quoted by M. D. Z. [Morton Dauwen Zabel], *Poetry* (Chicago), XVIII, no. 6 (September, 1936), 353.

[19] Anthony Blunt, "Another Superrealist," *The Spectator,* CLVII, no. 5,637 (July 10, 1936), 57.

attempts at delimitation are open to dispute. What is important is that mental representation (in the object's physical absence) provides, as Freud said, "sensations related to processes taking place on different levels of the mental personality, even the most profound." The necessarily more and more systematic exploration of these sensations is working towards the abolition of the *ego* in the *id,* and is thereupon forced to make the pleasure principle predominate over the reality principle. It tends to give ever greater freedom to instinctive impulses, and to break down the barrier raised before civilised man, a barrier which the primitive and the child ignore. The social importance of such an attitude, if one takes account of the general disturbance of the sensibility that it entails (shifting of considerable psychic burdens on to the constituent elements of the perceptions-consciousness system), on the one hand, and the impossibility of going back on the other, is incalculable.

And, stressing the revolutionary aspects of surrealism, he added:

We say that the art of imitation (of places, scenes, extrinsic objects) has had its day, and that the artistic problem consists to-day in bringing a more and more objective precision to bear upon mental representation, by means of the voluntary exercise of the imagination and the memory (it being understood that the involuntary acquisition of the material on which mental representation has to draw is solely due to exterior perception). The greatest benefit that surrealism has derived from this kind of operation up till now has been that of having succeeded in reconciling *dialectically* these two terms which are so violently contradictory for adult men: perception, representation; and in bridging the gap that separates them. Surrealist painting and construction of objects from now on permit the organisation of perceptions of an objective tendency. This tendency causes these perceptions to present a profoundly disturbing and revolutionary character in that they imperiously call forth, from exterior reality, something to correspond to them. One can predict that to a very large extent this something *will exist*.[20]

One must, incidentally, admit the validity and truth of Breton's final prophecy. Before too many years had passed, even the strangest and cruellest surrealist juxtapositions were to become realized in the destruction caused by the war.

Herbert Read, on the other hand, in his "Introduction" insisted on his customary distinction between super- and surrealism, the latter being no more than the reaffirmation of the former. His continuing efforts to ground surrealism firmly within the English romantic tradition carried consequences of which he seems not to have been aware: the particularly revolutionary value of surrealism is reduced by the degree that it can be shown to be little else than a special case of tendencies already present in the English tradition. The following statement from Read's "Introduction" to the Catalogue lacks, as do so many of his pronouncements on surrealism, the tough philosophical materialism of Breton's early pronouncements: where Breton finds revolutionary import in the liberation and free expression of the unconscious, in the supremacy of the id over the ego, Read seems to find little more than new and unusual subjects for art drawn from the freer activity of the "imagination":

In justifying such art the superrealist will point to the irrational art of the savages races, so powerful in its effects on the sensibilities of even civilised people. He will point to the strong appeal of various kinds of folk art, and of the unconscious art of children. He will point to the strange and disconcerting beauty of scribbles found on tempting walls, of objects found in un-

---

[20] André Breton, "Preface," trans. by David Gascoyne, *Catalogue of the International Surrealist Exhibition*, pp. 7–8.

accustomed places; he will demonstrate the fantasies of nature and will ask everyone to admit the vividness of their dreams.

In concluding his note on "The English Contribution," Read adds that it "is comparatively tentative, but our poets and painters have scarcely become conscious of this international movement. Now that it has been revealed in all its range and irrationality, they may recover, shall we say, the courage of their instincts."

Hugh Sykes Davies's lecture, "Biology and Surrealism," delivered at the New Burlington Galleries on June 26, marks a path that was to be followed by some of the adherents of English surrealism and a direction that was to lead Davies himself out of the movement. He opened with a statement that indicates a grasp of surrealism somewhat beyond Read's: "Surrealism is not a new style of painting, nor a new theory of art. It is concerned primarily with the condition of the human race." There follows an account of the development of sexuality and repression in the human being and a summarizing account that, again, shows that Davies understood Freud somewhat less naïvely than Read in his "Introduction" to *Surrealism*. "Repressions," he says, "are not only the result of education and social conditions, but also, and in the first instance, of the physical nature of man." The repressed unconscious can, of course, "give rise to a continual undercurrent in later years, a ceaseless feeling of undischarged tension; the unconscious phantasies can make use of the body itself, playing little dramas in which they find indirect satisfaction, but which cause illness and hysteria in the physical sense. Sometimes the unconscious so far obtains the upper hand that it substitutes its own phantasies completely for normal reality, and there follows a condition of delusion and paranoia." So far, Davies is treading on familiar ground, repeating more or less his essay of a few months earlier, "Sympathies with Surrealism." In the earlier essay, he drew some parallels between the satisfaction of human instincts afforded by dreams, myth, and art on the one hand and by hysteria and other psychic disturbances on the other, without pursuing the implications of these parallels. This time, he goes one step beyond his earlier speculations and at the same time parts company with surrealism. The conditions of hysteria and paranoia, the surrealists say, are considered aberrant only because they are seen from a narrowly conceived view of what constitutes "normality." From the surrealist point of view—and this is the whole point of Breton's *Nadja*—the "insane" are closely attuned to the real workings of the universe, precisely because in them, to use Davies's own words, "the unconscious so far obtains the upper hand that it substitutes its own phantasies completely for normal reality." In Nadja herself, Breton goes to great lengths to demonstrate that the distinction between her unconscious "fantasies" and "normal reality" is impossible to make. In short, for the surrealist, the fantastic becomes the real; this, of course, is the whole point of Dali's "paranoia." Davies, however, makes a somewhat different point, and in the process, distorts surrealism:

May I conclude by drawing your attention to the attitude taken by Surrealism to this human situation. . . . Through all the means at our disposal, through painting, through poetry, or through our scientific researches, we are engaged in the exploration of the unconscious, in its conquest and final synthesis with the conscious—a synthesis by which the surreal will become also the surrational. We propose an extension of our control over territories hitherto uncontrolled—the kingdom of the irrational within ourselves. And our purpose is this. As long as the world of dream and phantasy remains buried in the breast of each one of us, hidden, unseen, not understood, so long is it a potential danger. It is a private world, and when it invades the conscious life of any man who knows nothing of its strange shapes and images, he is helpless against it. He imagines that he alone in the world suffers from such feelings and such dreams. His loneliness provides the essential condition for his illness. We wish to make this impossible. We wish to make this private world public. We are to know one another's dreams, and to put an end to human loneliness in the face of this universal human situation.

Surrealism, then, in Davies's view, will serve as a kind of universal psychoanalysis that will show the sufferers of the human condition that they are not alone. It will have a certain therapeutic value, but since the malaise Davies describes is part of the "physical nature of man," that therapeutic value will be severely limited—surrealism will help, but it cannot cure, since not even the surrealists claimed that the human condition is a curable disease.

A mild surprise is that this speech was delivered at the New Burlington Galleries during the exhibition. There is no record of André Breton's reaction, but if Davies had been a French surrealist, he would without doubt have been drummed out of the movement there and then. Breton's English was notoriously poor and he may not have understood the speech, but excerpts from it appeared in the bilingual *International Surrealist Bulletin No. 4*, together with a French translation, and Breton is one of the signatories of the *Bulletin*. It is clear from this episode, among others, that Breton exercised no control whatever over the English surrealists and that they, in general, went their own eccentric ways. The individualism, eccentricity even, of the English was a factor in the whole history of the movement in that country; it is the reason given in the *Bulletin* for the fact that it took surrealism ten years to cross the Channel; it is one of the reasons given eleven years later for the failure of the movement in England.[21]

Although it did not appear until September, 1936, the *International Surrealist Bulletin No. 4* was prepared during the exhibition (it is dated July 7, 1936) and emphasizes English surrealist activity, which at the time consisted almost exclusively of the exhibition and reactions to it. Much space in the *Bulletin* is given over to a section carrying the following headings: "The Situation in England; The intellectual position with regard to Surrealism; The formation of an English group; Immediate activities." The first two items consist largely of an apology for the tardiness of the English in joining international surrealist activity. The tardiness, the statement insists, is not due to any intellectual or artistic backwardness, but to English individualism and tolerance which are rooted in three centuries of sectarianism in religion and "a continual confusion of politics by their fusion with the innumerable sects." This tradition of "pathological individualism," as the *Bulletin* calls it, permits endless confusions, equivocations and disguises: "We have left-wing priests, pacifist priests, communist priests, scientific priests." In short, the enemy is so protean that the opposition remains fragmented. English capitalism in particular is especially well adapted to play its deceptive role: "It is rich enough to be philanthropic, to set aside vast sums every year for petty alleviations of the social ills which it creates —every sort of kindly, patronising, comforting, soup-for-the-poor charity. This is made possible largely through 'our Empire.' If the capitalists were to starve large numbers of British workmen, and then shoot them down, the situation

---

[21] "Déclaration du groupe surréaliste en Angleterre," *Le Surréalisme en 1947* (Paris: Editions Pierre à Feu, 1947), pp. 45–47.

would be too clear. But they can starve and shoot down Indian workmen, using their labour to pay off English workmen, to maintain high wages here for the majority, while they starve a minority, the unemployed, in comparative security."

In artistic and intellectual activity, individualism is similarly responsible for the unwillingness of Englishmen to participate in communal activity which would limit "this crankiness." "Moral, ideological, and political irresponsibility is assumed to be the proper basis of English art." The English surrealists claim to have overcome these tendencies in themselves and are ready to act in concert against the drift toward fascism discernible in the government.

The statement ends with the announcement of a program of activities to propagate the surrealist doctrine: "numerous discussions" to take place during the coming autumn; an exhibition of objects to be held the next winter; an exhibition of the works of Henry Moore; the publication by Faber and Faber of Herbert Read's *Surrealism;* the production of a "large international anthology of Surrealism"; and the publication of a review. Only a few of these promises were kept.

One of the discussions promised by the *Bulletin* took place while the exhibition was still in progress. The Artists' International Association, a leftist grouping, had organized a debate on June 23, 1936, at Conway Hall, on the social aspects of surrealism at which Herbert Read read a paper. This speech, reproduced in the *Bulletin*,[22] provides an in-

---

[22] Except for Roger Roughton's statement in "Surrealism and Communism," *Contemporary Poetry and Prose,* no. 4–5 (August–September, 1936), p. 75, that the surrealists had been invited to join the A.I.A., and an announcement in the *New Statesman and Nation,* XI, no. 278 (June 20, 1936), 1011, that the debate was to take place,

structive contrast to Read's usual approach to surrealism: when he addressed the public at large, he tended, as we have seen, to dilute the revolutionary emphasis of surrealism and to stress those aspects of surrealism that are already present in the "English tradition"—in short, to emphasize what he called "superrealism." On the occasion of the Conway Hall debate, however, since he was addressing an informed, sophisticated audience with "revolutionary sympathies," he approached his subject from a much more orthodox point of view. What he stressed in this speech were precisely those materialist, revolutionary tendencies in surrealism that he deliberately underplayed or ignored on other occasions.

He opened his speech by acknowledging that the spectacular popular success of the exhibition did not mean that the thousands who visited the New Burlington Galleries had understood the significance of what they saw there. Most people, he said, "went there to sneer, to snigger, to giggle, and to indulge generally in those ugly grimaces by which people betray the shallowness of their minds and the poverty of their spirit. If the success of this Exhibition is significant, it is merely significant of the decadence of our culture." Surrealism, he added, "will only be successful in the degree to which it leads, not to social entertainment, but to revolutionary action." The particular contribution that surrealism can make to revolutionary action, he continued, is to reintegrate the human personality and the individual with his society. Just as the traditional views of the human personality make arbitrary divisions, so any form of art based

---

Herbert Read's speech reprinted in the *International Surrealist Bulletin No. 4* is the only surviving trace of this public event. I have been unable to discover who the participants in the debate were and what they said.

on a selected part of that personality is equally arbitrary. Classicism, which stresses the intellect; impressionism, which stresses the eye; naturalism, which stresses the understanding; expressionism, which stresses the feelings—are all "partial and incomplete forms of art, types of idealistic preference. If reality is to be our aim, then we must include all aspects of human experience, not excluding those elements of subconscious life which are revealed in dreams, day dreams, trances and hallucination. Such is the quite logical and quite materialistic claim of Surrealism."

Read continued with a presentation of the political and artistic aspects of surrealist doctrine, which unlike his other pronouncements on the subject, abandoned the familiar insistence on "superrealism" in favor of an orthodox view.

The *Bulletin* concludes with a few quotations from the press, deliberately chosen for their inaccuracy and ineptness in order to form a small *sottisier* which it was easy work to demolish. The reactions of the press, speaking broadly, lent themselves very easily to this kind of treatment. Very few of the newspapers of the day were willing to concede any serious intentions to the surrealists; they reacted almost entirely to the sensational aspects of the whole endeavor. A few headlines will provide a sample of the general tone: "A Shocking Art Show," "Girl Subjects of Surrealist Paintings" (*Daily Mail*, June 12, 1936, p. 13); "Cup and Saucer Made of Rabbit Fur!" "Terrifying Display" (*Evening News*, June 12, 1936, p. 6); "Needed Pork Chop to Complete Dress" (*Daily Mirror*, June 12, 1936, p. 2). There is not much point in reproducing the inanities of the reports in the daily press; but it is clear that the exhibition swept the London scene for several weeks during the summer of 1936: it became the subject of gossip columns, chatty news columns, letters to the editor, and even found its way to the sports page of the *Daily Herald* (June 16, 1936, p. 18). The *Daily Worker*, from which one might have expected some serious criticism of surrealism, limited itself to the fake proletarian manner of an obviously fake "Worker's Notebook": "The general impression one gets is that there is a group of young people who just haven't got the guts to tackle anything seriously and attempt to justify themselves by an elaborate rationalistic racket," a comment that ended with the obviously false statement that "the majority of those who attended the exhibition were the 'artists' themselves" (June 12, 1936, p. 4). Frank Rutter of the *Sunday Times* (June 21, 1936, p. 11) provided the item that wins first prize for ineptitude: "If Chirico, Nash, and Picasso are considered eligible as Surrealists, one would like to know why such painters as Wyndham Lewis and Wadsworth have been excluded." There is, unfortunately, no recorded answer from Mr. Lewis. The *Times* (June 12, 1936) was a good deal less than enthusiastic, but unlike most other dailies, it was willing to grant the exhibition some serious attention. Surrealism, it said, "would appear to be a 'curse-daddy' inversion, on true Freudian lines, of the 'kiss-mammy' art of our immediate ancestors." The *Times*'s art critic insisted that, contrary to Herbert Read's statement that "it is beside the point to talk of form and composition, of handling and handwriting," these are precisely the elements that are the mechanics of artistic composition, and it does not matter whether "you paint common objects of the seashore, or harps in the air . . . or flittermice in the campanile," what you do with them is the important question. On this point the critic of the *Times* found the surrealists wanting: "In this exhibition there are examples of the acrobatics . . . by which Mr.

Picasso seeks to conceal the fact that, though an eminent designer, he is not a painter." The *Times*, finally, accused the surrealists of a kind of artistic dishonesty, of consciously using "interesting hints of supernormal capacity" to make an effect. A more serious criticism, and one that was reiterated time after time, is that "there seems . . . to be a Surrealist stock-in-trade of objects which corresponds to the tambourine and the bouquet of flowers which slam the door in the face of psychological inquiries"; in other words, that the "curse-daddyism" has its deliberate clichés just as the "kiss-mammyism" of an earlier day had.

But for all their supercilious bafflement, the daily newspapers, even the worst, performed a signal service for the exhibition: they publicized it as no art show had ever been publicized; they devoted more space to it than the surrealists themselves could have hoped; they printed a great many photographs of the exhibits. The "Surrealist Phantom" was, of course, their favorite subject, but there were photographs also of works by Max Ernst, Roland Penrose, Edward Burra, and others.

Geoffrey Grigson in his autobiography reports a conversation he had with J. B. Priestley around the time of the exhibition which may be considered typical of honest John Bull's reaction to all these foreign goings-on. Priestley, according to Grigson, said: "As for Herbert Read—I hope he isn't a friend of yours—he is a nitwit. You could always take him in. . . . Did you go to that Surrealist opening? There was Herbert Read with all those Latin charlatans. Henry Moore's stuff was there. Henry Moore: he's lumpy. I don't know why all this modern stuff needs to be lumpy. What's there so attractive about eggy things?" In his own voice, Grigson adds, "It was not Mr. Priestley speaking. It was the public, honestly puzzled, not quite confident, successful,

generous, but generous to mediocrity and bitter to noncon-
formists of the small battalion." [23]

Art magazines were divided in their response to the exhibition. The editor of the conservative magazine *The Studio*,
C. Geoffrey Holme (August, 1936), devoted an editorial to
a protest against surrealism. The tenor of his opposition can
be gathered from the following:

Against the revival of imagination there is nothing to be said.
Against the Surrealist version there is much. . . . There are too
many "-isms" for the good of painting. Good painting is the
sincere effort of individuals. . . .

The type of imagination shown is repellent. The exhibition in
London abounded in literal monstrosities and cheap horrors.
These are a pathological study whether their producers were in
earnest or not. They may be ascribed to a deluded amateurism,
a striving for notoriety, or genuine craziness. The quality of
imagination is either feeble or vicious, sometimes both.

The *Architectural Review* (June, 1936), on the other
hand, in advance of the exhibition, printed an extremely
sympathetic article on surrealism which, although it said
nothing new or important, insisted that surrealism was of
great value in liberating the imagination, even for architects.
The sympathy of this periodical toward surrealism was expressed again a few months later (November, 1936) when
it ran a competition entitled "Holiday Surrealism" for the
best photographs "showing elements of spontaneous Surrealism, discernible in English holiday resorts." The results,
judged by Paul Nash and Roland Penrose, although not
particularly distinguished, are at any rate an index of the
interest aroused by the subject.

[23] Geoffrey Grigson, *The Crest on the Silver: An Autobiography*
(London: Cresset Press, 1950), p. 164.

The exhibition became the subject of the *New Statesman and Nation's* "week-end competition" for June 20, 1936, when it set the following problem: "Mr. Horace Walpole, late of Strawberry Hill, revisits England in 1936. We offer a First Prize of Two Guineas for an extract not exceeding 300 words for a letter of his written after *either* (a) a visit to the Surrealist Exhibition at the Burlington Galleries, or (b) a drive into the country." The results of the competition were disappointing: "Everybody took it for granted that Walpole would be filled with a sort of ghostly moral indignation. But would he? . . . These more-than-gothic phantasies would be right up his Arlington Street." The winning entry (July 4, 1936), by J. Molyneux Paul, was indeed poor, unimaginative stuff; it had Walpole writing: "I have had a most rare vision: I have been at the Surrealist Exhibition and how to tell you of it I know not. . . . You would be hard put to it to make a distinction between 'Reclining Woman' and 'Mansions of the Dead' without a catalogue." The joke, incidentally, is on Mr. Paul, since the catalogue would have been of no help either.

The weekly press was, again, largely unsympathetic. Hostility came from all quarters, from the Right as well as from the Left. Hugh Gordon Porteus, an ardent admirer of Wyndham Lewis and an avowed enemy of surrealism, had articles appearing in the *New English Weekly* both before and during the exhibition. His position, like that of most anti-surrealists, was simply that art, although made of unconscious elements, requires the control of the shaping intellect. Surrealism, on the other hand, taps the unconscious sources of energy directly, and is dangerous because it tempts the artist to tamper with the natural image-making process. Dali, Porteus says, is especially guilty of this particular transgression: "He does not *create* images; he paints pictures . . . of images consciously constructed, plastically worthless." [24] The very basis of surrealist art, its unconsciousness, Porteus claimed, destroys one of the great justifications of art, its cathartic properties. Surrealist art is too private to have more than a personal cathartic effect,[25] and, on this level, a Bushman's vision is preferable to a surrealist's because it is intelligible to the whole society.[26] By ignoring Freud's testimony of the impersonality of the unconscious, Porteus is prevented from seeing the logical connection between surrealism and communism: "Of all the strange paradoxes . . . none is more astonishing than that the Surréalistes, the most intensely subjective and individualistic artists, should embrace the political faith of the extreme left." He called Herbert Read to task for having, in the catalogue of the exhibition, classified Shakespeare with those artists whose imagination is not controlled by the intelligence, "But you have only to consider what would be the reactions of Sweet Will . . . to a glimpse at the . . . exhibits, to realize that Mr. Read is talking . . . through his hat." [27]

Anthony Blunt, the art critic of the *Spectator*, presents an interesting case, for he also wrote art criticism for the *Left Review* and contributed to that periodical's surrealist supplement (July, 1936). His principal objection to surrealism, in his *Spectator* review of the exhibition (June 19, 1936), was similar to Porteus's: that surrealism represents the last stage of the individualistic and subjective approach

[24] "Art: Notes on a Vexed Topic," *New English Weekly*, VIII, no. 11 (December 26, 1935), 215.

[25] "Art: The Surréaliste Exhibition," *New English Weekly*, IX, no. 10 (June 18, 1936), 193–194.

[26] "Art: The Higher Dream," *New English Weekly*, VIII, no. 13 (January 9, 1936), 253.

[27] "Art," *New English Weekly* IX, no. 13 (July 9, 1936), 253.

to art. Like Porteus, Blunt ignores the point that at the heart of surrealist doctrine is the belief that the subjective, probed to a sufficient depth, proves to be objective—this is the whole point of the surrealist doctrine of the object, of objective chance and objective humor. That surrealist art failed to demonstrate the objective value of the contents of the unconscious is a point worth arguing, but only in the context of its stated intentions. Instead of considering surrealist art from this point of view, Blunt emphasized the therapeutic value of surrealist art for the artist, and concluded that surrealists have moved from art to psychology. Surrealist art may have the secondary effect of helping "to clarify the subconscious of the spectator. How far they have gone away from art into psychiatry is shown by the inclusion . . . of 'found objects' which happen to perform the therapeutic function which the Superrealists demand from their paintings." Blunt is guilty of the same confusion as Porteus: can surrealist art be said to be individualistic and subjective if it has the effect of helping "to clarify the subconscious of the spectator"? How subjective can an object be that performs a therapeutic function?

Three weeks later (July 10, 1936), in a review of the Dali exhibit, Blunt reversed himself: "[Dali's] care for technique for its own sake is consistent with the doctrine of art for art's sake which on various occasions Breton has put forward and which is in a sense the logical end of Superrealism." Aside from the plain untruth of what Blunt attributes to Breton, we have here a further confusion: if surrealist art can be both subjective and therapeutic for the spectator, can it also be consistent with the doctrine of art for art's sake? Blunt finds that Dali is the most wholeheartedly bourgeois of the surrealists and has in common with them "the general non-revolutionary quality of extreme individualism and extreme subjectivity."

Another point that belies the surrealists' claim to be revolutionary, says Blunt, is the very fact of their success in London. It was not the proletariat that came to the New Burlington Galleries or that bought the Dali paintings, but the respectable highbrows for whom surrealism has snob value. But the success that surrealism was enjoying was not wholly due to its snob appeal, Blunt noted, "for there are signs that it is taking a deeper hold here than it achieved on the continent, and there are clearly many English people to whom it means a great deal." This appeal, he thinks, may be due to the repressive nature of English education: "it may be that after a life of good clean fun the sadism of *Soft Construction with Boiled Apricots* by Dali . . . or René Magritte's *Philosophic Lamp* . . . provides a healthy escape. Perhaps a travelling exhibition of Superrealism ought to be sent around all the public schools of the country." Mr. Blunt has obviously lost himself in a maze of contradictions: surrealist art is not art but therapy; it is consistent with the doctrine of art for art's sake; it is not revolutionary, but it is destructive of public-school values.

When he wrote for the surrealist supplement of the *Left Review* (July, 1936), Blunt made his objection to surrealism clearer, if not more cogent:

[Superrealism and Dada] both represent the best kind of art which a society in decay and chaos can produce, but the time has now come when we can expect art to be something more positive. If art is primarily an activity for the conveying of ideas, then Superrealism is a side track, and it is time that art came back to its true path. . . . A new art is beginning to arise, the product of the proletariat, which is again performing its true function, that of propaganda.

The same issue of the *Left Review* contains a cartoon showing visitors to the Surrealist Exhibition: they are the usual capitalist figures of communist caricature—the fat man with a bored, stupid expression and a big cigar; the haughty, supercilious, effete young man; and the horsy, bored, rapacious-looking woman in furs and jewels. The caption quotes Herbert Read's statement from the catalogue of the exhibition: "Do not judge this movement kindly. It is not just another stunt. It is defiant—the desperate act of men too profoundly convinced of the rottenness of our civilisation to want to save a shred of its respectability."

The third essay in the surrealist supplement of the *Left Review* (the first was Herbert Read's discussed earlier), "Surréalisme in Literature," by Alick West, does not deal specifically with surrealist art and had no particular connection with the exhibition.

The title of the essay is deceptive, for its subject is only indirectly literature. West bases his entire argument on a short quotation from Breton: "The word table was a begging word: it wanted you to eat, to prop or not to prop your elbows, to write. . . . In *reality* . . . a nose is perfectly in its place beside an armchair, it marries even the form of the armchair." But words, says West, do not behave as Breton claims. The word "table" in itself begs nothing, and it is only because we eat and write at a real table that the word begs.

The surréaliste demand for the liberty of the word really covers the demand for the liberty of the thing, the dream of a new society where everything would have a new function. That the demand for a new social order appears primarily as the demand for a new verbal order, is the first weakness of surréalisme; for it means that the liberation of words veils the acceptance of social conditions which gave them their meanings.

From the point of view that there is no connection between word and thing other than the purely denotative, this argument is perfectly acceptable; but this, of course, is not the surrealist view of language. In other words, West says, surrealism depends for its effect upon the existence of bourgeois standards and on the stilted, outworn way of looking at the world: "the nose perfectly in its place beside the armchair depends on the fact that the nose is not perfectly in its place beside the armchair, but on a person's face." Refusing to accept the surrealist view of language, West can say, logically, that "only from the bourgeois standpoint does surréalisme achieve its aim of reaching ultimate meaning by destroying all accepted meaning, of making the word into a god-scraper. From the proletarian point of view it is merely curious." West concludes that by opposing first the Moroccan war, then fascism, and by aligning themselves with the workers, the surrealists have tacitly admitted that reality is not "that mental sphere where all relations are fluid and all contradictions solved therein; reality is social struggle." And the path the surrealists should follow is clear: Aragon, the arch-heretic, has shown the way. In short, they should stop being surrealists.

One other comment from the Left, from Edgell Rickword, also emphasized the therapeutic effect of surrealism, but this time that effect is seen as harmful: "It is no accident that the Surrealist Exhibition . . . was thronged by excessively well-to-do people. The violence of the fantasy satisfied the sense of the necessity of criticising social reality, whilst effectively short-circuiting any impulse to action." [28]

The full-fledged attack on surrealism and its Freudian bases from the Left had to wait another year for the appearance of Christopher Caudwell's *Illusion and Reality*, which will be examined in the next chapter.

[28] Edgell Rickword, "Culture, Progress, and English Tradition," *The Mind in Chains*, ed. by C. Day Lewis (London: Frederick Muller, 1937), p. 249.

The most virulent and perhaps also the most stupid attack on surrealism came from Raymond Mortimer, who reviewed the exhibition for the *Listener* (June 17, 1936). He explained the origins of the movement in Paris bohemianism: "Would-be writers and painters, with a lot of 'artistic temperament' and very little talent. . . . Drink, drugs, sexuality in its most psychopathic forms, were the ostentatious relaxations . . . of this heterogeneous mob." The rest of his review seldom rises above this level. At the heart of surrealism is the desire to shock; its communist leanings are explained by the fact that France is a bourgeois country—in Russia the surrealists would presumably be Czarists; in short, they are revolutionaries for the sake of being revolutionaries. In painting, they represent a return to the Royal Academy tradition; the only difference is that they choose their subjects for their oddity or unpleasantness instead of their prettiness or sentimentality. Mortimer calls Magritte's "The Red Model," the famous painting of boots gradually turning into feet, the equivalent of Victorian paintings of boots with kittens climbing out of them. The only interest excited by a surrealist picture is that caused by surprise, but that lasts only an instant; beyond the initial surprise, surrealist art is tiresome, "for the unconscious is the least interesting part of a human being—analysis brings to light always the same monotonous old impulses of lust and anxiety and hatred." The only painters Mortimer found worthy of any commendation were Picasso, Klee, and particularly de Chirico, whose works have "the approved dream-like quality, but they are dreams organised by the consciousness."

This review, based entirely on personal prejudice, simply rejects surrealism out of hand, without any attempt to understand or explain what the surrealists were about. As such, it deserved no rebuttal or argument. Nevertheless, it elicited a response from Roger Roughton, the editor of *Contemporary Poetry and Prose*, who, given the nature and level of the discussion, was reduced to simple denials of Mortimer's assertions: no, the surrealists are not revolutionists for revolution's sake; no, surrealism cannot, because it is opposed to art for art's sake, be accused of returning to the tradition of the Royal Academy.[29]

Roughton's letter provoked another. Its author regretted that "a movement so sound and reasonable in its theory should have produced, so far, art of such small account," and that the unconscious, at the hands of surrealist painters, has proved so much less interesting than the conscious life which had hitherto supplied the artist's material. Of particular significance, the writer finds, is the fact that the best artist represented at the exhibition, de Chirico, is not, properly speaking, a surrealist at all. His particular distinction is that "though his work contains elements drawn from the dream world, they are incorporated . . . into a framework which clearly derives from the visible world around us. . . . The Surrealist Exhibition, in fact, has harboured, in what to many was the most distinguished work on view, a denial of its own principles." [30] What is amusing about this letter is that the characteristic of de Chirico's work that its author thinks is a denial of surrealist principles is the very quality that makes de Chirico a surrealist. The author of this letter is obviously a sensitive and sympathetic spectator; his misinformation about basic surrealist doctrine is a measure of

[29] Roger Roughton, Letter to the Editor, *The Listener*, XVI, no. 390 (July 1, 1936), 38.
[30] Alec Clifton-Taylor, Letter to the Editor, *The Listener*, XVI, no. 392 (July 15, 1936), 132.

the English surrealists' failure to make that doctrine more widely known. And David Gascoyne's popular *Short Survey* is probably the chief culprit in this regard.

Peter Quennell, who reviewed the exhibition for the *New Statesman and Nation* (June 20, 1936), regretted that no historical introduction to surrealism had been provided at the exhibition; if it had, the uninstructed visitor would have realized that what might seem a "fortuitous form of intellectual vagary is as old as the creative impulse itself, and that the love of the fantastic, singular and terrible, has its roots in the deepest recesses of the human spirit." But in spite of, or, perhaps, because of, his recognition of the fundamental truth of surrealism, Quennell thought the exhibition disappointing: as a tendency, surrealism may be interesting, but "this self-conscious delving into the unconscious, this extremely sophisticated attempt to recapture the primitive, this intellectual approach to the irrational" results in a "particularly portentous form of dullness." He much preferred "those natural Surrealist artists, the Marx Brothers and Mr. Walt Disney. What is the effect of a fur tea-set . . . or of M. Dali's famous 'Aphrodisiac Jacket' when it is compared to the fantastic effrontery of a Marx Brothers' film—that violent humour which saps the basis of reason and decorum?" But, paradoxically, in spite of its dullness, the surrealist movement can be "recommended as a stimulant to sluggish systems—a spiritual cathartic of which modern art, and British art in particular, stands very much in need. Certainly the crowd that assembled at the New Burlington Galleries showed signs of enjoying their liberation from the everyday world; for even British phlegm is not always proof against Surrealist fantasy." In other words, surrealist art is dull but stimulating.

Two of the important literary periodicals of the day, F. R.

Leavis's *Scrutiny* and T. S. Eliot's *Criterion* devoted serious, if critical, notices to surrealist art.

Richard March, in *Scrutiny* (December, 1936), subjected surrealism to a searching analysis based on the following premise:

> A piece of work only attains to the level of art when the workman, no matter how individual or even bizzare his methods may be, expresses something greater than himself, the terms of reference for which are outside the personal life. In the presence of such work the spectator is led into a hierarchy where the ordinary accidents of existence are no longer decisive. He becomes related to the totality of experience, the common heritage of the society of which he is a part.

Seen from the vantage point of this definition, surrealism is found wanting, for "the deliberate exploitation of the unconscious unrelated to any ulterior scheme, always leads back to a few dominating impulses in the human make-up." It is useless, says March, for the surrealists to refer to precursors like Brueghel, Bosch, Goya, Blake, because the "Surrealism of such a picture as 'The Temptation of St. Anthony' by Brueghel the elder is interesting precisely because of its relation to an explicit conception of life. The modern Surrealist, however, can with naive optimism be content with the prospect of 'the mind, on finding itself withdrawn from all ideas . . . occupying itself with its own life.' (Breton, *What Is Surrealism?*)" There is value in such an activity, to be sure—it "may be regarded as an attempt to *liquidate* the past," and "if the service [surrealism] is rendering is in the revolution away from materialism, it will have proved its worth." But as an end in itself, surrealism will prove sterile: "When you have wandered through those dead antique cities of Chirico . . . what then? . . . It is a pure and arbitrary assumption that the marvellous pursued for its own sake is necessarily beautiful or even interesting."

The surrealist, March concludes, is aware of the dilemma and has therefore allied himself with a rational scheme external to himself, and "in that spirit of fantasy that he practices with such success," has turned to dialectical materialism, but only because communism, too, is revolutionary and wants to liquidate the past; but "it must be plain that by its very nature this philosophy is antithetical to the ideals of liberty as envisaged by the Surrealist movement."

Roger Hinks, the art critic of the *Criterion* (October, 1936), on the other hand, saw clearly that surrealism is the necessary counterpart of dialectical materialism, for "absolute reason requires absolute imagination as its corollary." And it is precisely this aspect of surrealism that gives it its importance: "Surrealism has a myth . . . it is a social form of expression, and not merely a technique for putting across the personality. It claims to be the symbolic expression of dialectical materialism, a philosophy which, in its turn, undertakes to express the total consciousness of modern man." But just as an absolutely rational form of society is unattainable in practice, so the absolute imagination demanded by the early surrealists is unattainable and lacks significance. Dali is an example of the change in the surrealist attitude: his early work consisted of variations on Lautréamont's image of the chance meeting of the umbrella and the sewing machine on the dissecting table; some remarkable and suggestive juxtapositions resulted, but they were largely sterile to the spectator. His later work has changed: he is still preoccupied with the exact rendering of ordinary things, but the spectator's mind is sucked into his hallucinatory world; "he has exchanged the technique of rape for the technique of seduction"; the transitions between the ordinary and the extraordinary have become subtler. The difference between the early and the later Dali is like the difference between the nightmare and the dream: in the nightmare everything is monstrous; in the dream everything is familiar until the dreamer wakes up. This is the great virtue of art, that it can create images at once familiar and strange. Hinks quotes with approval Breton's statement that "the admirable thing about the fantastic is that it is no longer fantastic: there is only the real." But, Hinks says, Breton spoils this profound remark by exaggeration: "the marvellous is always beautiful, anything that is marvellous is always beautiful; indeed nothing but the marvellous is beautiful." This, says Hinks, is nonsense—we know the marvellous only through the ordinary, and "the beautiful is a mysterious amalgam of the marvellous and the ordinary." But more than being nonsensical, Breton's statement exposes the central and fatal weakness of surrealism: identifying the beautiful with the marvellous proves that "surrealism is only a parasite on modern civilisation, not the antitoxin to its toxin that the surrealists believe it to be. The principle of absolute non-conformity with the real world, which Breton claims as the central principle of surrealism, is as sterile as the absolute conformity of realism" which Breton denounces without seeing that as far as the imagination is concerned, any conformism is equally inhibitive. Breton's claim that only surrealism seeks to unify the duality of internal and external reality is a false one, for the "art of comparing two kinds of reality is . . . the essential feature of all creation without exception." Hinks's own position emerges finally as the usual, middle-of-the-road one: "I know that the imagination is not released by throwing the reason overboard; and I know that the reason withers if not besprinkled with the dew of the imagination."

Reactions to the exhibition may, then, be described as a mixed bag. They range from the stupid and the violent to the ironic and supercilious, to the intelligent but unsympathetic; there is, however, nowhere to be found a fully appreciative review of the exhibition or a fully sympathetic reaction to the surrealist endeavor. The opinions discussed here are, of course, only a sample, but, culled from the popular and important publications of the day, they are fairly representative. The exhibition did, without any doubt, have a considerable impact upon London; references to it continued to crop up with regularity during the next year or two.

In addition, the London exhibition stimulated interest in the works of individual surrealists and others associated with the movement. Between the summer of 1936 and the early years of the war, almost every important figure associated with surrealism, English and Continental, exhibited in one or more shows. Among them were Picasso, Ernst, Magritte, Miró, Tanguy, Delvaux, Duchamp, de Chirico, Man Ray, Klee, and Paalen.

4 | *English Evidence*

~~~~~~~~ David Gascoyne, remarkably precocious, emerged in 1936 as the leading, and perhaps the only, surrealist poet in England. In 1932, at the age of sixteen, he published *Roman Balcony and Other Poems,* and in the following year, a novel, *Opening Day.* His commitment to surrealism, although it seems wholehearted for the period under scrutiny, must be somewhat qualified. His answers to two questions of the *New Verse* "Inquiry" of October, 1934, indicate that at that early date in his career, he had some reservations about the surrealist program. To the question, "Have you been influenced by Freud and how do you regard him?" he answered:

I have never been directly influenced by Freud in my poetry, but I have been indirectly influenced by him through the Surrealists. To give oneself up at any time to writing poems without the control of reason is, I imagine, to have in a way come under the influence of Freud. I no longer find this navel-gazing activity at all satisfying. The Surrealists themselves have a definite justification for writing in this way, but for an English poet with continually growing political convictions it must soon become impossible.

Kathleen Raine, in her perceptive essay on Gascoyne, reads this as evidence that he was losing interest in surrealism as early as 1934 and that his productions of the next two years are to be regarded as aberrant.[1] It is true that by 1937, Gascoyne had abandoned surrealism and had returned to writing the kind of poetry he described in the New Verse "Inquiry." When asked "Do you think there can now be a use for narrative poetry?" Gascoyne replied, "What might be useful now would be a poem expressing the ever-rising feeling of crisis, anxiety and panic; a poem that would treat this feeling in a loose, universal and epic sort of way. I mean a poem narrating the contemporary Zeitgeist of Europe, or even of the world." Nevertheless, during 1935 and 1936, Gascoyne performed signal services for the surrealist cause with no indication that he was acting against his own preferences: he translated into English for the first time many poems of Eluard, Péret, Breton, Hugnet, Unik, Ribemont-Dessaignes, and Giacometti; in 1935 he wrote the first English surrealist manifesto and the Short Survey; in 1936 he helped organize the International Surrealist Exhibition, translated Breton's What is Surrealism?, and, together with Humphrey Jennings, edited and translated poems by Benjamin Péret which appeared under the titles A Bunch of Carrots and Remove Your Hat.[2] In 1936, also, a

[1] Kathleen Raine, "David Gascoyne and the Prophetic Role," Defending Ancient Springs (London: Oxford University Press, 1967), pp. 35–65.

[2] Published by Roger Roughton (London: Contemporary Poetry and Prose Editions, 1936). Contrary to appearances and published accounts, these two titles represent the same collection of poems except for minor differences. The first volume, A Bunch of Carrots, appeared with some blank lines which had been censored. The second volume, Remove Your Hat, with almost identical contents, carried the somewhat misleading note: "Second edition—revised, re-titled, uncensored; with three new poems." The note is misleading

volume of his poems, *Man's Life Is This Meat*, appeared.[3]
All but six of the poems, according to his prefatory note, are
surrealist. Miss Raine insists in her essay on a consistency
of development that may be too rigorous: it must not be
forgotten that Gascoyne was only eighteen years old when
he answered the *New Verse* "Inquiry" and no more than
twenty-one when he abandoned surrealism.

Since the poems labeled "surrealist" in *Man's Life Is This
Meat* constitute one of the few showpieces of English surrealism, they are worth some close attention. The impression
they create is that if they are surrealist, they are so at one
remove. They seem, rather than "pure psychic automatism"
issuing in words, to be verbal transcriptions of images seen
—and not all of these seen below the level of waking consciousness. There are none of the startling collisions of words
one has learned to expect from Breton, Eluard, Péret, and
others, but, instead, collisions of images that seem often
deliberately contrived. Gascoyne, to the degree that his
poems are the product of surrealist method, appears to have
fallen victim to the great danger Breton had warned against:
his poems are descriptions of images seen during the relaxa-
tion of consciousness or even descriptions of paintings; they

---

because the second edition omitted the two poems from which the
greatest number of lines had been censored and replaced them with
two new poems. It is uncensored in that it restored only one line
which had been deleted in the first edition. It is misleading to call
the volume uncensored if the editors have acceded to the censor's
wishes and replaced the offending poems. The note is inaccurate in
that the new edition contains only two new poems, the two that
replaced the heavily censored ones. It is difficult today to see why
these deleted lines should have caused offense: they are at worst
childishly scatological.

[3] David Gascoyne, *Man's Life Is This Meat* (London: Parton Press,
n.d. [1936]).

are not the true product of automatism. They often achieve the desired shock of the unusual juxtaposition, but they are not the real article; they do not, to use Herbert Read's image, travel along that geological fault that exposes the several layers of the human psyche in order to reach the depths of the unconscious; at best, they probe just below the first level. Gascoyne's procedure seems to have been, contrary to Breton's instructions, simply to choose a subject and then, by a process of free association, to permit images to cluster around that subject. These images appear to be the product of casual daydreams, not of profound probing into the unconscious. The first few lines of the first poem of the group he calls surrealist illustrate this point:

> Above and below
> The roll of days spread out like a cloth
> Days engraved on everyone's forehead
> Yesterday folding To-morrow opening

Aside from the Blakean echo (I . . . mark in every face I meet/Marks of weakness, marks of woe), the controlling image of this passage, "days spread out like a cloth," recalls very closely Reverdy's image "the day was folded like a white cloth," which Gascoyne had quoted in the *Short Survey* (p. 66). Even if Gascoyne's use of the image is an example of unconscious memory, one would have to conclude that in this instance, Gascoyne had not probed very deep, for it is doubtful that other poets' images can become part of one's unconscious, not if one takes the term "unconscious" in any serious Freudian sense.

This example is symptomatic: other of Gascoyne's poems are also illustrations of surrealism at one remove. For example, "Charity Week: To Max Ernst," opens with a striking image:

Have presented the lion with medals of mud
One for each day of the week

This is a deliberate description of one of the pictures in
Max Ernst's *Une Semaine de bonté* (1934), an album of
collages in seven parts, one for each day of the week. For
Sunday, the element is mud; the example, the Lion of
Belfort. Ernst's picture shows a lion-headed figure in military uniform with medals on its chest.[4] Max Ernst's picture
may have been produced by an automatic process; Gascoyne's image was not. The third stanza of this poem,

Hysteria upon the staircase
Hair torn out by the roots
Lace handkerchief torn to shreds
Their fragments strewn upon the waters

contains nothing that a deliberate, conscious process could
not have produced.

The poems entitled "Salvador Dali" and "Yves Tanguy"
are descriptions of works by these painters—if not of actual
paintings, then of imaginary ones in their styles. The first is
a rendition of typical Dali paranoiac images:

The face of the precipice is black with lovers;
The sun above them is a bag of nails; the spring's
First rivers hide among the hair.
Goliath plunges his hand into the poisoned well
And bows his head and feels my feet walk through his brain.
The children chasing butterflies turn around and see him there
With his hand in the well and my body growing from his head,
And are afraid. They drop their nets and walk into the wall
    like smoke.

[4] Reproduced in Marcel Jean, *The History of Surrealist Painting*,
trans. by Simon Watson Taylor (New York: Grove Press, 1960),
pp. 255–256.

The second is a typical Tanguy landscape:

> The fading cries of the light
> Awaken the endless desert
> Engrossed in its tropical slumber
> Enclosed by the dead grey oceans
> Enclasped by the arms of the night
>
> The worlds are breaking in my head
> Their fragments are crumbs of despair
> The food of the solitary damned
> Who await the gross tumult of turbulent
> Days bringing change without end

Another of Gascoyne's poems, from *Contemporary Poetry and Prose* (June, 1936), is of a similar kind. Entitled "The Very Image" and dedicated to René Magritte, it consists of a series of separate images that, if not in fact descriptions of paintings by Magritte, could very well be:

> An image of my grandmother
> her head appearing upside-down upon a cloud
> The cloud transfixed on the steeple
> of a deserted railway station
> far away
>
> An image of an aqueduct
> with a dead crow hanging from the first arch
> a modern-style chair from the second
> a fir-tree lodged in the third
> and the whole scene sprinkled with snow

The last line seems evidence that Gascoyne is describing and not experiencing.

The point of these comments is not that Gascoyne's poems are failures as poems. Some of them are, in fact, effective and successful juxtapositions of images, and the lines quoted above from "Yves Tanguy" are an excellent evocation of that painter's landscapes. These poems are not, however, surrealist in any true sense of the word.

Other poems are full of perfectly rational, even conventional images: from "Unspoken": "speech flowing away like water/With its undertow of violence and darkness"; "A wheel of fortune turning in the fog/. . . Back into the cycle of return and change"; from "The Truth Is Blind": "The light fell from the window and the day was done/Another day of thinking and distractions"; ". . . he saw the flaming sun/He saw the buildings between the leaves"; from "Educative Process": "A drop of dew sings psalms upon the hill/Anatomies of wonder opened at the first page"; "The glass on the table is empty and so are your eyes."

It is obvious that Gascoyne does not produce any of the violent juxtapositions that are common in Breton's verse. But not every poet who aspires to surrealism must have the same kind of verbal imagination as Breton; Gascoyne's, however, tends to be conventional, even stilted. He produces couplings of adjectives and nouns that would not be out of place in the most conventional Victorian poem: fevered breath, strident cries, cruel claws, oblivious dream, divided terrain, knotted hair, carnal lusts, pointing finger, sudden spasm, pure disgust—all from one poem, "Purified Disgust," which is not surrealist by any definition, although it bears that label:

> An impure sky
> A heartless and impure breathing
> The fevered breath of logic
> And a great bird broke loose
> Flapping into the silence with strident cries
> A great bird with cruel claws

Beyond the savage pretence of knowledge
Beyond that posture of oblivious dream
Into the divided terrain of anguish
Where one walks with bound hands
Where one walks with knotted hair
With eyes searching the zenith
Where one walks like Sebastian

. . . . .

How could we touch that carrion?
A sudden spasm saves us
A pure disgust illumines us
The music of the spheres is silent
Our hands lie still upon the counterpane
And the herds come home.

The technique of the first stanza is reminiscent of Baude-laire's "Spleen":

l'Espérance, comme une chauve-souris,
S'en va battant les murs de son aile timide
Et se cognant la tête à des plafonds pourris.

(Hope, like a bat, goes hitting the walls with
its timid wing and knocking its head against
rotten ceilings.)

The Baudelairean echo is symptomatic: what the poem does, instead of shocking us into seeing or being, as often the best surrealist verse succeeds in doing, is to present a series of images that are the equivalent of the emotion that the poem is about. This is the technique of the symbolists, of the imagists, and of the early Eliot, not of the surrealists, for it implies a certain distance from the matter of the poem, not an immersion in it.

This statement is true for Gascoyne's work only in a quali-fied sense; the technique of the total poem may be that of the symbolists or of the imagists, but individual images are sometimes effective in a way that approaches the surrealist, even if they are allegorical (as these lines from "The Truth Is Blind"):

> Love wrapped in its wings passed by and coal-black Hate
> Paused on the edge of the cliff and dropped a stone
> From which the night grew like a savage plant
> With daggers for its leaves and scarlet hearts
> For flowers—then the bed
> Rose clockwise from the ground and spread its sheets
> Across the shifting sands.

Another poem by Gascoyne, "The Cubical Domes," also contains an occasional image that has the true stamp:

> The slow voice of the tobacconist is like a circle
> Drawn on the floor in chalk and containing ants

or,

> For after all why should love resemble a cushion

but it also contains images that seem deliberately contrived for their absurdity:

> And then there is the problem of living to be considered
> With its vast pink parachutes full of underdone mutton
> Its tableaux of the archbishops dressed in their underwear.[5]

Gascoyne's poems to or about painters are the most obvious in this respect: in them he merely presents a previously seen or imagined thing. In poems that do not have so easily definable a subject, the effect is still the same: his images, almost always entirely visual, have no significance outside of their immediate visual effect; they have none of the visionary power that Breton's or Eluard's sometimes

---

[5] *Contemporary Poetry and Prose*, no. 2 (June, 1936), p. 34.

show. The inescapable impression that *Man's Life* creates is that Gascoyne *uses* surrealism, that he writes in a surrealistic style, despite his vehement insistence in his manifesto and *Short Survey* that surrealism is not a literary school or style. Perhaps this explains in part why he abandoned surrealism as soon as he did: as a style it proved unsatisfactory; he could do what he wanted more successfully in other ways. His next volume, *Poems, 1937–1942*, with the exception of an occasional violent image, shows no trace of surrealism. His later work moved toward a religious, perhaps even mystical, point of view. But one may say that even if he deserted surrealism not long after having become its champion, he did not entirely lose sympathy for some of its basic attitudes. In 1946, in the introduction he wrote to a volume of poems by Kenneth Patchen, he indicated that the dadaist attitude was still a valid position to assume against the world.[6] And in his later work, *Night Thoughts* (1956), Gascoyne returned to a kind of perception he learned from surrealism: he produces a dreamlike consciousness which by a confusion of inner and outer worlds finds the objective world full of "messages," heavy with meaning. As Miss Raine says of this poem, "We create the world continually in the image of our dreams; and see reflected in the outer, images of inner realities and preoccupations." [7]

The idea expressed by Miss Raine, that "we create the world continually in the image of our dreams," an idea that has its obvious affinities with the surrealist notion of the object, was the mainspring of what she calls "an English counterpart to surrealism (at all events of certain aspects of it) and an altogether original variant of the irrationalistic

[6] Kenneth Patchen, *Outlaw of the Lowest Planet,* selected and with an introduction by David Gascoyne (London: Grey Walls Press, 1946), pp. x–xiv.
[7] Kathleen Raine, *Defending Ancient Springs,* p. 47.

movement," that is, Mass-Observation.[8] Originally conceived by Charles Madge, a sociologist and poet; Tom Harrisson, an anthropologist; and Humphrey Jennings, Mass-Observation was a technique for recording what Miss Raine calls the "subliminal stirrings of the collective mind of the nation; through the images thrown up in such things as advertisements, popular songs, themes in the press, the objects with which people surround themselves (have on their mantlepiece, for example)." Miss Raine sees in this a kinship with the surrealist *objet trouvé* which embodies in the objective world desires first visualized in dreams or in the unconscious. Mass-Observation, then, attempted to combine a surrealist conception of the irrational with sociology. One of its founders, the anthropologist Tom Harrisson, had had, Miss Raine says, the novel idea of applying "methods of sociology hitherto employed only on savages to the English working class." The technique that was developed seems to have much in common with what later came to be known as "motivational research," although Madge and Jennings were primarily interested in what it would reveal about the imagination, or the functioning of a collective imagination.

The relationship of Mass-Observation to surrealism is, obviously, a tenuous one, although there is a similarity between it and the surrealist doctrine of the object. But to be quite accurate, Mass-Observation is a kind of surrealism in reverse. Whereas the surrealist sees in his objects—found or made—an objectification of inner states or desires, Mass-Observation assumes that the objects and images of our world are the concretization of inner states and seeks to recover those inner states by using the objects and images as signposts. Surrealism, to put it another way, wants to project the imagination onto the objective world in order to

[8] Information about Mass-Observation is scant. I am indebted to Miss Raine's account of it in *Defending Ancient Springs*, pp. 47–48.

transform it; Mass-Observation tries to recover the imagination that produced the vulgar objects and images of the everyday world. Although in theory Mass-Observation presented interesting possibilities, in practice, according to Ruthven Todd, who was peripherally involved with the movement, it posed insuperable problems. Whereas the results of motivational research or product surveys can be reduced to statistical information, the work of reconstructing the "collective imagination" expressed in vast numbers of Mass-Observation reports proved all but impossible, and the idea died very soon after its inception.

But if Mass-Observation failed in its stated aims, it did make possible,

a kind of poetic (or pictorial) imagery at once irrational and objective; and it was David Gascoyne who finally realized and perfected a kind of poetry (written also by Charles Madge and Humphrey Jennings) in which an imagery of precise and objective realism, gathered from the daily human (and therefore especially urban) scene, from the habitat of common man, is informed with a content not only supremely imaginative, but infused with the imagination of the collective mind of which it is an eloquent, if unconscious, expression; a listening to the dreaming . . . of a nation or a world, itself unaware of the purport of its own fantasies. Thus the poet reassumes the ancient role at once of national prophet, and reader of the auguries; not from entrails or yarrow-stalks, but from (literally) the "writing on walls," the seemingly fortuitous recurring images in the daily records. Anything and everything speaks to the augur attuned to its meaning. The two apparently irreconcilables are in such poetry brought together: imaginative inspiration, and a realistic objectivity.[9]

The debt this notion owes to surrealism is obvious.

[9] *Ibid.*

Humphrey Jennings, an early supporter of surrealism and one of the organizers of the International Surrealist Exhibition, left few published works. A few fragments and poems appeared in the thirties in the *London Bulletin, Left Review,* and *Contemporary Poetry and Prose.* After Jennings's death in 1950, Ruthven Todd printed a small collection of his poems on a hand press.[10] His vast anthology on the Industrial Revolution, "Pandemonium," remains unpublished; what information about him and his ideas is available must be gathered from the writings of people who knew him.[11]

Taking as his starting point Lautréamont's dictum that "poetry will be made by all," an idea adopted by the surrealists, Jennings based his ideas of the imagination and the poetic image on the concretization of imagination represented by the surrealist "object." But where the surrealist finds his images in the "real functioning of thought," that is, in automatism, Jennings thought that the image must be discovered, not invented; it must be sought for—visually in the external world, in literature, or in history. The surrealist image is impersonal in the degree that the unconscious is impersonal; for Jennings the image is impersonal by deliberate assumption: it communicates truth only in the degree that it is collective, public, and historical. "The imagination, according to Jennings, must test itself continually against historical actuality; for such actuality is itself an embodi-

[10] Humphrey Jennings, *Poems,* introduction by Kathleen Raine (New York: Weekend Press, 1951).

[11] Kathleen Raine, "Writer and Artist," *Humphrey Jennings, 1907–1950: A Tribute* (London: Published by the Humphrey Jennings Memorial Fund Committee, n.d. [1960]). Kathleen Raine, "Introduction," Humphrey Jennings, *Poems.* J. Bronowski, "Recollections of Humphrey Jennings," *Twentieth Century,* CLXV, no. 983 (January, 1959), 45–50. I owe the substance of my presentation of Jennings to Miss Raine.

ment of imaginative truth; for man creates his world continually in the image of his dreams. In this view . . . Jennings was indebted to Blake, who so vehemently declared
that the 'dark Satanic Mills' of industry are but an embodiment of the mechanistic thought of Bacon and Newton." [12]

A few lines from one of Jennings's best poems, "I See
London"—a deliberate echo of Blake's "I behold London"—
present images that seem copied from the paintings and
films of the surrealists but which were, for all their fantastic
aspect, in fact to be seen in London after an air raid:

I see a thousand strange sights in the streets of London
I see the clock on Bow Church burning in daytime
I see a one-legged man crossing the fire on crutches
I see three negroes and a woman with white face-powder
    reading music at half-past three in the morning
I see an ambulance girl with her arms full of roses
I see the burnt drum of the Philharmonic
I see the green leaves of Lincolnshire carried through London
    on the wrecked body of an aircraft.

Jennings seems, then, to be turning surrealism upside
down: he finds in the real, concrete object an image of the
collective imagination; the surrealist, on the other hand,
finds in his imagination (i.e., when he is in a state of automatism) an image which he seeks then to concretize in the
external world, in a painting, a poem, or an object. One of
the startling discoveries of surrealism, in the doctrine of
"objective chance," is that the objective world responds—
or corresponds—to the inner vision, that the alogical automatic mind (or the unconscious) has such subtle links with
the objective world that it can be prophetic of events in that
world. The most nightmarish juxtapositions in the surrealist

[12] Raine, *Defending Ancient Springs,* p. 50.

imagination—those troubling and poignant images in the canvases of Ernst, Magritte, Delvaux, in the films of Dali and Buñuel—proved all too prophetic of events in wartime London. If the Surrealist Phantom of the 1936 exhibition was a "made object" embodying one of Dali's "paranoiac" obsessions, the "ambulance girl with her arms full of roses" of Jennings's poem is a "found object," a ready-made concretization of the same obsession, removed from Dali's imagination onto the plane of the objective. Mass-Observation is an attempt to discover what imagination it is that projects its images onto the objective world; Jennings's poems use these images as embodiments of that collective, historical imagination; surrealism is an attempt to free that imagination from its traditional restraints so that it can freely express itself and transform the world.

Another event of importance occurred in 1936—the publication of *Thorns of Thunder*, a collection of poems by Paul Eluard in translations by Samuel Beckett, Denis Devlin, David Gascoyne, Eugene Jolas, Man Ray, George Reavey, and Ruthven Todd. George Reavey, the editor and publisher of the volume, wrote an "Editorial Foreword" which in the briefest manner defines surrealism:

"Everything can be compared to everything, everything has its echo, its reason, its resemblance, its opposition and its becoming everywhere. And this becoming is infinite." The systematic application of this concept to art is one of the main features of the Surrealist movement. Surrealism rejects the conventional imagery of traditional subjects and purely formal research (abstract art). It is primarily an art of dynamic images which discard the test of reality.[13]

[13] Paul Eluard, *Thorns of Thunder*, ed. by George Reavey (London: Europa Press and Stanley Nott, n.d. [1936]), p. vii.

and once again, surrealism has been reduced to a new kind of image-making device. Herbert Read wrote a very brief "Preface" for the volume in which he restated his familiar view that there is nothing particularly new about surrealism, that surrealist poets do what all true, i.e., romantic, poets have always done.

The book, or rather its preface and introduction, received a lengthy commentary from E. W. F. Tomlin in the *Criterion* (October, 1936). He took Read and Reavey severely to task for their claim that by discarding the test of reason a poet achieves imaginative liberation and rises *above* the level of rationality. This view implies that "poetic values are the highest values in a culture," as Read had said in his *In Defence of Shelley;* that the poet inhabits a higher intellectual plane than the scientist and philosopher; that aesthetic truth is the highest obtainable. "These three views," Tomlin says, "with their corollary that we must look to art for the solution of the problems of life, I regard as the major heresies of our time." Tomlin dismisses the claims made for Eluard by Read and Reavey: "Can we suppose . . . that such poetry as Eluard's springs simply from conformity to a theory. . . . Or are we entitled to maintain that the poetry of Eluard must be considered primarily as poetry and only secondarily as surrealist poetry?" Tomlin, finding it significant that Read did not mention surrealism at all in his preface, sees in this a tacit agreement with his own view that " 'in daring to be irrational,' in discarding the test of reason, the artist is merely daring to be an artist . . . asserting the inherent rights of the unfettered imagination." Tomlin, then, seems in agreement with Read that surrealism is little else than a reaffirmation of the "romantic principle."

The first number of *Contemporary Poetry and Prose* appeared in May, 1936, a month before the surrealist exhibition in London. The pompous title of this modest periodical may have been inspired by the same spirit that prompted Breton to name his dadaist magazine *Littérature*. The nine-teen-year-old editor, Roger Roughton, was a member of what he called the "loosely-constituted English Surrealist group," and, from the very first, the magazine reflected that interest, although Roughton insisted that the magazine was not an official surrealist organ and that it did not reflect the opinions of the group.[14] The magazine may, nonetheless, be considered a kind of semiofficial organ for the London sur-realists, who, until the appearance of the *London Bulletin* in April, 1938, were without a periodical of their own; many of its contributors were, if not outright surrealists, at least allied with them. But, perhaps in order to appeal to a wider public (Roughton published the magazine at his own ex-pense), the roster of contributors also included Wallace Stevens, William Empson, E. E. Cummings, Horace Greg-ory, Isaac Babel, St.-John Perse, and Dylan Thomas. But Roger Roughton was also a Communist, at the time perhaps the only wholehearted member of the Communist Party among the surrealists,[15] and his few editorial comments in the magazine deal directly with politics or related matters.

In his article, "Communism and Surrealism" (August–September, 1936), Roughton took up the question of the relation between the two movements. The English surrealist group, he announced, had just been formed and had issued the fourth number of the *International Surrealist Bulletin*. Roughton welcomed the desire to cooperate with the Com-

---

[14] *Contemporary Poetry and Prose*, no. 8 (December, 1936), p. 143.

[15] Information on this point is hard to come by; Gascoyne more than once expressed his leftist leanings ("If you are with us you are red"), but I have seen no statement that he was actually a member of the Party.

munists professed by the *Bulletin* because surrealism, "in so far as it can break down irrational bourgeois-taught prejudices [prepares] the mental ground for possible revolutionary thought and action." He praised Herbert Read's endorsement in the *Bulletin* of Breton's statement that "the surrealists entirely rely for the bringing about of the liberation of man upon the proletarian revolution," but he attacked Read for having said that the surrealist "generally claims that he is a more consistent Communist than many who submit to all manner of compromise with the aesthetic culture and moral conventions of capitalism." This, said Roughton, is a dangerous Trotskyist, "more communist than the communists" attitude: "those who, claiming to be communists, remain outside the party and criticize it, show not their independence but their irresponsibility." Similarly, if current conditions call for compromises in order to build a united front to oppose fascism, then such compromises must be accepted, even with the Christian churches, "for even though christianity is generally a weapon of counter-revolution, it still has a democratic rôle to play in certain circumstances, as can be seen in Nazi Germany." And, he concludes, "as long as the surrealists will help to establish a broad United Front . . . there is no reason why there should be any quarrel between surrealism and communism."

Two months later (November, 1936), the magazine published a "Declaration on Spain," issued by the "Surrealist Group in England" and signed by Hugh Sykes Davies, David Gascoyne, Humphrey Jennings, Diana Brinton Lee, Rupert Lee, Henry Moore, Paul Nash, Roland Penrose, Valentine Penrose, Herbert Read, and Roger Roughton (presumably all the members of the group). The Declaration called upon the British government to abandon its policy of nonintervention in Spain, a policy that, far from

expressing neutrality, indirectly encouraged the intervention of Germany and Italy, and to lift its ban on the sale of
arms to the Spanish Republic.

The same number of the magazine (November, 1936)
contained a typically ill-tempered attack by Ezra Pound
entitled "The Coward Surrealists." The title is clarified by a
statement that shows Pound's remarkable ignorance of surrealism: "The XIIth century had surrealism in plenty. A
brave man would admit it, and not run howling to cover
when asked to stand the comparison." As Roughton points
out in his rejoinder, and as is obvious from the most cursory
reading of surrealist statements, the surrealists have always
pointed to precursors (perhaps not those of the twelfth
century) in their desire to prove that their kind of irrationality had antecedents. Pound continues his attack:

When it comes to "breaking down irrational" (or rational for that
matter) "bourgeois prejudices" . . . the simple practice of using
WORDS with clear and unequivocal meaning will blast all the
London schools of economics; history and other bourgeois drib-
ble; without any -isms being needed as hyperdermic [sic].

The mere flight from and evasion of defined words and
historic fact is NOT sur- but SUB-realism; it is no more revolutionary than the dim ditherings of the aesthetes in 1888 which
supplied the oatmeal of the "nineties." A party wanting revolution instead of wishing to discuss blue china in mirrored alcoves
would face communization of product: it would face socialization of the means of exchange, it would at least be restive in
the presence of FALSIFIED history transmitted by employees
of the financiers. It might be as "immediate" as you like; in that
it need care no more than Manet for the title deed of the sun'd
haystack but it would not accept falsified clichés.

The intellectual timidity of the pseudolutionists gives me a
pain in the neck.

Roger Roughton rejoined in the same issue in a short article entitled "Eyewash, Do You?: A Reply to Mr. Pound." He agreed with Pound's last sentence, and explained that this was why he had written his editorial "Surrealism and Communism," from which Pound had quoted. The contribution to the revolution to be made by surrealism is, admittedly, a small one, Roughton said, and his editorial is to be considered a call to order, for "an overdose of Freudianism may lead, and has led, some surrealists to an individualistic, anarchic trotskyism." Even "maestro" Breton, Roughton said, is not free from this charge, for he "considers that now, now when democracy and socialism are fighting for their life against international fascism, is the time to publish an attack on the Moscow Trials and the Soviet Union." As for the use of words, Roughton answered, the *Communist Manifesto* and *Capital* are written in clear and unequivocal words and Pound is the proof of the inefficacy of that kind of revolution. "No," Roughton concluded, "the 'pseudolutionists' are rather to be found among the ex-patriate admirers of fascism and capitalist quackery."

Except for an attack on the Spanish rebels for the murder of Lorca and a plea for aid to antifascists in the October, 1936, issue these three statements were the extent of the political involvement of the magazine. Certainly the contents in no way reflected the editor's bias. However, one conspicuous absence from the roster of contributors—Herbert Read's—may perhaps be explained by Read's hostility to the Communist Party.

The second issue of *Contemporary Poetry and Prose* (June, 1936), a surrealist double number, appeared at the time of the opening of the exhibition. It contains poems by Eluard, Breton, Péret, Dali, Hugnet, Buñuel, and the

Belgian surrealist E. L. T. Mesens, who was to become
important in the English movement. The English contributions are scant: in addition to the two poems by Gascoyne
already mentioned, there are only a poem by Roughton,
one by Kenneth Allott, and two short pieces by children
aged five and seven.

Roughton's poem, "Animal Crackers in Your Croup,"
reads in part:

> I have told you that there is a laugh in every corner
> And a pocket-book stuffed with rolls of skin
> To pay off the bills of the costive
> To buy a new pipe for the dog
> To send a committee to bury a stone
>
> I have told you all this
> But do you know that
> To-morrow the palmist will lunch on his crystal
> To-morrow REVOLT will be written in human hair
>
>   . . . .
>
> To-morrow Karl Marx will descend in a fire balloon
> To-morrow the word that you lost will ask you home
>
>   . . . .
>
> To-morrow a child will rechristen our London as LONDON
> To-morrow a tree will grow into a hand
> Yes listen
> To-morrow the clocks will chime like voices
> To-morrow a train will set out for the sky

and from Allott, "Fête Champêtre":

> There was a fall of sawdust on the roofs of churches
> and there was a sudden interchange of sexes
> and no more children were born, but the dead rose
> and straddled their stones and cruelly mocked the living.

So everyone put on odd shoes and stockings
and went out on an orgy of window smashing

. . . . .

These two poems, together with the two by Gascoyne, make a rather poor showing for English surrealism. Allott's poem can be called surrealist only if violent images and superficial irrationality are the only criteria. Roughton's, on the other hand, succeeds in commmunicating a kind of ecstatic millenarian hope.

The magazine continued to publish surrealist works for the rest of its short life.[16] David Gascoyne contributed two short prose pieces, of which the following is an example:

But let us pause to consider the cause of the disturbance that is taking place at the end of the corridor. The waves have thrown up the remains of a small vessel on to the sanded floor, and among the tattered casks and the crumbs of the ship's biscuits one can see a dissevered head that is trying to speak to the assembled multitude. . . . It is covered with sunspots and will undoubtedly break into flame at the end of a quarter of an hour or so. Lay your hand on the massive forehead and you will feel the gradual movement of the birds that are imprisoned underneath.[17]

The attractive phantom of the exhibition, Sheila Legge, proved that she had a more substantial existence than that of an apparition by contributing a short prose piece.[18]

One of Hugh Sykes Davies's rare surrealist poems appeared in the November, 1936, issue. Entitled simply

[16] Ten numbers in all were published. With no. 9 (Spring, 1937), the magazine changed to quarterly publication, but only one more number (Autumn, 1937) appeared.

[17] "The Light of the Lion's Mane," *Contemporary Poetry and Prose*, no. 8 (December, 1936), pp. 160–162.

[18] "I Have Done My Best for You," *ibid.*, p. 165.

"Poem," it is a careful and highly effective piece of work. It starts quite simply:

> In the stump of the old tree, where the heart has rotted out,
>   there is a hole the length of a man's arm, and a dank pool
>   at the bottom of it where the rain gathers, and the old
>   leaves turn into lacy skeletons. But do not put your
>   hand down there to see because
>
> in the stump of old trees, where the hearts have rotted out

and by very gradual and subtle alterations and seemingly insignificant additions to the catalogue of objects in the stump of that tree, builds to a climax of horror:

> . . . and if you ever put your hånd
> down to see, you can wipe it on the sharp grass till
> it bleeds, but you'll never want to eat with it again.

Whether this is, strictly speaking, surrealist, is a difficult question—there is nothing startling about the language or the imagery, but it succeeds in transmuting completely ordinary items into objects of terror, and achieves, in a small way, that synthesis of internal and external states.

In addition to a number of poems, Dylan Thomas contributed three short stories to the magazine, "The Burning Baby," "School for Witches," and "The Holy Six," which are among his works showing surrealist influence. Since Thomas, however, presents an important and special problem in his relation to the whole subject of surrealism, he will be treated in the next chapter.

Roger Roughton himself published much of his work outside of *Contemporary Poetry and Prose;* a frequent contributor to *Poetry* (Chicago), he won that magazine's Harriet Monroe Lyric Prize for 1937. The *Criterion* published some of his verse in April, 1936, and an allegorical short story, "The Sand under the Door" in October, 1937, which proved prophetic of his suicide in April, 1941, at the age of twenty-four.[19] Another allegory, "The Human House," appeared posthumously in *Horizon*.

In November, 1936, it will be recalled, Herbert Read's *Surrealism* appeared; Read's own contribution to that volume has already been discussed. Hugh Sykes Davies's essay "Surrealism at This Time and Place," is instructive about the basic attitudes of English surrealists. His fundamental point is the same as that of almost all English writers on surrealism: "We, the Surrealists in England, have not heard a message from France in a cloud of fire. Surrealism is the natural and inevitable product of historical forces; it is not inspired, it is caused. . . . It is the purpose of this essay to show . . . how our position follows inevitably from a proper understanding of the historical movement in England." The present moment, Davies says, can be understood only as a development from the past, and from the nineteenth century in particular; in order to understand the nineteenth century, the eighteenth must be studied, and so on. The particular poetic crisis that the nineteenth century faced was the result of the debasing of poetry at the hands of the classicists to the level of mere diversion and ornament; it had lost whatever power to communicate truth it had ever possessed.

Coleridge's work, Davies says, "was determined primarily by the violent reassertion of poetic activity which we call romanticism," and his task in restoring poetry to a level higher than that of a "cosmic cosmetic" was to abolish the

[19] "Notes on Contributors," *Horizon*, IV, no. 19 (July, 1941), 8; David Gascoyne, "An Elegy: R. R. 1916–41," *Collected Poems* (London: Oxford University Press, 1965), pp. 68–70.

materialist contrast between reality and fantasy, to restore to human desires the status of facts, and to show that poetry conforms to the nature of the human mind itself. On the psychological level, Coleridge's solution involved the distinction between delusion and mania, a distinction parallel to that between fancy and imagination. The great examples of imagination in poetry all have the quality of mania or, in our modern terminology, paranoia: for example, Lear, Coleridge says, "spreads the feeling of ingratitude and cruelty over the very elements of heaven"; Wordsworth, impelled by his sense of guilt, projects his feeling onto his famous huge mountain peak which "As if with voluntary power instinct/ Upreared its head." Upon this experience Wordsworth built his whole mythology, and for Coleridge, this projection of inner upon outer states, this maniac system, became the power that informed all truly imaginative poetry. In Wordsworth's mythology, and this is its importance, Davies says, "subject and object, man and nature, are unified and made one; in it, therefore, we find a true knowledge, the coincidence of man and the world."

Coleridge, then, had abolished the distinction between reality and fantasy; and poetry, instead of being an ornament or a distortion of reality, became the only true approach to that reality. Surrealism, of course, has come to the same conclusions; it, too, attempts to unify human feeling and external objects. Similarly, in the areas of political and social freedom, surrealism continues the work of the English romantics, and can, therefore, correctly be considered the prehensile tail of romanticism, as Breton has called it.

At Davies's hands, surrealism becomes the only possible conclusion of the process of English literary history; it is never clear from his discussion why this should be so; why, for example, it should not be T. S. Eliot's idea of tradition that is the correct one. It too has its roots in the literary past, and its relevance could be demonstrated by a procedure analogous to the one Davies uses to demonstrate the irrefutable relevance of surrealism.

Breton's contribution to the volume, "Limits Not Frontiers of Surrealism," [20] is a highly condensed presentation of fundamental surrealist doctrines, and since Chapter 1 is an elaboration of these, there is no need to review them. One important point, however, must be stressed concerning this particular essay. Discussing the vogue of the *romans noirs,* i.e., the Gothic novels, Breton says that "the attention of humanity in its most universal and spontaneous form as well as in its most individual and purely intellectual form, has here been attracted not by the scrupulously exact description of exterior events of which the world was the theatre, but rather by the expression of the confused feelings awakened by nostalgia and terror." The substitution of romantic scenery for realistic scenery in these novels, Breton insists, was not deliberately determined by their authors; rather, the style of the Gothic novels "may be considered pathognomic of the great social troubles in which Europe was enveloped at the end of the eighteenth century." For Breton, the truth of this is evidenced by the automatic origin of *The Castle of Otranto,* described by Walpole in his famous letter to William Cole (March 9, 1765). The task of surrealism, Breton says, "is the elaboration of the *collective myth* belonging to our period in the same way" as the Gothic novels belong to theirs:

Human psychism in its most universal aspect has found in the Gothic castle and its accessories a point of fixation so precise

[20] This essay is conveniently reprinted, in a different translation, in Justin O'Brien, ed., *From the NRF* (New York: Meridian Books, 1959), pp. 83–95.

that it became essential to discover what would be the equivalent for our own period. . . . However, Surrealism is still only able to point out the change from the period of the "roman noir" to our time, from the most highly charged emotions of the miraculous *apparition* to the no less disconcerting *coincidence*, and to ask us to allow ourselves to be guided towards the unknown by this newest *promise*.

Breton is talking of *surrealism* and its promise; Read and Davies were discussing *superrealism*, to borrow Read's term, and in doing so, they were destroying that promise. Put another way, the objection to Read and Davies as surrealists is that they ignore what Breton calls "the change . . . from the most highly charged emotions of the miraculous *apparition* to the no less disconcerting *coincidence*"; for them the ghost remains on its romantic battlements, the coincidence never really becomes proof of "objective chance." If, in their historical survey, they do not actually commit the genetic fallacy, they very nearly do so. They are simply interested in demonstrating the "eternal truths" of surrealism, in codifying and categorizing it. For Read, surrealism corroborates his own aesthetic bias; for Davies, it is an illustration of Coleridge's ideas. Paul Nougé, the Belgian surrealist, made a similar point in a different context when he warned against the danger of taking doctrines and theories as "truths" rather than tools: "What is to be thought of the poor beginner who, under the pretext of surrealism, devotes his attention solely to the dream-world, the appearances of automatism, and who proposes to reduce every Surrealist undertaking to certain elementary formulas about dreams, delirium, and the mechanics of the unconscious?" [21] Al-

[21] "A Warning," *London Gallery Bulletin*, no. 1 (April, 1938), pp. 5–6.

though he did not name Read and Davies, Nougé's comment applies to them.

Soon after the publication of *Surrealism*, Read and Davies together replied to an attack by A. L. Lloyd in the *Left Review* (January, 1937), and their reply must rank high among the oddities of the movement. Lloyd had used the occasion of a review of Herbert Read's *Surrealism* to accuse the movement of social irresponsibility:

The Surrealist is caught in the trap of individualism in this way: try as he may, he can do no more than sublimate the narcissism of the bourgeoisie. . . . If Surrealism were revolutionary, it could be of use. But Surrealism is not revolutionary, because its lyricism is socially irresponsible. It does not lead fantasy into any action of real social significance. . . . It has no bearing on proletarian problems, gives no twist towards social responsiblility. . . . These frivolous games of automatism and newspaper-clipping-creation, of goosy ghost-hunting and a hazardous preoccupation with chance . . . can play no part in making the proletariat conscious of its social and revolutionary responsibilities.

In their rejoinder in the February, 1937, issue of the *Left Review*, Read and Davies objected to the term "lyrical impulse" because it belongs in bourgeois terminology and is associated with inspiration, with religious and idealistic assumptions. They continued to use it because Lloyd had, but they make it clear that by it they mean "dream-activity." In rebuttal of the charge of irresponsibility, they said:

We are convinced that at present it is extremely dangerous to allow the lyrical element to combine with our intellectual positions. Our interest in the lyrical impulse is motivated . . . by our belief that if it is not isolated, studied, and brought under rational control, it will remain a source of danger to our reason.

For the moment, then, we isolate the lyrical impulse, not because we are anti-rational, but because we wish to preserve a clear reason.

This statement puts Read and Davies squarely in the camp of those for whom the value of surrealism is largely cathartic and therapeutic, but therapeutic in a way that is subversive of the very aims of surrealism. That either Read or Davies should have continued to be associated with the movement after having stated this position is one of the minor curiosities of literary history.[22] Davies, in fact, dropped out of sight soon after. What is almost as odd as the statement itself is the fact that no English surrealist objected to it anywhere in print.

The London Gallery opened a show of surrealist objects at midnight, November 25, 1937, and to serve as catalogue for that exhibit published a small book of poems and reproductions.[23] Herbert Read, in a foreword, provided a definition of the object that demonstrates once again the distance that separates the English from the French on this important point, as on so many others. Read saw in the surrealist doctrine of the object little more than an example of primitive animism, and once again, a serious and demand-

[22] In a letter to the author (June 10, 1964), Sir Herbert stated that he did not recall making the statement and thought that Davies probably wrote it and got him to add his signature. He added, "I am . . . puzzled by the statement, which is contrary to all I have ever believed in. I have talked about reconciling reason and romanticism, but even then my definition of reason is not rationalistic." Since the statement accords so closely with the position enunciated by Davies in "Biology and Surrealism," Sir Herbert was probably correct in attributing it to Davies.

[23] *Surrealist Objects and Poems* (London: London Gallery Editions, n.d. [1937]).

ing surrealist doctrine was diluted to serve smaller ends. The whole point of the surrealist object—the proof it provides of the connection between internal and external states is lost in Read's familiar attempts to subsume surrealism under "superrealism." The unfortunate result of this dilution is that the object now becomes an aesthetic subject.

The poems in the book do little to raise the level of performance; it is only by virtue of the loosest of definitions that they can be called surrealist. For example, Read's "A Poem for Spain":

> I only hear the sobbing fall
> of various water-clocks
> and swift inveterate wail
> of destructive axe.
>
> Lorca was killed, singing,
> and Fox who was my friend.
> The rhythm returns: the song
> which has no end.

David Gascoyne contributed several short prose poems, one of which reads, in part:

It is well nigh impossible to describe in words the natural beauties of this country. The hills are bathed in a glow of the most subliminal tranquility, like that which is given out by the innocent eyes of children, milky and diffuse. . . . It became quite clear that this light was given out not . . . by a cluster of stars, but by five enormous and distinctly outlined eyes, which hovered gravely, motionless and without blinking in the sky for about ten minutes . . . and then faded away like a cloud.

Grace W. Pailthorpe, a psychologist for whom surrealist expression was a form of therapy and who later theorized on

this subject, contributed the following bit of Freudian
naïveté:

Don't go! Don't go! Don't go there!
'Tis only a dead man's bones.
You wouldn't wish to see that—
a corpse and putrefaction.

          .   .   .   .   .

You pale. Why so? Your father's far away
in distant lands—
What can it be that you should pale at the corpse of an old man?

He is old, is he?
Then that's good, it can't be of whom I thought,
He can't be dead.

The award of the Royal Medal for Poetry to W. H. Auden
in 1937 was the occasion for an incident at the show of surrealist objects. An anonymous exhibit consisting of a glass
witch ball arrived at the London Gallery. It had smart
painted moustaches of various colors stuck around it; on
top, a paper frill held a pig's trotter which in turn held a
cigarette. The object was accompanied by a newspaper
clipping: "Auden Receives Royal Medal." It was not
shown.[24]

Paul Nash, the leading English surrealist painter, who
had shown several "interpreted natural objects" at the surrealist exhibition the preceding year, wrote a short article
explaining his use and understanding of the object for the
magazine *Country Life* (May, 1937). For him, as for Read,

---

[24] Julian Symons, *The 'Thirties: A Dream Revolved* (London:
Cresset Press, 1960), p. 92; *New Verse*, no. 28 (January, 1938), p.
14.

the object has none of the meaning and associations that it has for the surrealists; again, what importance the object has lies in its animism. Most of the article is devoted to an exposition of animism, a subject that the readers of *Country Life* could not be expected to know, and Nash concludes with his own theory:

To obtain personal distinction, an object must show in its linea-ments a veritable personality of its own. . . . But the surrealist has a deeper thought: first that by finding you create it; second, that it has always been yours, living . . . in the unconscious until the accident of your perception gave it birth. . . . My own use of the object pictorially and in making groups or interpreting natural objects is inevitably imaginative. But I do not allow the prompting of the unconscious to lead me beyond a point of defensive control, *in support of certain aesthetic convictions.*

One thing is clear, however. . . . The more the object is studied from the point of its animation the more incalculable it becomes in its variations; the more subtle, also, becomes the problem of assembling and associating different objects in order to create that true irrational poise which is the solution of the personal equation [Italics added].

Aside from the obscurity of the last clause of this statement, it is clear that, once again, the import of a surrealist dis-covery is being debased for aesthetic purposes, for solving the *personal* equation, whatever that may be.

Paul Nash had been a member of "Unit 1," a group founded in 1933 and devoted to the structural principle in art and the imagination free from metaphysics. In 1936, however, he accepted an invitation to participate in the surrealist exhibition, where, certainly, the principles of de-sign and structure seemed the remotest of objectives. Her-bert Read saw no contradiction between Nash's earlier de-clared principles and his adherence to surrealism: "A declaration in favour of the structural principles does not necessarily exclude the tangible elements of the imagination. A painter so dedicated to the *genius loci* as Paul Nash was never likely to compromise this aspect of reality." [25] Although Nash had, as early as 1911, painted pictures which anticipated Magritte—his "Vision at Evening" shows a disembodied girl's face floating in the sky, her hair merging into clouds—it was primarily his interest in natural objects, animism, and the "spirit of place" that brought him to surrealism. He explained himself some of the effects of certain localities on him:

It is unusual in English surrealism for the place to provide the phenomenon. In the case of Swanage we owe so much to those eminent Victorian surrealists, Mowlem and Burt, the makers of Swanage, and the process of Pelion upon Ossa, that the significance of the original site is dubious. But here in the Avon Gorge, I had no doubt whatever that it was the natural features and spirit of the place that inspired irrational dreams. That mighty rift in the landscape, the effect of volcanic eruption or the pickaxes of giants, the convulsive, varicosed rocks, the impenetrable woods, the tortuous trees and, withal, beneath, the sundering waters of the Avon; these elements brewed a magic for the imagination which mounted to the brains of prosaic engineers, unsettling their equilibrium and releasing into their troubled thoughts poetic visions and schemes of paranoia.[26]

Swanage was a favorite subject of Nash's—he described its ugliness and incongruity, and its resemblances to canvases by de Chirico and Ernst. "The Giant's Stride," the bridge that spans the Avon Gorge described in the passage

[25] Herbert Read, *Paul Nash,* "The Penguin Modern Painters" (Harmondsworth, Middlesex: Penguin Books, 1944), p. 13.

[26] Paul Nash, *Outline: An Autobiography and Other Writings,* preface by Herbert Read (London: Faber and Faber, 1949), p. 241.

above, struck him as having "an unhappy air like the dream of an ambitious mind, never quite realised." The idea that elements of the site "brewed a magic for the imagination" and released "poetic visions and the schemes of paranoia" is closer to Wordsworth's notions of the influence of site than to the surrealist idea of paranoia. For the surrealist, it is the mind that projects itself on the external world and reinterprets it, not the external world, fantastic though it be, that inspires the mind.

Christopher Caudwell's *Illusion and Reality*, probably the best English Marxist analysis of literature, appeared post-humously in 1937. Caudwell rejected the simplistic view of art as propaganda held by the writers of the *Left Review* and by the contributors to C. Day Lewis's symposium, *The Mind in Chains.*

Poetry, and art in general, are no doubt utilitarian for Caudwell, but not on the superficial level understood by his simpler condisciples. For Anthony Blunt of the *Left Review*, art has only one function, that of propaganda; [27] for Edward Upward, no modern book can have value "unless it is written from a Marxist or near Marxist viewpoint." [28] Caudwell's more generous view permits him to find value even in books not written from a Marxist position. Poetry, he claims, "cannot be separated from the society whose specific human activity secretes it"; [29] it represents "an adaptation to external reality . . . an emotional attitude toward the world. It is made of language and language was

[27] "Rationalist and Anti-Rationalist Art," *Left Review*, II, no. 10 (July, 1936), vi.

[28] From *The Mind in Chains*, quoted by W. Y. Tindall, *Forces in Modern British Literature* (New York: Vintage Books, 1956), p. 44.

[29] *Illusion and Reality: A Study of the Sources of Poetry*, 2d ed. (London: Macmillan, 1944), p. 44; first published in 1937.

created to signify otherness, to indicate portions of objective reality shared socially" (p. 214). And, of course, from the Marxist point of view, the heart of that objective reality is economic production. Man's anarchic instincts are at variance with social reality, and the purpose and value of poetry is that it "moulds the instincts to reality, and is therefore useful, for it does not protect the reader from reality but puts him in good heart to grapple with it" (p. 219). Poetry, then, far from being an escape from reality, results in a heightened consciousness of ourselves and our relations to reality (pp. 262–263).

Surrealism, from Caudwell's point of view, tries to avoid contact with reality and reverses the progressively sharper perceptions of reality that poetry affords and is, therefore, reactionary. It is the perfect expression of the bourgeois illusion of what constitutes freedom. From the Marxist point of view, freedom, as Engels has said, is the recognition of necessity, and necessity is social and economic in nature. The bourgeois poet tries to avoid that necessity by turning to fantasy or, in the case of the surrealist, to the unconscious, hoping to find there his freedom. But, says Caudwell, as Freud and others have shown, the free association which is the basis of surrealist technique is far from being free; it is, on the contrary, much more compulsive than rational association: "In rational association images are controlled by a social experience of reality—the consciousness of necessity. In free association the images are controlled by the iron hand of the unconscious instincts" (p. 110).

Caudwell is forced to admit the existence of more than one necessity: there is "the social experience of reality—the consciousness of necessity," a necessity moulded by the inevitable dialectical process, the realization of what constitutes freedom; and there is the "iron determinism of unconscious necessity," the necessity of the instincts and of the dream. The recognition of two kinds of necessity leads Caudwell into an ontological difficulty: on what basis is the one called "reality" and the other "illusion"? Unable to deny the evidence of Freud, Caudwell must admit that there is a connection between dream and thought, but in order to accord the status of reality to one and not to the other, he is forced to insist that there is a discontinuity between the two and to resort to the "leap": "As soon as a mentation becomes conscious, it makes a qualitative leap and enters the sphere of free will. Conscious mentations are different in quality from unconscious precisely because they are conscious. Consciousness is a real material quality and not an epiphenomenon; it is the quality of freedom in mentation" (p. 170). The difference between the two kinds of necessity, then, is that one is conscious and free, and the other unconscious and the slave of the instincts. But this does not explain how consciousness arises, and when Caudwell attempts to do so, he is forced into a curious circular account: "Consciousness is the product of association: not of herd association which is mediated by the instincts, but by association for economic production which is mediated precisely by consciousness—by specific adaptations of the psychic instincts" (p. 171).

Caudwell, in short, denies one of the basic Freudian premises—the continuity between the unconscious and the conscious, and the consequences of that premise, that conscious, rational processes are based upon unconscious, irrational ones, that the unconscious is the foundation stone of all of man's constructs, including civilization. Caudwell starts from the other end—from the structure of society, which, properly understood, is economic and rational; but when he comes to the individual member of that society,

man, he cannot, by definition, admit the reality of the irrational, anarchic unconscious, and the continuity between
the conscious and the unconscious. But since society is
made of men, some continuity must exist, and the gap must
be bridged by a leap which is itself irrational.

Poetry, in Caudwell's scheme, issues from the societal organization, that is, reality; but he was too sensitive to poetry
to claim that it was entirely rational: "Poetry flows from
reality down to the instincts, stopping only on the last out-
post of perception where it encounters the instincts face to
face" (p. 220). Dream, on the other hand, "flows from the
instincts to the boundary of reality, at the limit of attention,
and stops there, short of actual achievement, because it
stops short of action" (p. 220). The dream must be denied
ingress into reality and cannot be allowed to influence
reality, contrary to Freud's evidence. Since Caudwell cannot deny the dream all value, he is reduced to allowing it
only a biological function, that is, to enable the sleeper to
continue sleeping (pp. 176–177). However, he extends this
biological function of the dream by suggesting that by "ex-
perimenting ideally with possible realities and attitudes
towards them [the dream] paves the way for such changes
in reality. Dream prepares the way for action; man must
first dream the possible before he can do it" (p. 182). But
this extended function of the dream, Caudwell realizes, runs
counter to the discontinuity between the conscious and the
unconscious that he has postulated, and the dream, therefore, must become something other than it is: "The 'remedy'
for the illusory character of dream is not to abolish dream
but to so enlarge and extend it that it becomes increasingly
close to the realization it is made to anticipate; to fill it
more full of life and reality and vivid content. Once again
freedom is extended by an extension of the consciousness of

necessity. This programme calls for the socialization of dream" (pp. 182–183). The dream, in other words, must cease to be dream. How this is to be done Caudwell does not say.

The surrealist is barred from Caudwell's republic because he refuses to face social reality, because he is the "bourgeois rebel [who] attempts to shake himself free of the social ego and to escape into the world of dream where both ego and external world are personal and unconscious" (p. 253). Surrealism, Caudwell says, is "the apparent return of a realism which is . . . fictitious, because it is not the real, *i.e.* social external world which returns, but the unconscious personal world" (p. 253). But the denial of reality to the "unconscious personal world" is predicated, we have seen, on the discontinuity between the unconscious and conscious facets of the human personality, a premise which led Caudwell into serious difficulties.

It would appear that Caudwell's rejection of surrealism is based—like that of so many critics of the movement—upon either a misunderstanding of surrealist doctrine or a refusal to give that doctrine serious consideration. Caudwell sees surrealism as a regressive turning to the unconscious as an escape from the real world; nowhere does he discuss the theoretical justification for this turn to the unconscious, a turn which claims to do precisely what Caudwell said needed to be done—to socialize the dream. For what else is the meaning of Lautréamont's dictum, which the surrealists never tire of repeating, that "poetry must be made by all, not by one"? Actually, the surrealist turning to the unconscious, far from representing a turning away from reality, intends to discredit "bourgeois" reality, and claims—at least theoretically—to reintegrate the human unconscious with external reality from which it has been dissociated, thereby extending freedom by extending the consciousness of necessity. It succeeds, at least in theory, where Caudwell fails: in bridging the gap between the unconscious and the conscious, between the individual and society.

In his final chapter, Caudwell's argument takes a surprising turn, and, destroying much of what he has said, corroborates a basic tenet of surrealism:

Of the future one can only dream. . . . Yet to dream is not to associate "freely" but to have certain phantasies, a certain reshuffling of memory-images of past reality blended and reorganized in a new way, because of certain real causes in present reality. Even dream is *determined,* and a movement in dream reflects perhaps a real movement into daylight of material phenomena at present unrecognised. That is why it is possible to dream with accuracy of the future—in other words, to predict scientifically (p. 270).

The illusory dream, the product of unconscious necessity, can, then, accurately foreshadow events in the real world. Since Caudwell is far from postulating a supernatural cause for this, he is echoing rather closely the surrealist doctrine of objective chance.

The manifestations of surrealism in England, and particularly the appearance of Herbert Read's *Surrealism,* provided, in 1938, the material for an interesting study of the psychological bases of surrealist aesthetics. In two articles in the *British Journal of Psychology,* W. R. D. Fairbairn, drawing almost exclusively upon the illustrations in Read's volume, elaborated an aesthetics that accounts, from a psychological point of view, for some of the characteristics of surrealist art; then, basing himself on the surrealist notion of the "object," he developed what he called "the ultimate basis of aesthetic experience." [30]

The foundation stone of Fairbairn's approach is an analogy between what Freud called the "dream-work" and its equivalent in the production of art, what Fairbairn calls the "art-work." Just as the "dream-work" precedes the formulation of psychological states into the visual images of the dream and transforms the latent into the manifest content of the dream, so the art-work "precedes the emergence of the creative fantasy into the artist's consciousness; and the creative fantasy which emerges is thus analogous to the 'manifest content' of the dream. . . . Art-work thus provides the means of reducing psychical tension in the artist's mind by enabling his repressed urges to obtain some outlet." In Freud's theory of the psychical structure, the role of the repressing censorship is attributed to the "ego-ideal" or "super-ego"; the dream-work, then, is seen as "a function of the ego which thereby modifies fantasies engendered by the instinctive id-impulses in deference to the demands of the super-ego." And, logically, the stronger the demands of the super-ego, the stronger the repression and the more dream-work is required in the formulation of the dream. If the analogy hold between dream and art, then the stronger the demands of the super-ego, the more "art-work" will be required in the production of a piece of art. Comparing da Vinci's "Madonna" in the Hermitage Museum with Miró's "Maternity," reproduced in Read's *Surrealism,* Fairbairn notes that da Vinci's painting shows considerable art-work, whereas Miró's, "like most Surrealist works of art, shows

[30] W. R. D. Fairbairn, "Prolegomena to a Psychology of Art," *British Journal of Psychology,* XXVIII, no. 3 (January, 1938), 288–303; and "The Ultimate Basis of Aesthetic Experience," *ibid,* XXIX, no. 2 (October, 1938), 167–181.

comparatively little. It requires no very profound study of Surrealist works of art to convince us that the comparative poverty of the art-work they display is directly related to the pressure of unconscious fantasy combined with weakness of repression. . . . The comparative poverty of [the surrealists'] art-work seems to justify the view that Surrealism does not provide us with art of a very high order. . . . There can be no doubt that art-work, like dream-work, is dependent upon repression, and that without repression no high achievement in art is possible." The same is true of Dali's pictures, in which "there is, so to speak, a low co-efficient of repression in relation to the strength of the unconscious urges expressed; and the result is that the art-work is comparatively meagre." Fairbairn notes that "as repression is overcome in the course of psycho-analytical treatment, dream-work becomes progressively simplified until a point at which the significance of the symbol becomes apparent"; the same is true in Dali's pictures, in which the development of symbolism is easy to trace, as for example, his persistent image of the chest of drawers which symbolizes the female body.

Drawing upon Melanie Klein's work with children, Fairbairn notes that destructive fantasies are often accompanied by fantasies of restitution: "Their function is to provide some reassurance regarding the integrity of the love-object." The "principle of restitution," he adds, "can be seen to underlie all the strivings of man after the perfect, the ideal, and the absolute. . . . Since the chief source of inner tension is to be found in the pressure of destructive urges, and since artistic activity both relieves this inner tension and is essentially creative, we are justified in concluding that the principle of restitution is the governing principle of art." Seen from this point of view, classical art is primarily restitutive; modern art, however, shows a tendency to "tear to pieces," although the principle of restitution is at work also: the pieces are put together again, even if in an unfamiliar order. Art, then, is not only a sublimated expression of repressed urges, but "also a means whereby *positive values* are created in the service of an ideal. The ideal served is the super-ego; and the creation of positive values is an act of restitution on the part of the ego."

Fairbairn's view of art, in its broad lines, accords fairly closely with the surrealists'. They would, however, undoubtedly disagree with his statement that classical art is primarily restitutive: for them the art of earlier periods is the expression of the divided personality since it is primarily rational. Their claim, of course, is that they have brought the irrational into consciousness as one of the elements in the restitutive process. This reservation apart, if one replaces the word "restitution" with "synthesis," a substitution that does no violence to Fairbairn's view, it becomes immediately clear that his analysis is very close to that of the surrealists.

The Hegelian idea of "synthesis" is the subject of Fairbairn's second article, ambitiously entitled "The Ultimate Basis of Aesthetic Experience." Starting with the surrealist "found object," he notes that this represents "the most primitive form of artistic creation" since in this form the object is merely framed more or less as it is found; the "made object" is then a slightly more complex product of artistic creation. But if the object represents a primitive form of artistic creation, it is far from simple from the psychological point of view because it is "not simply something that was there all the time and is now revealed; for, since its significance is dependent upon its capacity to represent a wish fulfillment, it does not exist apart from the

act of discovery itself; and the discovery represents a creative act on the part of the artist." As Fairbairn had noted
in his first article, surrealist art is distinguished by a marked
poverty of "art-work"; the found object, then, represents
"the demands of unconscious urges with an unusual poverty of disguise." But even for the surrealist, a certain
amount of disguise is necessary in order for any object to
function as a "found object," for, as Breton noted in *What
Is Surrealism?*, "one's pleasure is always partly accounted
for by the lack of resemblance between the desired object
and the *discovery*." The disguise is what permits the beholder to participate in the discovery and to enjoy the shock
of recognition that is the basic requirement for the success
of the object. For, as Fairbairn noted in his first article and
repeats in the second, "when the artist's super-ego is weak
and his suppressed urges are really 'urgent,' these urgent
urges express themselves in the work of art with a minimum
of disguise. The effect of such a work of art is to provoke
an excessive emotional reaction in any beholder whose
super-ego is more exacting than that of the artist, and whose
need for the disguise of repressed urges is greater. So far
from saying too little, such a work of art says too much. It
says more than the beholder's super-ego will tolerate. . . .
It is, so to speak, too like the real thing. This applies, so far
as most people are concerned, to Surrealist works of art in
general." The surrealist object that is sufficiently disguised,
then, can provide the proper bridge between the urge and
its symbolic satisfaction; it provides a further link in that
in its discovery, the finder operates as both artist and beholder at the same time; it represents, as Fairbairn says,
*"an intermediate point between the attitude of the artist
and that of the beholder."* Fairbairn's entire aesthetic becomes an extension of this point: "Aesthetic experience

may . . . be defined as *the experience which occurs in the beholder when he discovers an object which functions for him symbolically as a means of satisfying his unconscious emotional needs.*" In this definition, of course, by "object" Fairbairn means any work of art that the beholder beholds and not just a surrealist "found object." However, his debt to the surrealist doctrine of the object is clear and inescapable; and when he restates his theory in Hegelian terms, his definition of the aesthetic experience becomes almost identical with Breton's definition of surreality:

We may say that aesthetic experience depends upon the resolution of an antinomy created by the simultaneous operation of the libido (the life principle) and the destructive urges (the death principle). In the resolution of this antinomy the demands of the libido may be said to constitute the thesis, the pressure of the destructive urges the antithesis, and restitution of the synthesis. . . . What constitutes aesthetic experience within the field of art is the capacity of the work of art to represent such a synthesis for the beholder.

In 1938, Edward Upward published *Journey to the Border,* a novel whose principal subject is a critique and rejection of surrealism. Its repressed hero, an unnamed tutor, becomes aware of the psychological origins of his own and society's illnesses. Another character, Gregory Mavors, tries to teach him the cure for his dissatisfaction: "Reason is death. . . . Unreason is life. . . . Unreason is the language of desire." [31] Filled with desire freed from reason, the tutor experiments with his power: "He had wanted the bowls on the tables to be silver, and his Desire, freed at last from reason, had made

[31] Edward Upward, *Journal to the Border* (London: Hogarth Press, 1938), p. 147.

them silver." But he is still not convinced; would his unreason "always succeed with human beings . . . who might
themselves choose to reason and to ignore the voice of his
Desire?" His mentor, Mavors, replies, "The man who has
released his Desire, will always prevail over the man who
tries to keep his Desire in chains . . . the man who reasons
is divided against himself, and the more vital part of him, his
Desire, must take the part of his unreasoning opponent, of
the man whose Desire is free. Therefore your power to
change human beings will be no less than your power to
change inanimate objects." With his desire now completely
freed, the tutor journeys to the border of sanity and becomes entangled in a vast hallucination that threatens to
destroy him; but just before he passes over the border, the
voice of sanity restrains him: "You ought to learn first of all
that your problems cannot be solved in the mind alone, nor
can they be solved in the heart, in the emotions. They must
be dealt with in the external world. . . . You must take
action—living, practical action." The voice of sanity teaches
him that in his delusions he had completely overlooked "the
real external world," that his sense of power was merely
another delusion. Warning him of the dangers of the life
of the imagination, the voice tells him he must face reality.
The only way out of his dilemma, out of his repressed life,
is "the way of the workers. You must get in touch with the
workers' movement." Mavors, his first mentor, is revealed
at the end to have been a member of a fascist group plotting
to take over the country.

This novel, a strange, sometimes brilliant mixture of
Freud, Kafka, and surrealism, is, in the last analysis, little
more than an allegory of the opposition between the illusion of bourgeois art and the reality of Marxism.

In 1938, Montague Summers in *The Gothic Quest*, a verbose and eccentric study of the Gothic novel, directed a few poorly aimed shafts at the surrealists in an attempt to show that they understood nothing of the true import of the genre. Since his animadversions have already been thoroughly criticized,[32] there is need here only to provide a sample that will make clear the tenor of his attack. To disprove the surrealists' contention that the Gothic novel is the expression of a subversive impulse, Summers points out that Horace Walpole was a gentleman; that Mrs. Radcliffe was personally genteel, shy, and conservative; and that Matthew Gregory "Monk" Lewis liked the company of dukes and duchesses and basked in their familiarity. Commenting on Gascoyne's statement in the *Short Survey* that surrealism aims "to dispose altogether of the flagrant contradictions that exist between dream and life, the unreal and the real, etc.," Summers shows that all "Romantic" writers have dealt with the fantastic, that Aeschylus makes mountains speak, makes Brute Force into a person, has Father Ocean conversing; that Shakespeare gives Bohemia a wild sea-coast; that Dryden shows us Granada besieged; that Ariosto shows us impossible things; and asks, pointedly, "In what sense is Surrealism strange or modern or new?"[33] He dismisses automatism by pointing out its dangers:

On their own showing the Surrealists are devoted to automatic writing, which is in itself a very dangerous experiment. They also lay great stress on dreams, and emphasize that messages be received through dreams. It is devoutly to be hoped that the

[32] J. H. Matthews, *Surrealism and the Novel* (Ann Arbor, Mich.: University of Michigan Press, 1966), pp. 23–27.

[33] *The Gothic Quest* (London: Fortune Press, 1938; reissued New York: Russell & Russell, 1964); the quotations below appear on pp. 408 and 412 respectively.

Surrealist visions in this kind do not resemble only too nearly those "somnia et noctium phantasma" from which night by night at Compline we pray to be delivered and assoiled. We must be very careful even in art and literature lest—if I may venture to apply in this connexion a vital phrase of S. Augustine — "dormienti falsa visa persuadeant quod vigilanti vera non possunt."

He invokes St. Augustine once again to dispose of the entire surrealist claim:

In spite of the doctrine which the Surrealists proclaim so loudly and in so many words, in spite of their dreams and visions, their "pure" poetry, their *collage* and *frottage*, their myths and symbols, their slogan "L'image est une création pure de l'esprit," and all the rest, the fundamental weakness, nay, the very rot which cankers the whole movement, would seem to be a crass materialism. "Supremacy of matter over thought," one of their leaders has announced to be an essential principle of their scheme. They are unmystical, unromantic. They deny the super- natural. Yet everything, in the last analysis depends upon the supernatural, since as S. Augustine tells us, God is the only Reality.

In the spring of 1938, *Transition,* in one of its periodic questionnaires—this one devoted to the dream—asked the following questions:

1. What was your most recent characteristic dream?
2. Have you observed any ancestral myths or symbols in your collective unconscious?
3. Have you ever felt the need for a new language to express the experience of your night mind?

T. S. Eliot replied politely that "Questions 1 and 2 are really matters I prefer to keep to myself. The answer to number 3 is definitely *no.* I am not, as a matter of fact, particularly interested in my 'night-mind.'" Herbert Read, however, answered more fully with the essay "Myth, Dream, and Poem," [34] which amplified a suggestion first tentatively made in the "Introduction" to *Surrealism*—that sometimes in the dream "we find . . . the day-world transformed and occasionally this new reality presents itself to us as a poetic unity." In the new essay, Read records two experiences in verse writing. In the first poem, he attempted to transcribe a dream with indifferent success; the result was a failure because it did not "nearly express the peculiar vividness and significance of the dream" (p. 106), largely because the conscious, elaborating mind had interposed itself between the dream and its transcription. The second poem differs from the first "in that it had no precedent experience such as a dream, but was itself the experience. . . . The poem was written automatically, without hesitation or revision, in a state of trance" (p. 111). As a poem, it was no better than the first, but after studying it, Read found that it embodied "a myth which exactly expressed Freud's theory of the two instincts which control all life—the instincts of Eros and Death" (p. 114). In other words, the mind in a state of trance is in touch with the profound unconscious truths about human life, the truths that are expressed in myths. Poetry, that is poetry not produced by the conscious mind, is, then, a species of myth, and is "the mediator between dream and reality" (p. 115). Art becomes "the only objective evidence we possess of whatever superreality is cosmic and eternal" (p. 116).

Read in this essay clearly demonstrates his awareness of a distinction he avoided in his "Introduction" to *Surrealism,* the crucial distinction between the description of an experi-

---

[34] Reprinted in *Collected Essays in Literary Criticism* and *The Nature of Literature;* all page references are from the latter.

ence and the experience itself. Nevertheless, Read still does not come all the way to the surrealist position: he recognizes that the automatic mind comes in contact with certain eternal truths expressed in images and myths; he does *not* accept the surrealist view of the necessary connection between the automatic mind and the external world. Like Jung, Read implies a mystical bent; his view lacks the tough materialism of the surrealist position. The difference between Read and the surrealists may be expressed in a visual metaphor. The process as Read sees it is a vertical one: the mind in a state of trance, plunging deep into the collective unconscious, comes up with an image or myth that expresses an eternal truth about man or the cosmos; for the surrealist, the process is horizontal: the mind in true automatism expresses the manifest content of the unconscious, the truth of which is corroborated in the external world by "objective chance." There is in the surrealist view no talk of external truths, of myths in the sense that Read understands them; there is, rather, the idea of a necessary connection between the internal and the external world. The point of automatism for the surrealist, is not that it permits the mind to plunge into the region of eternal truths, but that it reveals the connection between inner and outer realities.

Read demonstrated once again in this essay that his commitment to surrealism was far from complete, that in spite of his talk of dialectical materialism, his view of the world was far from materialistic. The experiments described in this essay could easily become exhibits in Maud Bodkin's *Archetypal Patterns in Poetry;* they could never take their place with Breton's "Tournesol" and Victor Brauner's prophetic paintings as surrealist proof of the connection between dream and reality.

On March 16, 1938, a discussion sponsored by the Artists' International Association took place between supporters of realism and of surrealism. Two years earlier the A.I.A. had invited the surrealists to join the Association,[35] and a similar public discussion had been announced.[36] The hard core of the A.I.A. was made up of three men who wrote regularly for the *Left Review:* James Boswell, James Fitton, and James Holland. In spite of its indirect association with the *Left Review,* the A.I.A. was not identified with the Communist Party, but rather with what may be loosely termed social realism, although its members willingly exhibited together with surrealists and abstractionists.[37] Two members of the A.I.A., Graham Sutherland and Robert Medley, did, in fact, have pictures in the International Surrealist Exhibition.

The surrealists had never accepted the invitation to join the Association. The discussion of March, 1938, pitted the outstanding members of each group against one another: Anthony Blunt, Alick West, Graham Bell, and William Coldstream on the one side; Herbert Read, Roland Penrose, Julian Trevelyan, and Humphrey Jennings on the other.

Each side claimed victory in the debate. Randall Swingler, editor of the *Left Review,* wrote that the realists "carried the day . . . by their humility and honesty. . . . Their aggressive opponents, the Surrealists, are betrayed by their very vociferation, the pretentious flourish of any pseudo-

---

[35] Roger Roughton, "Surrealism and Communism," *Contemporary Poetry and Prose,* no. 4–5 (August–September, 1936), p. 75.

[36] The only evidence that this discussion actually took place and its only surviving trace is the speech by Herbert Read delivered at the Conway Hall on June 23, 1936, to which reference has already been made (see above, pp. 148–150).

[37] Julian Symons, *The 'Thirties,* pp. 96–97.

philosophical, pseudo-psychological, pseudo-literary pseudo-phraseology which has nothing to do with art, as people with a complete despair and sterility as regards the practice of art." [38]

Herbert Read reported in the *London Bulletin* (April, 1938) that "we are partisans of the Surrealists . . . but no unprejudiced observer could describe the affair as anything but a rout. . . . We have tried to remember anything contributed to the debate by Graham Bell [and] William Coldstream . . . but there is only the stammer and the sweat. On the other side Roland Penrose contributed some very cool and convincing aids to extra-retinal vision; Julian Trevelyan revealed himself as a brilliant dialectician, and Humphrey Jennings made some extremely important statements on the nature of automatism."

The accounts of the discussion repeated the usual arguments. Swingler asserted that surrealism is the result of the artist's fear of looking at the real world: looking instead into his own bowels, he finds what is of interest only to the alienist or the pathologist: "When artists have the confidence to look outside their own protective circle and discover something about the larger social relations . . . then Surrealism will die a natural death and Realism will prove to be . . . the basis of real painting." Then painting will serve its real and obvious function, as it does in the U.S.S.R. and in Spain.

Read was brief and contemptuous: the realists "are reduced to talking about the camera and Courbet. Actually, of course, our English Realists are not the tough guys they ought to be, but the effete and bastard offspring of the Bloomsbury school of needlework."

[38] Randall Swingler, "What Is the Artist's Job?" *Left Review*, III, no. 15 (April, 1938), 931.

To date, the nearest thing to an English surrealist periodical had been *Contemporary Poetry and Prose*. But even this magazine, although sympathetic to the surrealists, cannot be considered an official organ. Moreover, it had ceased publication with its tenth number (Autumn, 1937). In April, 1938, the London Gallery, one of the principal promoters of surrealist art in London began a magazine that was to be the quasi-official surrealist publication in England. E. L. T. Mesens, one of the organizers of the Surrealist Exhibition of 1936, became a director of the London Gallery and the editor of the *London Bulletin*. Together with René Magritte and Paul Nougé, Mesens had been one of the leaders of the Belgian surrealists, had directed the surrealist publishing house in Brussels, Editions Nicolas Flamel, and edited the Belgian surrealist magazine *Documents 34*.

The purpose of the new periodical, first called the *London Gallery Bulletin*, was to supply the catalogues for the shows at the London Gallery and several other galleries which were principally devoted to what may loosely be termed "advanced" art—the Mayor, Zwemmer, and Guggenheim Jeune galleries. In addition, the *Bulletin* printed appreciations and explications of the artists involved. For example, the first number, devoted to the René Magritte show at the London Gallery, contained a poem on Magritte by Eluard and articles about him by Read and others; this show, incidentally, marked Magritte's introduction into England. The second number of the magazine (May, 1938) was devoted to Joan Miró, who was having a show at the Mayor Gallery. Other numbers were devoted to Tanguy and Picasso. But the magazine, which at first seemed intended to promote surrealism, soon expanded its scope and publicized other than surrealist art. For example, its double number on "Living Art in England" (January–February, 1939), prepared in conjunction with an exhibition at the London Gallery, covered a wide range of artists—from the constructivists Naum Gabo, Piet Mondrian, and Barbara Hepworth, to the surrealists Eileen Agar, Conroy Maddox, and Henry Moore, to several painters labeled "independents": Paul Nash, Julian Trevelyan, and Ithell Colquhoun. As if to show its catholicity, the magazine printed essays on Ben Nicholson and constructivism by Herbert Read.

Although the magazine was ostensibly devoted to a wide range of artistic expression, its sympathies were clearly surrealist. The post of assistant editor was filled, in succession, by Humphrey Jennings, Roland Penrose, George Reavey, and Penrose again. Jennings and Penrose were among the most faithful members of the London surrealist group. Jennings was later excommunicated for having done work that earned him the Order of the British Empire and accepting the decoration, but Penrose remained faithful to the end. Most of the articles and editorial comments of the magazine were concerned with surrealist matters.

One such article, "The Scientific Aspects of Surrealism," by Dr. Grace W. Pailthorpe (December–January, 1938–1939), painter and psychologist, raised an issue of some importance to English surrealism. Dr. Pailthorpe, with the assistance of Reuben Mednikoff, an English surrealist painter, had been performing a series of "scientific" experiments that demonstrated the therapeutic value of surrealist art. Surrealism and psychoanalysis, she claimed, share the common goal of freeing "the psychology of the individual from internal conflict so that he or she may function freely." Painting in the traditional manner, she said, expressed the unconscious desire to paint according to parental wishes; painting freely, or surrealistically, on the other hand, may, in the unconscious, mean the making of a mess. Traditional painting is equated with "early enforced restrictions on the infant's excretory functions," with inhibited fantasy life and repressed imagination; painting freely, then, is the expression of the full freedom of the imagination.

The exact nature of Dr. Pailthorpe's experiments is not clear from her brief account, but it presumably involved analyzing several paintings produced automatically by herself and her collaborator. One of these analyses is here given in full; not much is lost by not having the picture itself reproduced:

The little figure standing on a jaw-bone represents the artist. It has a claw finger on each hand with which it can scratch. It is pointing to its ear and to its belly to indicate where it wants to scratch. The jaw it is standing on is the mother's face. The small figure climbing up behind the jaw is again the same little person and so is the monkey on the ball shape above. This ball represents the mother's head and the back of the jaw the mother's shoulder. The picture is saying, "I have two irritating places for which I can get no relief except in being held close to the mother's head, neck and shoulder."

Since no other information is supplied, the "scientific" value of this kind of analysis is doubtful, to say the least. Dr. Pailthorpe admits readily that every unconscious creation is not a work of art, but she insists that "where complete freedom has been possible the results are perfect in balance, design, colour, rhythm, and possess a vitality that is not found anywhere else than in Surrealism." On the basis of her experiments, she concludes that surrealism, "if followed wholeheartedly to its final goal, has the power to bring happiness to all humanity."

It is obvious that in her demonstration of the scientific aspect of surrealism, the picture has been reduced to the level of symptom, and psychoanalysis to the level of simple equation-making. Presumably, the free expression of the untrammelled imagination, either in painting or in "making a mess"—and the two are equivalent in her system—is what will bring happiness to mankind. But what is puzzling in her approach is her view of psychoanalysis; one can agree with her statement that psychoanalysis "strives to free the psychology of the individual from internal conflict," but not with her contention that the goal of psychoanalysis, like that of surrealism, is the "liberation of man"—not if by psychoanalysis she means the Freudian variety, and there is no indication that she means any other kind. It is clear from even the most cursory reading of Freud that the whole purpose of his therapy is to reconcile man to the demands of reality, not to free him from these demands. It was precisely on this point that the surrealists had parted company with Freud.

There is, of course, nothing fundamentally new in Dr. Pailthorpe's approach. Since surrealist art has its origin in automatism, it would of necessity express the content of the unconscious. But it is perhaps indicative of the unscientific nature of her experiments (despite her claims) that Dr. Pailthorpe did not analyze any pictures not painted by herself or her collaborator. The reason for this, she said, is that the analysis would not be reliable. The whole experiment leaves one with the impression that she is recommending some kind of parlor auto-analysis as the way of achieving happiness for mankind. Some of the analyses she supplies are so facile that one wonders whether the pictures were not painted for the sake of the analyses.

Parker Tyler wrote from America to protest against Dr. Pailthorpe's "mummified and perverted" approach, an approach "to be feared and deplored." [39] The most telling point

[39] "Letter from Parker Tyler to Charles Henri Ford," *London Bulletin*, no. 17 (June 15, 1939), p. 21.

against Dr. Pailthorpe, however, was made in a reply to her article by Baron Werner von Alvensleben. Freud, the Baron reported, had been invited by Breton to contribute to a collection of dreams that Breton was getting ready for publication. Freud replied that "a collection of dreams without supplementary associations, without knowledge of the circumstances, says nothing to me and I fail to see how it can say anything to others. . . . Obviously the manifest dream exhibits all the diversity of the products of the intellect." [40]

Dr. Pailthorpe replied to the Baron by reasserting that "freed fantasy will vitalize everything it touches in life," [41] but she did not counter Freud's statement, nor in any way justify her simplistic approach, nor yet clarify the connection she had made between psychoanalysis and surrealism.

This article illustrates once again the attitude of so many English participants in the movement, that is the avoidance of what surrealism was about in order to make it serve some other purpose: aesthetic, literary, or, in this case, "scientific."

The *London Bulletin* published little verse other than translations of poems about the painters exhibiting at the moment. Among the exceptions are poems by Herbert Read, Kathleen Raine, Ruthven Todd, and Djuna Barnes, but their connection with surrealism does not go beyond an occasional violent or unusual juxtaposition of images. A few short prose pieces by Ithell Colquhoun and Robert Melville come closer, although even here, the striking imagery seems deliberately produced. For example, from "Suburban Nights," by Robert Melville: "Occasionally a white glove fell and at

[40] Quoted by Werner von Alvensleben, "Automatic Art," *London Bulletin*, no. 13 (April 15, 1939), p. 22. Freud's letter is published in *Cahiers G. L. M.*, 1938.

[41] "Letter to the Editor," *London Bulletin*, no. 17 (June 15, 1939), p. 23.

such a time a long, low cry ran with sudden twists along the ground and rose into the air at the end of the street" (January–February, 1939). A poem by Hugh Sykes Davies (May, 1938) marked his last appearance as a surrealist. It is an attempt to achieve an effect using the device of repetition with variation, but unlike an earlier poem in the same manner in *Contemporary Poetry and Prose,* it does not succeed. It starts rather simply:

> It doesn't look like a finger it looks like a feather
> of broken glass

and grows progressively more violent:

> It doesn't look like a finger it looks like a feather
> with broken teeth

and ends with an unearned conclusion:

AND ANYTHING YOU SEE WILL BE USED AGAINST YOU

The *London Bulletin,* like *Contemporary Poetry and Prose,* was not, then, a magazine devoted exclusively to surrealism; it was intended to serve the purposes of the London Gallery, and that was publicizing exhibitions. Only the last number, which appeared after a hiatus of one year, can be said to be truly surrealist; published, not by the London Gallery but by the surrealist group in England, it was prepared in conjunction with the exhibition "Surrealism To-Day" held at the Zwemmer Gallery in May–June, 1940. Concerned primarily with the exhibition, it contains articles and poems about the artists involved: de Chirico, Henry Moore, Paul Delvaux, and Yves Tanguy; in addition, it published an impressionistic article on the surrealist object by Conroy Maddox, several poems by Mesens, and an article on Monk Lewis by Pierre Mabille.

Besides issuing the *London Bulletin,* the London Gallery

sponsored a publishing house, London Gallery Editions, which, under Mesens's direction, produced several books of surrealist interest. The catalogue of the exhibition of objects, *Surrealist Objects and Poems,* was its first publication. The second was Roland Penrose's *The Road Is Wider Than Long,* an "image diary" of a journey to the Balkans in the summer of 1938. Illustrated with photographs by the author and printed in a variety of colors and type faces, the diary is a long, semi-surrealist poem, whose opening lines read:

> They breathe with the night
> in houses whose marble veins
> are washed with sail cloth
> whose carpets are covered with olives
> whose gardens begin under the sea
> they breathe with the sun
> enemy the SUN closes their eyes
> the day of summer lasts
> until the earthquake hatches
> from the dream of heat
> the dream of cold.
> Let us through
> lift your four striped arms
> and let us through
> we need dancing
> young grass
> children to sing for rain [42]

Other volumes published by London Gallery Editions included Eluard's *Poetry and Truth, 1942,* translated by Mesens and Penrose, and Mesens's *Troisième front.* The former was later to be the center of a quarrel among surrealists.

[42] Roland Penrose, *The Road Is Wider Than Long* (London: London Gallery Editions, n.d. [1939?]), n.p.

André Breton's visit to Mexico in 1938 produced a new manifesto entitled *Pour un art révolutionnaire indépendant* which appeared over his and Diego Rivera's signatures; some years later Breton admitted that his collaborator had been, not Rivera but Trotsky, whom Breton had visited in Mexico.[43] The manifesto affirms once again the principles of freedom in the service of the revolution. But the revolution, from the surrealist point of view, must begin with individual freedom, and this, we have seen, involves the liberation of the individual unconscious from moral, political, and social restraints. The manifesto draws upon psychoanalysis to demonstrate that it is only by bringing the repressed elements of the human personality into harmony with the ego, and not by repressing them further, that man can be emancipated. The corollary of this view is that art cannot submit to external or alien directives whose purposes are purely pragmatic and whose ends are extremely short-lived. The artist must be free to choose his themes and to explore them in total freedom. To those who wish to force art to submit to any discipline that goes counter to its means, the manifesto opposes the motto, "Complete licence in art." If the revolution must erect a *socialist* system on the material plane, on the intellectual plane it must establish and insure an *anarchic* system of individual liberty. The rallying cry of the manifesto is "No authority, no constraints, not the slightest trace of commandments, of orders."

The consequence of this cry for liberty is, of course, a rejection of totalitarian restraints, be they from the Right or the Left. Both Nazi Germany and Stalin's U.S.S.R. are

---

[43] Reprinted in *Documents surréalistes* (Paris: Club des Editeurs, 1948), vol. 2 of Maurice Nadeau, *Histoire du surréalisme*, pp. 372–378. Breton's admission was made in *Entretiens, 1913–1952* (Paris: Gallimard, 1952), p. 190.

attacked in similar terms: both attempt to impose restraints upon the free exercise of artistic impulses. The rejection of solidarity with the ruling caste of the U.S.S.R. is especially strong because that caste claims to embody the revolutionary hopes, but actually, so far from representing communism, is its most perfidious and dangerous enemy. The manifesto ends by calling for the formation of a Fédération Internationale de l'Art Révolutionnaire Indépendant (F.I.A.R.I.).

The English surrealist group received the text of the manifesto from Paris, together with the statement that the French surrealists expected the formation of an English section of the F.I.A.R.I. A meeting took place at the London Gallery, but the English group could come to no agreement. Those who were committed to the Third International were of course shocked by the violently uncompromising attitude expressed by the manifesto, even though Breton's attitude toward Moscow was well known. Some were reluctant to speak so openly against the U.S.S.R. for fear that such a polemic might at some later date play into the hands of the opposition. The thorny problem of the relation of surrealism to communism, which had caused so much dissension in and so many defections from the ranks of French surrealists, seems in England to have been characteristically brushed aside. The tenor of the meeting, according to one of the participants, seems to have been, "Why bother with politics; let's just get on with being painters." The London group had to report to Paris that it had been unable to agree upon a plan of action.

According to Conroy Maddox, a member of the London group, the collapse of English surrealism can be dated from this meeting; not all activity ceased, but the group ceased to function as a group.[44]

[44] Letter to the author, May 22, 1964.

The London group faced another crisis shortly afterward; a meeting which took place in late 1939 or early 1940 in a Soho restaurant was to have serious consequences for the English movement. Every important figure associated with English surrealism was present: Herbert Read, Roland Penrose, E. L. T. Mesens, Humphrey Jennings, Jacques Brunius, Ithell Colquhoun, Eileen Agar, Edith Rimmington, S. W. Hayter, A. C. Sewter, Dr. Grace Pailthorpe, Reuben Mednikoff, John Banting, Gordon Onslow-Ford, Charles Howard and others.[45] Attempting to form a more closely knit organization, Mesens, who had taken the leadership of the group, read a number of propositions to which those who wished to remain members had to subscribe. The more important and controversial points were:

1. Adherence to the proletarian revolution.
2. Agreement not to join any group or association, professional or other, including any secret society, other than the surrealist.[46]
3. Agreement not to exhibit or publish except under surrealist auspices.

Unable to subscribe to these points, Herbert Read was expelled from the group. Although he could not, as a professional writer, subscribe to the third point, Read believed that the charge against him was primarily political and proceeded from the militant Communists in the group. He was accused of collaborating with the "establishment"—

---

[45] No records of the meeting seem to exist; I have had to rely on the memory of participants which, after three decades, is somewhat less than exact.

[46] The prohibition against joining secret societies seems to have been directed against those who, like Ithell Colquhoun, were interested in pursuing occult studies. Mesens, unlike Breton, Seligman, and other continental surrealists, was opposed to this facet of surrealist activity.

the British Council, for example—and of close association with T. S. Eliot and the *Criterion*. As a professed anarchist, he was politically suspect to the doctrinaire Communists,[47] although the surrealists' alliance with the Communist Party was, he says, "a matter of words rather than deeds. . . . I was never aware of any reciprocity on the part of the communists." [48]

Others were also expelled: Dr. Pailthorpe and Mednikoff rejected the third point; Eileen Agar, a member of the neo-realist "London Group" of artists, could not agree to the second and third points; Ithell Colquhoun, objected to the purely verbal political commitments of the surrealists and, wanting to be free to pursue her occult studies as she saw fit, rejected the first and second points. She objected to the third point also because it meant, in effect, not publishing or exhibiting at all since there was, at the time, no surrealist gallery or publication (the London Gallery closed in 1940; the *London Bulletin* ceased publication in the same year).

Eileen Agar subsequently retracted her objections and was permitted to retain her dual membership. But as a result of their objections, Herbert Read, Dr. Pailthorpe, Reuben Mednikoff, and Ithell Colquhoun were not invited to participate in the "Surrealism To-Day" exhibition held at the Zwemmer Gallery in June, 1940. Herbert Read remained on friendly terms with individual members of the group, but he dated the end of his association with the surrealist group from this meeting.[49]

The group show "Surrealism To-Day," held at Zwemmer's in the spring of 1940 was organized in honor of Gordon Onslow-Ford, the English surrealist painter, who had left Paris

[47] Letter to the author, April 25, 1966.   [48] *Ibid.*, June 10, 1964.
[49] *Ibid.*

and returned to England at the outbreak of the war. The show, unfortunately, opened in June while public attention was directed elsewhere; it consequently attracted little notice and closed very soon. Buchan, a regular contributor to the *Left Review,* gave the show a passing glance, dismissing it unqualifiedly:

For a short time the Surrealist movement discovered much new material for the artist. Certain ways of seeing and painting that they invented had a liberating influence on painting as a whole. The show at Zwemmer's, however, showed no advance, and in most ways was a retrogression. If this is all the Surrealists have to say after nine months of war they would be better advised to remain silent.[50]

William Plomer gave the show a favorable review in the *New Statesman and Nation* (June 29, 1940), praising the surrealists' antidefeatism and unequivocal opposition to Nazism. Striking a note that was to become frequent in comments on surrealism, he said that once again nature had imitated art: "The high explosives which are going off everywhere were detonated first in the unconscious. . . . In total war the incongruous has already become the commonplace. . . . Dali's melting watches, flesh beset by ants, disintegrating tripes in Libyan evenings, chests of drawers embedded in torsoes, are now features of many a landscape."

Thomas McGreevy, usually very conservative, noted the congruence of surrealist images and world events in a surprisingly favorable review of the exhibition:

From the traditional point of view these paintings and sculptures may have been outrageous but they did not leave the visitor in-

[50] Buchan, "Wanted: a Goya," *Poetry and the People,* no. 20 (June, 1940), p. 23.

different. They amused or annoyed him—or both. Which could only mean that in their own odd way they had actuality, that they were the expression of a phase of imagination which may be presumed to be still active.

In view of the fact that when the exhibition opened the most ghastly of wars was raging about [Paris] it is strange that these works should not seem out of date. Clearly, the movement must, from the beginning, have been something more than an outbreak of Parisian frivolity. . . . One cannot help wondering whether the surrealists did not instinctively sense whither the European society in which they lived was tending, and whether their movement was not, in fact, a criticism of that society, a mirror in which it either did not recognise itself or did not choose to recognise itself.[51]

Cecil Beaton, a few years later, struck the same note in a description of a Libyan battlefield strewn with hundreds of half-buried, neatly folded shirts—the remains of a clothing store—and the carcasses of burnt-out tanks: "The Surrealists have anticipated this battle ground. In all their paintings, now proved to be prophetic, we have seen the eternal incongruities." [52]

The English surrealist group continued to meet at the Barcelona Restaurant in Soho during the war. These meetings were attended by the painters Robert Baxter, Emmy Bridgewater, John Banting, and, occasionally, Lucien Freud; the writers E. L. T. Mesens, Jacques Brunius, Serge Nin, and the Turkish poet Feyyaz Fergar; the cartoonist Philip Sansom; later, in 1943, the poet and translator Simon Watson Taylor joined the group, and in 1945, the jazz singer and

[51] "London's Liveliest Show," *The Studio*, CXX (October, 1940), 137.

[52] Cecil Beaton, "Libyan Diary," *Horizon*, VII, no. 37 (January, 1943), 38–39.

cartoonist George Melly. Although the coming of the war considerably curtailed surrealist activity, it did not extinguish it entirely. In addition to the "Surrealism To-Day" exhibition, Mesens organized a surrealist exhibition at the Oxford University Art Society in autumn, 1940, and a series of art shows, in December–January 1940–1941, with lectures tracing the development of fauvism, cubism, dadaism, and surrealism at the Dartington Art School in Devonshire.[53] In London, however, with the closing of the London Gallery and the cessation of publication of the *London Bulletin*, surrealist activity came to a virtual standstill, largely, it would appear, because of the inactivity of Mesens who had assumed the leadership of the group. In late 1940 or early 1941, however, the painter and poet Toni del Renzio joined Mesens's group and infused it with new life. In March, 1942, del Renzio issued a new magazine, *Arson*. Unfortunately, only one number appeared because of lack of funds and stringent paper rationing. Mesens had no hand in the production of the magazine although he is named in the dedication; del Renzio did, however, have the support of John and Robert Melville and Conroy Maddox who had moved to Birmingham at the outbreak of the war. Dedicated to every leading surrealist in the world, *Arson* reprinted the text of the interview granted by Breton in New York to *View* in November, 1941. The interview is important for its reaffirmation of surrealist principles and activity in a time of crisis, and for suggesting possible areas of new surrealist endeavor. To the interviewer's question, "Do you think that a Third Manifesto of Surrealism is in order?" Breton replied, "Absolutely." However, Breton never went beyond issuing a prolegomenon to a third manifesto, and for this failure he was severely criticized by del Renzio a few years later.

[53] Marcel Jean, *The History of Surrealist Painting*, pp. 335–336.

In addition to the interview, *Arson* contained a number of reproductions of paintings, mainly by the English surrealists John Melville, Eileen Agar, Toni del Renzio, Gordon Onslow-Ford, Emmy Bridgewater, Conroy Maddox, but also by de Chirico and André Masson; an article on Masson by Robert Melville; a fragment of de Chirico's *Hebdomeros;* and Nicolas Calas's important essay, "The Light of Words." No verse was published in *Arson* for the simple reason, the editor said, "that we do not believe there is a single line approaching the nature of poetry being penned in English" (p. 32). Brief reviews of periodicals dismissed John Lehmann's *Penguin New Writing* with the comment, "We are convinced of Mr. Lehmann's ignorance of two terms: a. new; b. writing," and Lehmann's *Daylight* with "we prefer the night," and "To such a Lehmann we would prefer a priest even." An exhibition of paintings sponsored by the A.I.A. was similarly dismissed as "dead," except for a few contributions by John Banting and Eileen Agar. Ithell Colquhoun was attacked for her "admission of endeavouring to do in painting what the 'New Apoplexy' is doing in literature."

Nicholas Calas's essay, "The Light of Words," is important for analyzing the crisis in surrealist poetry, a crisis that consists of the fact that "the game of discovering new combinations of unconscious images has proved less rich in possibilities than had at first been hoped." Unconscious images, he noted, have a tendency to recur and to cluster around the same sex-complexes: "What in 1925 was bold and original gave ten years later the effect of intolerable repetition." The reason for the crisis, Calas claims, is that surrealism was influenced not only by Freudian theory, but also by the method of psychoanalytic treatment; poets, he says, "have exaggerated the poetic value, not of the unconscious image, but of the free-association method." The flow of freely associated words in psychoanalysis is controlled by the practitioner and is directed toward the past with the purpose of effecting a cure. The poet's words, on the other hand, are not directed by an external agent; if the poet turns to the past, it is in order to make something present—the poem—so that the movement is toward the future. The poet seeks "to place, in the time dimension (which he often presents in the form of futurity), a compensation for an activity in space which for one reason or another he avoids, because it pains him too much. The poet appeals to a different time because he is maladjusted. . . . It is because every poet refuses to submit to present reality that he is a rebel." The poet, then, oriented toward the future and in rebellion against present reality, must become an explorer, and "all discovery is the result of exceptional lucidity; the poet's eye is not a glass reflecting light . . . but a torch of radiance." The poet becomes a hero who "speaks to open the way to action; he understands the function of speech; he is conscious of his power over words: while the victim speaks only to express his derangement, and to *confess*." Calas asks, then, that poets turn away from the confessional, which is by definition oriented toward the past, that they look to the future, that they understand that the past is prologue. This brief account of Calas's essay cannot do justice to his brilliant analysis of the poetic image and to the closeness of his argument, but it will suffice to indicate the direction of his thought.

The rift that had occurred in the ranks of the English surrealists as a result of Mesens's dictatorial demands in 1940 was now to bear serious consequences for the movement. Soon after his attack on Ithell Colquhoun in *Arson*, del Renzio met her and fell in love. Miss Colquhoun, it will be recalled, had refused to subscribe to Mesens's demands and had left the group, and del Renzio's association with her, consequently, cost him Mesens's favor.[54] Since del Renzio was highly articulate and profoundly committed to surrealism, his differences with Mesens took on the proportions of a major split in surrealist ranks, although del Renzio, after gaining the temporary support of the Birmingham group, remained alone in his opposition and constituted a splinter group of one.

A surrealist exhibition held at the International Art Center in November–December, 1942, provided the first public, though mute, evidence of the split. It was del Renzio who organized the exhibition and not Mesens as in the past. Roland Penrose, although he later sided with Mesens, lent paintings from his superb collection for the exhibition, which included pictures and objects by Dali, Ernst, Klee, Masson, Tanguy, Picasso, Magritte, Paalen, Agar, Colquhoun, del Renzio, Maddox, and Melville. Del Renzio wrote a brief foreword for the catalogue, which made the usual claims for surrealist art, but which also showed evidence of the influence of Calas:

[These pictures] must inspire to action by their revelation of what the future holds. In the magic of their paint the pictures divine not the mysteries but the marvels of what ought to be, what will be. . . .

[54] I owe this information to Miss Colquhoun. Mesens has ignored all inquiries. Sir Roland Penrose has replied that the quarrel was of no interest "except as a purely personal matter." Mr. del Renzio, in 1964, wrote that he did not know why Mesens had attacked him, but he corroborated Miss Colquhoun's account. I have been unable to find any reasons for the quarrel other than those given by Miss Colquhoun. Some former members of the group have suggested, however, that an element of personal jealousy may have been involved because del Renzio's independent activity presented a challenge to Mesens's leadership.

We must create a new world outlook, a new myth. To create we must destroy, must oppose. To oppose demands liberty, the liberty of the militant. By opposition can we resolve the antithesis the responsibility-liberty [sic]

OPPOSE. Comrades, our watchword is REVOLT.[55]

The rift was further widened when del Renzio rather than Mesens edited a surrealist section for *New Road, 1943* at the invitation of the editors, Alex Comfort and John Bayliss. This he did in a highly provocative manner. In the brief introduction he wrote for the surrealist section, del Renzio attacked those who "claim for themselves *transformation*" (the name of an annual devoted first to the New Apocalypse and later to "Personalism"), those who "only now understand ruins and visions" (obviously a reference to Stephen Spender), those who "cannot appreciate the profound moral difference . . . between Picasso and Joyce," those who "still subscribe to the central European school of aesthetics that handed victory to the Nazis" (Herbert Read?). Only the surrealist, he claims, hears the music in the word "freedom": "to the shadows of men that the petty-minded mistake for 'great,' it is a fearsome word that betrays only too well the insincere. . . . The surrealist voice records its miracle, revealing metamorphosis, initiation, monogamy, freedom, through alienation of sensation, objective hazard, *humour noir.*" Del Renzio emphasized the "sexual element in the unconscious reality of the Surrealist Group," an attitude stressed by Breton in *L'Amour fou,* by Calas, and characterized by Engels as the most revolutionary—"the monogamic tendency."

Aragon is next attacked because "his sexual attitude, to

[55] Toni del Renzio, "Foreword," Catalogue to the Surrealist Exhibition held at the International Art Center, London, November 27 to December 15, 1942.

say nothing of his miserable practice, was incompatible with the monogamous attitude of the group." Del Renzio notes in passing that "it is only to be expected that our intellectuals should rave over the recent poems of Aragon. His attitude sexually and politically was in accord with theirs. We should like to inform the reader that he has just signed a manifesto with Déat." [56] And finally, "it is perhaps this same incompatibility [as Aragon's] that has removed from our midst, in this country, those wretched creatures who were mistakenly allowed within Groups and who, in the fashionable years, were loudest in their profession of a bastard creed that they were pleased to call Surrealism." It is unclear whom del Renzio is including in this final condemnation, but one may assume that, in all probability, Mesens is one of them; the absence of his name from the list of contributors to the surrealist section is a glaring one.

Del Renzio concluded by announcing the forthcoming issuance of a third manifesto by Breton. This manifesto, he said, will define "the sexual nature of the Surrealist unconscious reality and its rôle in the life of the Surrealist Group and the members of that group," and the "New Myth, monogamy . . . intimately related to liberty . . . by revelation, by initiation. The problem of liberty . . . is the great problem of our time. . . . We alone dare to evaluate liberty." [57]

Since lucidity is not the outstanding virtue of del Renzio's prose, and since Breton never issued the promised third manifesto, the sense of del Renzio's comments on monogamy and its revolutionary value is far from clear; the nature and

[56] Arthur Calder-Marshall accused del Renzio of slander on this point in *Tribune*, no. 357 (October 29, 1943), p. 15.

[57] Toni del Renzio, "The Light That Will Cease to Fail," *New Road, 1943*, ed. by Alex Comfort and John Bayliss (Billericay, Essex: Grey Walls Press, 1943), pp. 180–183.

object of his attacks were clear enough, however, and reaction was not long in coming.

The contributions to the surrealist section of *New Road, 1943* are centered upon del Renzio's idea of the "New Myth," although even this is not clear: excerpts from Breton's "Prolegomena to a Third Manifesto," a reprint of Lionel Abel's foreword to the first issue of the American surrealist review *VVV*, and a brief note on myth by Ithell Colquhoun. In addition, several articles on theoretical matters were included: an essay on Tanguy by Calas, one on de Chirico by Robert Melville, an essay on anxiety by Kurt Seligman, and autobiographical notes by Max Ernst. The section, perhaps symptomatically, contained very little original work: a short prose piece by Leonora Carrington; another by Ithell Colquhoun; another, not surrealist by any standard, by Brion Gysin; a few poems by Aimé Césaire, Valentine Penrose, Charles Henri Ford, Georges Hénein, and del Renzio.

Perhaps the most genuinely surrealist piece of work in the anthology is Leonora Carrington's "The Bird Superior: Max Ernst":

Fear, in the form of a horse and dressed in the furs of a hundred different animals, leaps into the kitchen throwing up a shower of sparks under her hooves, the sparks turn into white bats and flit blindly and desperately around the kitchen upsetting pots, tins, bottles and phials of astrological cooking ingredients which crash to the ground in pools of colour. The Bird Superior ties Fear to the flames of the fire by her tail and dips his feathered arms in the colour. Each feather immediately begins to paint a different image with the rapidity of a shriek (p. 194).

Horizon was one of the very few literary magazines published in England during the war, and since it had shown some interest in surrealism, the Mesens–del Renzio feud was continued in its pages. The October, 1943, issue contained a scathing review of del Renzio's little anthology ("The unbelievably scrappy Surrealist section reflects nothing more than its editorial vulgarity"[58]) and a violent letter to the editor concerning del Renzio, which is here reproduced in full:

Astonishing as it may seem, there are always nonentities for whom Surrealism is a means of arrival. The latest attempt of this kind is the so-called "Surrealist Section" in *New Road 1943*. Sheltering beneath a quotation from Breton, a spam-brained intellectual institutes the Barnum of Surrealism.

"The discoveries of surrealism," he writes, "made at the risk of our lives . . ."

We wonder how, when and where this gentleman has risked his life in bothering to compile this small anthology. This is not the first time that a buffoon has smuggled himself into the surrealist wagon. It is not very important.

But we owe it to our surrealist friends in the U.S.A., Mexico or in French colonial territory to bring to the notice of the British public that they are not responsible for the wrigglings of this gentleman. Profiting by their ignorance of him, of their lack of knowledge of the English language, he has taken advantage of their distance to involve them in his grotesque manifestation. We in England formally refuse to associate ourselves with this caricatural and bewildering publication.

(Signed) J. B. Brunius
E. L. T. Mesens
Roland Penrose

In his reply (December, 1943), del Renzio rejected "the assumption by these gentlemen of an *ex cathedra* infallibility" on the grounds that two of them, Mesens and Pen-

[58] Ivor Jacobs, "Auden Aftermath," *Horizon*, VIII, no. 46 (October, 1943), 288.

rose, had "publicly compromised themselves with the moribund versification of that dismal renegade, Eluard," by translating Eluard's *Poésie et vérité, 1942*.[59] And, with a good deal of truth, del Renzio accused Mesens and the others of having "skulked in silence, sitting as a deadweight upon a movement that is alive and has demanded a voice," for, with the few minor exceptions noted above, Mesens had been largely inactive since 1940.

"Literary Idolatry," an article by Arthur Koestler published in the socialist weekly *Tribune* (November 26, 1943), provided the occasion for another outburst from Mesens and Brunius. Koestler heaped scorn on English critics who enthusiastically praised anything French; he called trashy three recent French books which had been greatly praised: Gide's *Imaginary Interviews*, whose message, he said, "was like the Emperor's new clothes: nobody dared to confess that he could not see them." Aragon, whose *Le Crève-Coeur* had been similarly acclaimed, was not, Koestler insisted, the hero the publisher's blurb made him out to be; his ideas on the subject of rhyme and versification, furthermore, were absurd. Vercors's *Les Silences de la mer*, extravagantly praised both in England and America, he called psychologically fake and politically reactionary.

Mesens's and Brunius's reply, entitled *Idolatry and Confusion*, intended for *Tribune*, was published as a leaflet by London Gallery Editions (1944) when that magazine rejected it. In it, the authors echoed Koestler's complaints about the lack of attention paid in England to important French writers and attacked those English critics who had praised the patriotic war poetry of Eluard and Aragon—Naomi Mitchison and Kathleen Raine in particular. The

[59] Paul Eluard, *Poetry and Truth, 1942*, trans. by E. L. T. Mesens and Roland Penrose (London: London Gallery Editions, 1944).

only texts in French of any importance—completely ignored in England—they said, were Georges Bernanos's *Lettre aux anglais*, Breton's interview in *View* (reprinted in *Arson*), Breton's "Prolegomena to a Third Manifesto," his "Situation du surréalisme entre les deux guerres" (a speech to the students at Yale University, reprinted in *VVV*, New York), and Denis de Rougemont's *La Part du diable*. English critics, they complained, have paid attention only to Vercors's *Les Silences de la mer*, "about which there has been such a commotion only to conceal its distressing emptiness," and which has since been accused of being indirectly sympathetic to Nazi Germany.

Mesens defended his translation of Eluard's *Poésie et vérité, 1942* from del Renzio's attack on the grounds that it contained nothing of a patriotic nature. Brunius and Mesens then turned their guns on Toni del Renzio, whose name at their hands underwent several interesting metamorphoses: Mr. Ranci del Conno, Mr. Conci el Rondeau, Mr. Vomi du Pinceau. Del Renzio, who, in his letter to *Horizon*, had referred to Eluard's "moribund versification," was now told that "at the most there can be found in Eluard's work since 1920 a single poem using rhyme or metre. This poem is called 'L'Egalité des sexes.' . . . And what, in any case, does Mr. Conci el Rondeau know of the reasons the surrealists had for using rhyme or not. Attempting to make up to André Breton, having vaguely learnt that he is in disagreement with Eluard, and not knowing with what Breton reproaches him, the Sergeant of the 'King' of Poland, the Rosicrucian Knight, attacks at random." [60]

The attacks on Aragon and the reference to Eluard's

[60] A reference to an eccentric character seen in London, a New Zealander of Polish origin who claimed to be the rightful king of Poland and whom del Renzio had befriended.

"moribund versification" are explained by the fact that during the war, a kind of reactionary literary wave was sweeping over France, reactionary both in form and content. A collection of patriotic poems, mostly in regularly rhymed verse, was clandestinely published under the title *L'Honneur des poètes*, and later attacked by Benjamin Péret in 1945 in a pamphlet entitled *Le Déshonneur des poètes*. The two leading exponents of the new mood were former surrealists, Aragon and Eluard. Their crime, as far as the surrealists were concerned, was that they had allowed patriotic and propagandist motives to override more profound needs. The surrealists' rallying cry of "resistance," by which they meant resistance to all bourgeois conformism and values, including patriotism, had been debased by Aragon and Eluard into "resistance" to the political enemy, Nazi Germany. The "total war" that the surrealists had declared against all opponents of freedom (see the F.I.A.R.I. manifesto) was being severely compromised by the performance of Aragon and Eluard who, as faithful Communists, were putting their art at the service of political propaganda. None of the three authors mentioned by Mesens and Brunius —Breton, Bernanos, or de Rougemont—could be said to glorify the various conformities which seem appropriate in time of war, and this explains why they were largely ignored by English critics who found much to praise in what the surrealists considered reactionary works, Aragon's *Le Crève-Coeur* and the anthology *L'Honneur des poètes*. In his attack on the last-named and on the entire tendency, Péret pointed to the large number of poems in the volume which linked Christianity and nationalism as if they wished to demonstrate that religious and nationalistic dogma had a common origin and an identical social function. In truth, Péret said, wars like the one just fought were made possible

only by a conjunction of all regressive forces. The participation of poets in this is, for Péret, precisely where their
dishonor rests.[61]

Aside from the "dishonor" embodied in this literature from
the surrealists' point of view, the tendency to praise anything French had the depressing effect of elevating the
second-rate to the first rank. Two years later, after the heat
of the moment had dissipated, Anthony West, who had none
of the surrealists' bias, wrote:

The resistance literature is, politically speaking, a fine manifestation of France's powers of endurance and recovery, but it is
very doubtful stuff as literature. The admirers of France, who
stop nothing short of idolatry, wriggle on their bellies in self-
abasement before it, crying that it is the only considerable work
that has been produced in the last five years. But when one reads
such poems as *Les Yeux d'Elsa* or the much touted *Silence de la
Mer* [sic] one recognises very moderate talent.[62]

Toni del Renzio, in April, 1944, issued a manifesto, *Incendiary Innocence,* which redefined the surrealist position,
measured Aragon's failure against that position, and, in
passing, heaped some abuse on Mesens. The crisis facing
poetry, del Renzio says, can be summarized in three assertions: first, that Aragon's "collapse" is symptomatic not of
an exclusively French situation, but of an international
"failure of nerve"; second, that no solution for the crisis
"can be offered by pretending any longer that 'resistance,' in
its ephemeral sense, is a substitute for the subtle and in-

[61] Benjamin Péret, *Le Déshonneur des poètes* (Paris: Le Terrain
vague, 1945; reprinted by Jean-Jacques Pauvert, 1965).

[62] Anthony West, "The Precious Myth," in *The Mint: A Miscellany
of Art, Literature and Criticism,* ed. by Geoffrey Grigson (London:
Routledge and Sons, 1946), p. 66.

formed *resistance of poetry*"; and third, that poetry cannot be abstracted "from the chain of commitments in the 'real world,' in that poetry cannot be recognised but as irrevocably, of its own nature, tending to transform the world."

These statements, he insists, must be understood to mean that the poet, as poet, cannot "be reduced to merely embellishing such political banalities that epigones of Stalin and of Kropotkin may benevolently permit"; and that, on the other hand, the efforts to create a "pure poetry" will serve only "the ugly interests of reaction." Poetic integrity does not survive in the face of war and death, and the contributions to *L'Honneur des poètes* serve only to emphasize "the shame of poetry." Eluard, for example, "pitiably drags image after image from his former glory to make some eighty-five lines of nothing new on liberty"; a similar collapse is evident in England, in Eliot's "Little Gidding," in Spender's "inability to see ruins before bombers created them" or to convince his readers of "visions," in the New Apocalypse, the New Romanticism, "the new whatever is old, outworn or misunderstood, so far has the process obtained in severing *the sign from the thing signified.*"

Surrealism alone, del Renzio claims, has faced this crisis and, alone, has supplied a solution to it—automatism. Del Renzio then briefly outlines the five main points of surrealist doctrine:

1. The unconscious alone "can furnish the valid basis for the appraisal of human motives," and automatism, as the way into the unconscious, is "the first visible example of a general reform of methods of knowledge."
2. The existence of that *"spiritual plane* whence perception by opposites shall cease."
3. The resolution of the contradictions between human and

natural necessity, that is, the recognition that chance is objective, "a manifestation of extreme natural necessity which finds its way into the unconscious."

4. The recognition of humor as a means of defense and of attack, of surmounting the "traumas of exterior reality."

5. Alienation of sensation which makes of surrealism a means of occultation, of *"intervention into mythic life,* which in the form of a work of art prefigures accurately and in strict order certain *facts* destined to be realised in the real world."

As a consequence of this position, del Renzio says, surrealism has directed its attention "to the need for a cosmological outlook, the rediscovery of the appetite for universal knowledge," and to the problem attendant upon "the inflation of words." The general "failure of nerve" earlier referred to is now defined as "the deadly collapse into the confusion resulting from the separation of the symbol from the thing for which it stands." Therefore, he adds, "Surrealism cannot consider it enough to present as a poem just a series of pedestrian puns and doubtful jokes." He insists, however, that he does not mean this comment to apply to the humor of Marcel Duchamp, but "to the banality of . . . Monsieur Sous Merde d'Ane" (an anagram for Edouard Mesens). Insisting, finally, upon "the deep and genuine occultation of Surrealism," the " 'hermetic' immersion in metaphysics," del Renzio points to the occultists, to Christian Rosencreutz especially, as having supplied "the *form* as well as the *content* of some of [surrealism's] boldest . . . assertions.[63]

So far, del Renzio seems to be completely orthodox; he has in fact, said nothing that Breton had not said. However,

[63] *Incendiary Innocence,* "An Arson Pamphlet" (London: privately printed, 1944).

he makes one more assertion that brings him dangerously close to an idealism consistently rejected by Breton: "What is more and more clear is that *materialism* becomes a weapon only so long as reality, no more and no less than any other perception, is seen to be but a symbol." This raises a difficult and slippery point, but Breton has said often enough that the aim of surrealism is to effect a synthesis between the internal and external worlds; this does not mean the dissolution of the external world implied in del Renzio's statement. Breton's interest in the occult is based on the belief that occultism provides a different way of looking at and into reality than that of the rational sciences; it is not based, I believe, on any desire to deny the reality of the external world in favor of another, wholly nonmaterial reality of which the external world is merely the symbol. Breton, in spite of his growing interest in hermetism and magic, had not abandoned his fundamental materialism. It is probably ideas of this kind that earned for del Renzio the title of "Rosicrucian Knight" from Mesens.

There is, however, no indication in the text itself that del Renzio considered himself at variance with orthodox surrealist doctrine. He repeatedly asserted his devotion to Breton: in *Arson*, in his letter to *Horizon,* in his introduction to the surrealist section of *New Road, 1943*, in *Incendiary Innocence*. In fact, the outstanding characteristic of del Renzio's commitment to surrealism is a purity so great that even Breton was found wanting when measured against it a few years later. But in spite of del Renzio's orthodoxy at this time, Breton considered him responsible for having split the London group. Mesens, as the only one with sufficient influence and access to funds to keep a group going, remained the head of the official London group.[64]

[64] From a letter from Miss Colquhoun, November 22, 1961.

One of the last manifestations of group activity by the English surrealists was the bilingual pamphlet, *Message from Nowhere,* edited by Mesens and published by London Gallery Editions in November, 1944. In retrospect, it is difficult to see what the "message" was, for the pamphlet, in the manner characteristic of many English surrealist publications, is retrospective rather than prospective. Pride of place is given to a short excerpt from "The Position of Surrealism between the Wars," the speech given by Breton to students at Yale University in 1942, in which Breton once again answered the "gravediggers" who had proclaimed the death of surrealism. Much space is given to an "Homage to Alfred Jarry," consisting of some rather pedestrian translations of poems. Among the new works offered is some violently anticlerical verse by Mesens and Brunius, an antiwar poem by Roland Penrose, some poems by Patrick Waldberg, Simon Watson Taylor, Feyyaz Fergar, and others. More interesting from the historian's point of view are the "Epitaph" by Ken Hawkes and the "Correspondence re 'Idolatry and Confusion.'" The former is a brief attack on del Renzio and the surrealist section he had edited for *New Road, 1943,* an attack that included the serious charge that the section had "consisted of unauthorized translations of work by members of the international surrealist movement." The "Epitaph" concludes with a brief account of a surrealist poetry-reading given in early spring, 1944, by del Renzio and Ithell Colquhoun (Mrs. del Renzio) at the International Arts Centre, Bayswater. The meeting was attended by a number of French, Belgian, American, and British surrealists "who were determined to prevent the further discrediting of the movement by this quaint couple. The Charwoman [sic] of the meeting refused to read the letter of protest from one of our friends." The meeting was disrupted by noise from the audience, three-quarters of which left after the first half-hour. "Mr. del Renzio's only vocal supporter was a gentleman of military appearance whose moustaches bristled when he shouted at E. L. T. Mesens 'I know you are no gentleman, Sir!' " [65]

The correspondence about *Idolatry and Confusion* consists largely of letters congratulating the authors of that leaflet for their attacks on Aragon and Vercors. Osbert Sitwell wished that they "had dwelt a little more on the intrinsic *worthlessness* of Aragon's verse"; E. M. Forster was "delighted to find that [the leaflet] confirmed my misgivings about Vercors. I have never got on with Aragon either. You are quite right"; Stuart Gilbert apologized that he was cut off from literary currents in North Wales and did not really understand the controversy; A. Calder-Marshall hoped to see some cogent answers to the argument put forth by *Idolatry and Confusion;* Herbert Read, Henry Treece, Conroy Maddox, and Robert Melville all voiced agreement with it. Alex Comfort, the editor of *New Road, 1943,* declaimed responsibility for the views expressed by del Renzio in his "surrealist section" of that volume. In answering this last comment, Mesens and Brunius repeat the serious charge made by Ken Hawkes in "Epitaph," that del Renzio had collected the material for his anthology "without asking either authors or publishers authorizations, in cutting some texts in the most absurd and unscrupulous way." Mr. del Renzio has admitted Mesens's and Brunius's charge, but he explains that "the publishers of *New Road* had undertaken to write all the authors but owing to the wartime difficulty of communication it was a frequent practice to publish even

[65] In a letter to the author (May 15, 1964), Mr. del Renzio said that the account of the meeting as given in *Message from Nowhere* is essentially correct.

without having received permission. Moreover, believing myself to be a part of the international surrealist movement and since the section of *New Road* was supposed to be a manifestation of that movement, I didn't feel I was doing anything quite as dastardly as was afterward made out." [66]

Three years later, the English surrealists made rather extravagant claims for *Message from Nowhere* in their "Déclaration du groupe surréaliste en Angleterre" which formed part of the catalogue of the 1947 International Surrealist Exhibition in Paris. *Idolatry and Confusion,* they claimed, had rallied the scattered membership of the English group; the fruit of this regrouping was *Message from Nowhere.* The quality of the fruit, unfortunately, does not testify to the health of the tree. So much space is given over in English surrealist publications to retrospective glances at the past glories and to insistences of continuing vitality, and so little to the evidences of such vitality, that one must conclude that by 1944 the movement in England, for a number of reasons, was moribund.

In the early 1940's the name Leonora Carrington began appearing in surrealist documents with increasing frequency. Primarily a painter, she published a number of short prose pieces that are a strange blend of childish fairy-tale and paranoid terror. Her first story, *La Maison de la peur,* written in French after she had lived in France only a few months and full of anglicisms and errors, has a speaking horse that takes the heroine to the house of Fear where the following scene greets her:

Devant nous sur une très grande lit incliné d'une façon roman était la patronne, la Peur. Elle resemblait légèrement à un cheval

[66] Letter of May 15, 1964.

en beaucoup plus laide, sa robe de chambre était fait des chauvesouris vivante coudre ensemble par leurs ailes. D'après la façon dont ils remuaient on dirais qu'ils ne ce plaisaient pas.[67]

Other stories, written in English, have a suggestiveness reminiscent of the best de Chirico canvases. Her masterpiece, however, is "Down Below," an account of her descent into madness and her treatment in a Spanish insane asylum following her escape from France in 1940. This piece has been compared by Pierre Mabille and Maurice Blanchot to Nerval's *Aurélia*.[68]

Leonora Carrington has been extravagantly praised: "The greatest English surrealist poet, and, without any argument, one of the four or five greatest poets of . . . surrealist tendency on the international scene." [69] But so few of her writings are at present available that neither agreement nor disagreement with this estimate is possible. Her paintings, which have been shown in every major surrealist exhibition since 1937, occupied a prominent place at the 1960 International Surrealist Exhibition in New York.

On September 3, 1945, Sonia Araquistaín, the twenty-year-old daughter of Luis Araquistaín Quevedo, the Spanish ambassador to Paris in 1936–1937, committed suicide by jumping nude from a third-story window of a house in Bayswater. The suicide led to a public inquest during which the prosecutor "found an unhoped-for opportunity of spitting on

[67] Leonora Carrington, *La Maison de la peur,* preface and illustrations by Max Ernst (Paris: Collection "Un Divertissement," 1938), n.p.

[68] Leonora Carrington, *Une Chemise de nuit de flanelle,* trans. from the English by Yves Bonnefoy, preface by Henri Parisot (Paris: Librairie Les Pas Perdus, 1951), n.p.

[69] Claude Serbanne, "Surréalistes étrangers—panorama," *Les Cahiers du Sud,* no. 280 (1946), p. 397.

everything poetic in this world." [70] It was revealed at the inquest that she had studied Freud and been peripherally associated with the surrealists; it seemed to Toni del Renzio that she had been a "surreal" person and should be recognized as such. "For me," he says, "the image of this girl who mounted the stairs nude before her fatal leap leant a lucidity to the works of Delvaux." [71] At Georges Hénein's suggestion, he planned a collection of drawings, poems, and other writings inspired by her defiant gesture, on the model of *Violette Nozières,* a collection dedicated to a young girl who had murdered her father. Del Renzio, however, was unable to obtain sufficient cooperation from other surrealists, probably because of Mesens's hostility to him, and the project, unfortunately, came to nothing. [72]

Among other events of surrealist interest in the years immediately following the end of the war was the exhibition "Surrealist Diversity" at the Arcade Gallery in London in October, 1945, a small exhibition which brought together one, or at most two works by each of the following: Arp, Brauner, de Chirico, Delvaux, Dominguez, Ernst, Giacometti, Klee, Magritte, Miró, Paalen, Picasso, Man Ray, and Tanguy, in addition to a few lesser known artists.

In 1944, Feyyaz Fergar, a Turkish poet who wrote primarily in French, became associated with the London surrealists. In July, 1944, he edited *Fulcrum,* an ephemeral magazine which issued one number only. The roster of its contributors includes the names of E. L. T. Mesens, Henry Treece, J. B. Brunius, Valentine Penrose, Edith Rimmington, James Kirkup, Simon Watson Taylor, Sadi Cherkeshi and Fergar himself. A sample of its contents is provided in

[70] Georges Hénein, *ibid.,* p. 394.   [71] Letter of May 15, 1964.
[72] From letters from Miss Colquhoun and Mr. del Renzio.

the following piece entitled "Automatic Writing" by Edith Rimmington:

When the music of the touch hangs well then the oasis, the chair and the gasp as the tall chimneys shatteringly deliver death. The hair waves back on the shore of white pickled bones, reluctantly returning to the dun of to-morrow, empty of the fury of yester-day. The starfish is dead in the empty box and the prone logs dream go-astray until the glare cut short their sojourn and return-shocks them to the drag a chain.

The following year, Fergar together with Sadi Cherkeshi edited a somewhat longer-lived magazine, *Dint*, which issued two numbers. The first consisted almost entirely of verse of vaguely surrealist tendency; the second contained also some very very short stories, and some automatic texts by Fergar. One of the stories, "O" by Sadi Cherkeshi, is given here in full:

"This extraordinary event of every day being the same. Keep away Loved One, keep away. Or else I will round you, make you perfect."

After saying this, he approached her and erased the features of her face with his hand.—His hand a condor's wing.—His arm a muscular column.—His muscles of flexible marble.—With calcified feathers of fingers he moulded her curves and angles out of shape. She became perfectly round and lit with a blood-red glow. Then she started to grow and when she reached the size of his love and hate, which was great, he ran round her a minute speck.

There was only one opening left on her roundness and this resembled a mouth and all her purple veins were centred here. Through this opening he entered and left his arm out and then slowly oh! slowly so slow a calcified hand slowly vanished into her roundness. The opening rounded up, closed, disappeared.

Now a globe of blood-red glow wanders the domain of time and space perfectly round, complete.

Fergar's "Automatic Text" is given in full:

Now I want to go straight. The colony of my roots is restless. Far, far away are the tubes of my masturbation mirrored by all the prisms in the world. My oscillating metronome rejects all viscous lullabies and drinks its own cobra-blood swollen to the highest pitch.

    Cut, Cut, Cut, Cut,
      Cut, Cut, Cut.

It is difficult, from the vantage point of the present, to see why these pieces were thought worth publishing.

With the exceptions already noted, group activity of the London surrealists was limited, during the war years, to regular meetings at the Barcelona Restaurant in Soho and to occasional quarrels with Tambimuttu's *Poetry London* group on Wednesdays in the Horseshoe pub on Tottenham Court Road. The meetings at the Barcelona Restaurant were usually chaired by E. L. T. Mesens or Jacques Brunius and consisted of a lot to drink, dinner, surrealist games ("exquisite corpse" and collective pictures), and recitations of poetry. One event which awoke memories of the great dada outrages of the 1920's was the surrealist raid on the Café Royal in 1942. But even this was an anti-climax, for no one seems to have been outraged or even interested.[73]

By this time, the London surrealists had become a very loose group which no longer required adherence to a code as a prerequisite for membership, except in the most general way: one could not, for example, be both a Roman Catholic

[73] George Woodcock, "Elegy for Fur-Covered Horns: Notes on Surrealism in England," *Limbo* (February, 1964), p. 52.

and a surrealist. After a period of revitalized activity in the early years of the war, stimulated by the presence in London of a number of Paris surrealists, the meetings at the Barcelona toward the end of the war had acquired a very strong nostalgic flavor. Surrealism was already then, for the English in particular, a thing of the past.[74]

In 1946, Simon Watson Taylor published the last production but one of the English group as a whole, *Free Unions Libres,* an anthology of material collected during the war. While he was preparing the collection, Mr. Taylor's apartment was raided by the police who were looking for an anarchist friend of his. The manuscript of *Free Unions* was confiscated because the raiding policemen, unable to make out the contents, thought it was in code. The manuscript was returned shortly after by a Special Branch detective who asked if he could join the group.

The English surrealists had not had a regular outlet for their productions since the *London Bulletin* had ceased publication in 1940, except for the single number of *Arson,* the unrepresentative surrealist section of *New Road, 1943,* which was not the expression of the English group, *Message from Nowhere,* and *Dint* and *Fulcrum,* which seem to have been peripheral to the activities of the London group. *Free Unions* was the first such outlet for material produced during the war, and yet the editor found room, within the narrow compass of forty-eight pages, to publish a translation of a few scenes from Jarry's *Ubu Roi,* an excerpt from Charles Maturin's *Melmoth the Wanderer,* a fragment from Sade's *Philosophie dans le boudoir,* a long poem by Mesens dating from 1931, and a confused, puerile essay on T. S. Eliot's

[74] From interviews with participants in these meetings: Conroy Maddox, George Melly, and Simon Watson Taylor.

"Little Gidding." All of this testifies to the poverty of the material available, an impression that is strengthened by such productions as these:

> If your brains
> were wool
> You could not knit a sock

> If your brains
> were thread
> You could not manipulate a sewing machine

> If your brains
> were dynamite
> You could not blow off the top of your head [75]

or:

The first light of dawn winked suddenly with a sign and a grey hand-clasp; all the wild flowers of the fields were sleeping drunkenly or climbing fences under the protection of the armed scouts of the darkness. A day exploded among the distant hills, as guilty as a burst paper-bag, and the tree shivered with fear and emotion.[76]

or:

The history of Christianity is the history of a creeping sickness, for submission and obedience before the fear-imagery of priest-craft humanity is offered the dubious honour of being clasped to its filthy bosom.[77]

The editor's hope that "these pages, the evidence of a creative, organic existence lived by individuals amid fossilized

[75] George Melly, *Free Unions,* ed. by Simon Watson Taylor (London: privately printed, 1946), p. 38.
[76] Simon Watson Taylor, *ibid.,* p. 18.
[77] Conroy Maddox, "Notes on the Christian Myth," *ibid,* p. 14.

. . . conceptions of life . . . may serve to cast some light on the contemporary landscape . . . allowing others to distinguish once and for all the living from the dead," is, unfortunately, not fulfilled. The editor, Simon Watson Taylor, left the surrealist movement in 1951 to become one of the leading lights of the College of Pataphysics.

Breton's *Young Cherry Trees Secured against Hares* was published in 1946 by A. Zwemmer in a translation by Edouard Roditi. The book attracted almost no attention, except that del Renzio used his review of it and of two other works by Breton, *Fata Morgana* (1942), and *Arcane 17* (1945), to point to a deepening crisis in surrealism and to accuse Breton of hedging on certain crucial issues.[78] The crisis centered upon the problem of the relation between the conscious and the unconscious in surrealism. Both Nicolas Calas, in "The Light of Words" (1942), and André Masson, in "A Crisis of the Imaginary" (1945),[79] had pointed to the dead end to which uncritical automatism had led, and had both called for increased conscious control as a means out of the impasse created by the monotony and limitations of unconscious symbols. Calas had called for "lucidity," and Masson had, in fact, broken with surrealism on this issue. In 1942, Breton had spoken of the need for a third manifesto, but had gone no further than issuing prolegomena to that manifesto; and now, in 1947, del Renzio says, "It is more than disconcerting that Breton should . . . pronounce only equivocations on these issues where his associates disagree."

[78] Toni del Renzio, "André Breton a-t-il dit passe," *Horizon*, XV no. 88 (May, 1947), 297–301.
[79] Calas in *Arson* (1942); Masson in *Horizon*, XII no. 67 (July, 1945), 42–44.

In his later work, Breton had shown an increasing pre-occupation with the symbolism of alchemy, magic, and hermetism. This, of course, indicates a direction away from the personal unconscious toward the traditional and, in some measure, objective. The equivocation of which del Renzio complains consists of Breton's refusal to deal with this new direction in his theoretical considerations. In his practice, del Renzio says, Breton is showing increasing concern with the objective, traditional symbol; in his theory, however, he still clings to his commitment to unconscious automatism.

Another point of contention between del Renzio and Breton is the fact that Breton, in spite of his earlier pronouncements on monogamy, had divorced his wife Jacqueline in the United States and married the *femme-enfant* of *Arcane 17*. This, for del Renzio, is another betrayal of revolutionary surrealist doctrine.[80] Breton, then, instead of facing issues squarely and taking unequivocal positions on the problems facing the movement, says *passe* and continues to play his old role of high priest, still surrounds himself with disciples, still utters "the same exclusions and initiations to . . . a different group." And, del Renzio concludes, "Perhaps it is a desire not to be conscious of his situation that conditions so rigidly [Breton's] attachment to the unconscious and his failure to appreciate all that the conscious can achieve." [81]

The International Surrealist Exhibition of 1947, held in Paris at the Gallerie Maeght, was the occasion for the last appearance of the English surrealists as a group. They issued

[80] del Renzio himself was divorced from his wife in 1948.
[81] del Renzio, "André Breton," p. 301.

a "Declaration" which is more an apology for the failure of surrealism in England than a positive affirmation of principles.[82]

Among the reasons given for the failure of surrealism to take firm hold in England is, primarily, the fact that irrationality has always been an element of English culture; that English thought and even English daily life have never been ruled by a "logic of a coercive nature"; that in English education the place which in France is reserved for Corneille and Racine is taken by the Elizabethan dramatists and the romantic poets; that "nonsense" and fairy tales are the staples of English children's reading. All this explains why there are in England so many precursors of surrealism—from Cyril Tourneur, Swift, Blake, and Coleridge, to Lewis Carroll—and so few intentional surrealists. In addition, the form of Christian moral oppression is different in England from that in France. Whereas in France the enemy is the sharply defined, monolithic Roman Catholic Church, in Protestant England, the enemy attacks man from within himself and is, in itself, divided and superficially liberal. The need, therefore, to band together in order to oppose oppressive forces is less obvious in England than elsewhere. Further, the decentralized character of English society, in contrast to the concentration in France of all intellectual activity in Paris, makes the formation of cohesive groups difficult.

The declaration proceeds then to a series of denunciations and exclusions of the kind that have always been a feature of this sort of surrealist document. Henry Moore is damned for having gone without warning from surrealism to the

[82] "Déclaration du groupe surréaliste en Angleterre," *Le Surréalisme en 1947* (Paris: Editions Pierre à Feu, 1947), pp. 45–46.

making of sacerdotal ornaments and having, in consequence, fallen into monotony and into the miserable vulgarization of his "reclining figures." Herbert Read, whose eclecticism has reached staggering proportions, is next, followed by David Gascoyne, whose mystifications have left him foaming at the mouth, and Humphrey Jennings, who has been decorated with the Order of the British Empire. There are more, the declaration says, but their names are not known outside of England.

In spite of these difficulties and defections, the declaration goes on, certain of the signatories have, in the face of militarism, patriotism, and censorship, kept the surrealist flame brightly burning. Their intervention took the form of pamphlets and letters to the press. *Idolatry and Confusion*, in particular, rallied the scattered membership of the group; Mesens's *Message from Nowhere* and the anthology *Free Unions* are cited as the evidence of this regrouping.

The declaration, signed by John Banting, Robert Baxter, Emmy Bridgewater, F.-J. Brown, J. B. Brunius, Feyyaz Fergar, Conroy Maddox, George Melly, Robert Melville, E. L. T. Mesens, Roland Penrose, Edith Rimmington, Philip Sansom, and Simon Watson Taylor, concludes with a reaffirmation of devotion to surrealist principles as stated by Breton in his interview in *View*, his prolegomena to a third manifesto, his "Position of Surrealism between the Wars," and in Benjamin Péret's *Le Déshonneur des poètes*.

For all its talk of activity and regroupings, the declaration is a tacit admission of the failure of the English surrealists to maintain any kind of productive cohesiveness. Had an active, productive group existed during these years, there would have been no need for regroupings. Further, the evidences of such regroupings—*Message from Nowhere* and

Free Unions—are, we have seen, faint indications indeed of vitality. Some of the reasons for the failure of surrealism as a movement in England are given in the "Declaration"—reasons, incidentally, very similar to those given in the *International Surrealist Bulletin No. 4* for the lateness of the English in adopting surrealism—but others of which the "Declaration" does not speak have been adduced by former members of the group: the principal reason for the failure of the movement in England, as indeed of most other non-French groupings, was the lack of a leader with the genius and magnetism of Breton. Mesens tried to fill the role, but without success. One of the effects of this lack was that, in England at any rate, no first-rate talents were attracted to the movement. English surrealism did not produce its Eluard, its Péret, its Crevel. It did attract some writers who, as we shall see in the following, took from surrealism what they could use, but none who actually were or remained surrealist. Those who could have given the English movement its own direction and importance—Herbert Read, Hugh Sykes Davies, and Humphrey Jennings—saw surrealism merely as a special example of something else which interested them more; the effect of their contribution to surrealism was to dilute rather than affirm the special point of view offered by surrealism. Their endeavor, while certainly a legitimate one, had, in the end, the effect of making surrealism seem little more than an eccentric variation of what had always been available in English romanticism. There is, of course, a good deal of truth in this view: had there been a real need for the special contribution of surrealism, no amount of excuses and explanations—the lack of inspired leadership, the lack of café life similar to the Parisian, the excessive individualism of the English, the war,—

would have been sufficient reason for the failure of the movement. Had there been a need, it would have been filled.

In 1951, speaking primarily about surrealist art, Herbert Read accurately summarized the situation:

The break-up of the Surrealist Movement as a direct consequence of the Second World War is an historical event which has never yet been adequately explained. . . . This is a complicated problem not unconnected with the general political disillusionment that took place during the war—for there was always a close connexion between surrealism and communism. But in England . . . surrealism never crystallised into an independent group of distinct character—most of our surrealists kept a foot in some other camp, and never fully committed themselves to that "automatism" of creative activity which André Breton has always made the criterion of a surrealist attitude in art. Francis Bacon, though he has never, to my knowledge, called himself a surrealist, is probably the most consistent surrealist among us. Others who might claim the title are too consciously fantastic. Nevertheless there are characteristics in the art of painters like John Armstrong, Francis Bacon, Edward Burra, Robert Colquhoun, Mervyn Evans, Tristram Hillier, Louis le Brocquy, Roland Penrose, Robert MacBryde, Ceri Richards, Julian Trevelyan, John Tunnard, Keith Vaughan, and Bryan Wynter, and sculptors like Adams, Chadwick, and McWilliam which, given coherence and scope, might have constituted a vigorous surrealist movement in England. That this did not happen was due to anti-organizational traits in the English character rather than to any absence of appropriate talent.[83]

More recently, however, Read adduced somewhat different reasons for the failure of the movement in England:

[83] Herbert Read, *Contemporary British Art* (Harmondsworth, Middlesex: Penguin Books, 1951), pp. 34–35.

I still believe that the cause of the "failure" of the whole movement was not the war as such, but the attempt to place the movement *au service de la révolution.* There was a fundamental contradiction (not of the kind that can be dialectically resolved) between the political program of the Communist Party and Breton's (to me so sympathetic) libertarianism. . . . I still think that the only political counterpart of surrealism is anarchism, and if that had been recognized from the beginning the movement would have had more logical coherence and a longer life. Hegel was our real enemy, and how in any case does one reconcile automatism and the dialectical process? [84]

[84] Letter to the author, April 25, 1966. The last sentence is somewhat confused: automatism is not reconciled *with* the dialectical process; it is reconciled *by* the dialectical process with its opposite.

5 | *Fringes and Influences*

~~~~~~~~ Surrealism in England had considerable influence on the writing of verse and, to a much smaller degree, of prose. It is well, when discussing influences, to remember André Gide's warning that "influences do not create anything; they merely awaken what is already there." [1] We have already seen that the principal theoreticians of surrealism in England, Herbert Read and Hugh Sykes Davies, were primarily concerned with demonstrating the truth of this observation. But other forces and tendencies than those discussed by Read and Davies were at work in England which were reinforced by the impetus of surrealism. These concerned especially the doctrine of the poetic image.

The ground had been well prepared in England for the incursion of surrealism. Earlier in the century, imagism, reinforced by Freud's analyses of dream-imagery and the doctrines of French symbolism, had put a heavy burden on the image. Replacing statement and description, the image became the principal vehicle for poetic communication.

In elaborating their conception of the image, T. E. Hulme

---

[1] Quoted by Enid Starkie, *From Gautier to Eliot: The Influence of France on English Literature, 1851–1938* (London: Hutchinson, 1960), p. 12.

and Ezra Pound, reacting against the loose rhetorical moralizing and sentimentalizing of the popular Edwardian and Georgian poets, rejected the current view that the poet is primarily concerned with expressing his "personality," that is, that conscious part of him that describes feelings and constructs moral positions on those feelings. Instead, Hulme insisted on "dry, hard classical verse," on brevity, concreteness, and precision of expression, on images rather than discourse. However paradoxical this may appear, Hulme's ideas are a consequence of Bergson's anti-intellectual philosophy, of which Hulme was the foremost propagandist in England. For Bergson, the only reality is in the "flux of phenomena," not in intellectual concepts; and intuition, not the rational intellect, is the means to knowledge. Intellect may provide "approximate models," but it is only by intuition that one can know the "flux." In the realm of language, Hulme thought, abstractions and conventional rhetoric may provide "approximate models," but images are the direct expression of the flux. Poetry, in which "each *word* [is] an image *seen*, not a counter," [2] is then the only means of communicating reality. It is this view that led Pound to say, "It is better to present one Image in a lifetime than to produce voluminous works." [3]

But Pound's definition of the image as "that which presents an intellectual and emotional complex in an instant of time" [4] makes clear that the image as finally crystallized in the poem is not a purely unconscious product, but the re-

[2] "Notes on Language and Style," *Further Speculations by T. E. Hulme,* ed. by Sam Hynes (Minneapolis: University of Minnesota Press, 1955), p. 79.

[3] "A Few Don'ts by an Imagiste," *Poetry* (Chicago), I, no. 6 (March, 1913), 200–201.

[4] *Ibid.*

sult of the fusion of intellect and emotion. This idea leads directly to T. S. Eliot's definition of the "undissociated sensibility" as one that possesses the "essential quality of transmuting ideas into sensations, of transforming an observation into a state of mind," a sensibility in which "there is a direct sensuous apprehension of thought, or a recreation of thought into feeling" ("The Metaphysical Poets"). This, in turn, has its obvious affinities with surrealist principles: where Eliot was concerned with what seemed to him the artificial division between thought and feeling, the surrealists worried about the distinction, equally artificial, between reality and dream, between conscious and unconscious. The nature of the concern is the same, only the degree differs: Eliot wants to reintegrate the poetic sensibility; the surrealists, because they reject the distinction between art and life, the entire human personality.

The theories of Freud and the practice of Joyce, further weakening the bond between the two members of the image, went so far as to attack the integrity of the basic unit of language, the word. We have already examined some of the consequences for language of Freud's theories, particularly of the *Interpretation of Dreams*. Joyce, like the surrealists, leaned heavily on Freud's theories, and although he was not a surrealist, his method has obvious similarities to theirs. His conscious creation of his hero's unconscious has already been mentioned, but even the language of *Finnegans Wake* has analogues with surrealist practice: just as his fluid words change meaning under scrutiny and his puns are "quadrivial," so Dali's images are double or triple, and "the same picture can represent different images at the same time." [5]

T. S. Eliot, whose work is the meeting point of many of

[5] Marcel Jean, *The History of Surrealist Painting*, trans. by Simon Watson Taylor (New York: Grove Press, 1960), p. 217.

these tendencies, is not a surrealist by any definition. He has, in fact, stated his opposition to surrealism: "Our instincts of tidiness imperatively command us not to leave to the haphazard of the unconscious what we can attempt to do consciously" ("The Function of Criticism"). But this rejection leaves a wide field of operation for the unconscious, for, as many of Eliot's critical observations show, there is much that we cannot "attempt to do consciously." As C. K. Stead has shown in his remarkable study, *The New Poetic*, Eliot's ideas of the "impersonality" of the poet have been mistaken for a call for a new classicism, whereas properly read, they indicate a desire to escape, not from the self, but deeper into the self in order to release the poet from his own rational will.[6]

Stead shows that even in his early essays, Eliot was struggling to express satisfactorily a distinction between the operation of the conscious mind and what is unconsciously offered up to the conscious mind to work on. Eliot repeatedly returned to the idea that the poet's conscious mind must be preoccupied with technical matters, with "meaning," in order to allow material from the deeper unconscious levels to rise to the surface. At certain heightened moments, when "strong habitual barriers" are broken down, the unconscious elements rise to the surface unimpeded, providing material which represents "the depths of feeling into which we cannot peer," material that remains obscure even to the poet. Moments like these, Eliot says, have their analogy with mystical experience.[7] This is an idea that Eliot had explored once before, in his essay on Pascal's *Pensées*

[6] C. K. Stead, *The New Poetic: Yeats to Eliot* (New York: Harper Torchbooks, 1964), chapter 6.

[7] T. S. Eliot, *The Use of Poetry and the Use of Criticism* (London: Faber and Faber, 1933), pp. 144 and 148.

(1931): "It is a commonplace that some forms of illness are extremely favourable, not only to religious illumination, but to artistic and literary composition. A piece of writing meditated, apparently without progress, for months or years, may suddenly take shape and word. . . . He to whom this happens assuredly has the sensation of being a vehicle rather than a maker."

Probably sensing that he was coming very close to surrealist doctrine, Eliot added a qualification immediately after the passage just quoted: "I have no good word to say for the cultivation of automatic writing as the model of literary composition." But the only difference between the process that Eliot has described and automatic writing is that, as Stead notes, in the former case "the material has obviously been incubating within the poet for a long time." But this, I believe, is a distinction without much difference: the unconscious material that is tapped in automatic writing has doubtless also been incubating for a long time, as any reader of Freud's dream analyses knows.

It is not my purpose here to demonstrate that Eliot was a surrealist in spite of himself, but that both he and the surrealists owe a debt to a common source. Eliot's "objective correlative"—i.e., "a set of objects, a situation, a chain of events which shall be the formula of [a] particular emotion" —has its obvious similarities to Pound's "Image"; both in turn, it seems to me, are not unlike the surrealist "made object" which, we have seen, is essentially a concretized image. All three depend upon a descent into the "flux," the "deeper" levels of the mind, the unconscious.

Unless we are willing to dismiss Eliot's accounts of the creative process and insist, as many of his commentators have done, on the prose meaning of his poems, we must grant that Eliot's images are the result of the process he has described. They must be seen, then, as objective correlatives for what would otherwise be inexpressible. It is interesting in this context that many of these images in his poems of the 1920's seem verbal equivalents of images in surrealist paintings:

Dead mountain mouth of carious teeth
> (*The Waste Land*, l. 339)

A woman drew her long black hair out tight
And fiddled whisper music on those strings
And bats with baby faces in the violet light
Whistled, and beat their wings
And crawled head downward down a blackened wall
> (*The Waste Land*, ll. 377–381)

. . . the surface of the blackened river
Is a face that sweats with tears
> ("The Wind Sprang Up at Four O'Clock")

. . . breastless creatures under ground
Leaned backward with a lipless grin.
Daffodil bulbs instead of balls
Stared from the sockets of the eyes!
> ("Whispers of Immortality")

The sight of a prostitute in a doorway evokes the memory of

A twisted branch upon the beach
Eaten smooth, and polished
As if the world gave up
The secret of its skeleton,
Swift and white.
A broken spring in a factory yard
Rust that clings to the form that the strength has left
Hard and curled and ready to snap.
> ("Rhapsody on a Windy Night")

These are fairly obvious on the visual level even if the "meaning" is elusive. But there are larger and subtler effects in Eliot's poetry that approximate those of surrealism. These involve a technique similar to that of telescoping disparate elements into a single image, but on a larger scale. These effects are achieved by the juxtaposition of contexts and the distortions of perspective that have an affinity with the technique of "photo-montage"; this, in turn, has its ancestry in the condensed dream-images analyzed by Freud and finds an echo in the collage of surrealism.

The whole *Waste Land* is such a juxtaposition which produces a kind of dream-perspective: images from all history and literature flow through the universal consciousness of Tiresias. To achieve these fusions Eliot sometimes resorts to a device not very different from the surrealist method of interpreting objects. By subtle alteration of a borrowed line of poetry, Eliot telescopes contexts otherwise disparate; for example, by changing "the king my father's wreck" from *The Tempest* to "the king my brother's wreck" in the *Waste Land* (l. 191), Eliot brings together the world of *The Tempest* and the world of the grail legends.[8] Similarly, by "interpreting" images or objects, the surrealists attempt to fuse the conscious with the unconscious: the fur-lined tea-set is the obvious instance. A photograph interpreted by Dali is a striking example of the method: horizontally, the photograph shows a group of African natives before a hut; vertically, the same configuration changes into a face.[9] However, since the *Waste Land* came several years before some of these techniques were developed by the surrealists, we

---

[8] Cleanth Brooks, *Modern Poetry and the Tradition* (Chapel Hill, N.C.: University of North Carolina Press, 1939), p. 152.

[9] Reproduced in Marcel Jean, *The History of Surrealist Painting*, p. 217. Cf. Jacob Korg, "Modern Art Techniques in *The Waste Land*," *Journal of Aesthetics and Art Criticism*, XVIII (June, 1960), 456–463.

must conclude that Eliot was not influenced by them, but that both he and they found a common source elsewhere, probably in Freud's analyses of dream-images.

The verse of Edith Sitwell shows some of the same freedom of imagery that surrealism has rendered almost commonplace. Miss Sitwell says that when she began to write, during the years of the *Georgian Poetry* anthologies, "change in the direction, imagery, and rhythms in poetry had become necessary," [10] and, in order to direct and provide for that change, she edited her own yearly anthology, *Wheels* (1916–1921). The technique of the *Wheels* group has been described as follows:

The initiate regards an object fixedly until its leading characteristics have become blurred; then, in place of these, he grafts the leading characteristics of some other object which, not having been regarded at all fixedly, is in consequence bright and fresh. Thus he may cause the sea to lose its distinguishing colours, noises and surges, and become remarkable for its amber portals, its parrot plumes and its tight monkey-skin.[11]

Miss Sitwell's own practice is the embodiment of this technique; I have selected a few examples upon which she has commented herself. "Said King Pompey," a poem from the early *Façade* (1922), contains this image:

> . . . the hairy sky that we
> Take for coverlet comfortably

"Hairy sky" is an image one might expect in a Dali painting, but Miss Sitwell has an explanation that removes the image

[10] Edith Sitwell, "Some Notes on My Own Poetry," *The Collected Poems of Edith Sitwell* (New York: Vanguard Press, 1954), p. xv.

[11] E. G. Twitchett, "Poetry Chronicle," *London Mercury*, XX, no. 116 (June, 1929), 204.

from the realm of the surreal: "I was speaking of streaks of dark cloud in a hot summer sky, and I meant, too, that now everything, even the heaven, seems to be of an animal, a material, nature." [12]

"Aubade," another poem from *Façade*, contains the lines,

> Flames as staring, red and white,
> As carrots or as turnips, shining
> Where the cold dawn light lies whining.

Miss Sitwell's explanation of the last line is that to her, "the shimmering movement of a certain cold dawn light upon the floor suggests a kind of high animal whining or simpering, a half-frightened or subservient urge to something outside our consciousness." One suspects, however, that the rationale is a result of the line and that "whining" suggested itself, perhaps automatically, as a rhyme for "shining."

Again from *Façade*, "Dark Song" contains the line "The fire was furry as a bear." This poem, Miss Sitwell says, is "about the beginning of things and their relationships—the fire that purrs like an animal and has a beast's thick coat (the crumbling, furry black coal)." But for a similar image, "Furred is the light," from another poem, "Madame Mouse Trots," Miss Sitwell has a different explanation: "I was thinking of misty moonlight." In the same poem, the following image appears:

> Hoarse as a dog's bark
> The heavy leaves are furled

and Miss Sitwell explains that "certain leaves have a rough and furry texture and jut violently from their branches." But she says nothing about why the leaves are furled like

---

[12] "Some Notes," pp. xx–xxxviii.

a hoarse bark, unless we are to assume that their jutting from the branches is as violent as a bark. In either case, the explanation is not satisfactory, although the image is, and I suspect that Miss Sitwell was as surprised at the image as her reader, and is no more able than he to supply a completely rational explanation for it.

One more image and explanation—from "Père Amelot": "the image 'hen-cackling grass' refers to quaking grass, and it was suggested by the fact that the color and dusty aspect of the pods are like the color and dustiness of a hen, are dry and have markings like those on a hen's legs, and, as well, by the fact that the shaking movement resembles, for me at least, the quick dry sound and dipping movement of a cackling hen." Again, it would appear that the image suggested the reason, for it seems unlikely that a poet would work in the manner that Miss Sitwell's explanation suggests. What is more likely is that the image suggested itself in that mysterious automatic way familiar to poets and that, after the fact, its rightness became evident. I am not here suggesting that Miss Sitwell is a surrealist poet or that she writes automatically. I am suggesting, however, that these striking images—and many more like them—were produced by a process other than the one she describes, and that that process is akin to that of the surrealists, with results akin to those of surrealist method.

The similarities between some of her images and those of dadaist and surrealist verse, in fact, led Miss Sitwell on more than one occasion to launch ill-tempered attacks upon surrealism and its supporters. In the course of one of her periodic skirmishes with Geoffrey Grigson, editor of *New Verse,* she attacked him for having opened his pages to such works as Giacometti's "Poem in Seven Spaces," upon which she comments, "I wish there had been more spaces: in short, I wish there had been nothing except space." [13] She took the opportunity of the 1937 Northcliffe Lectures, which she and her brothers delivered at the University of London, to renew the attack. Her dismissals of the endeavors of surrealism deserve no attention, for they consist only of quotations from the surrealists and her own contemptuous snorts. She did, however, feel the need to defend herself against charges of dadaist tendencies:

It was at about this time that my brothers and I began to write, and the Dadaist nonsense . . . was seized upon, immediately, as a rod with which to belabour us. It was decided that we were doing the same thing as the Dadaists, and the fact that we were doing nothing of the kind made no difference to the attackers.

My poems in especial were singled out as Dadaist, and this was, I imagine, because I was writing exceedingly difficult technical exercises. . . . The fact that the surrealists for the most part have not even a rudimentary technique,—indeed *boast* that they have no technique, made no difference to these critics." [14]

The case of W. H. Auden is at once simpler and more complex. Although not a surrealist poet, he has availed himself of certain surrealist devices in order to make his didactic points. Having set himself the task of diagnosing the illness of modern bourgeois society, he depends heavily upon Freudian strategies. This means that he has to create the unconscious of that society, as it were, in order to subject

[13] *Aspects of Modern Poetry* (London: Duckworth, 1934), p. 37.
[14] "Three Eras of Modern Poetry," in Osbert, Edith, and Sacheverell Sitwell, *Trio: Dissertations on Some Aspects of National Genius* (London: Macmillan, 1938), pp. 162–163.

it to his probe. This involves a kind of pseudo surrealism: availing himself of Freud's discoveries, he deliberately constructs dream-images that will serve as symptoms of the disease he is attempting to expose. As Stephen Spender says, "He consciously invents dreams and depicts actuality in the language of unconscious fantasies. In this way he has transformed the poetic role from that of the poet withdrawn into a world of wishful fantasies into that of the poet interpreting or creating dreams, writing a commentary on his epoch in a language of dream-fantasies and symbols."[15]

A favorite device of Auden's is the catalogue of objects that have no rational connection with each other; the purpose of this is to suggest that a dream-logic holds these objects together in the bourgeois unconscious and that, therefore, they possess a significance denied to rational products. For example, from an early poem, "1929":

                          . . . we know that love
Needs more than the admiring excitement of union,
More than the abrupt self-confident farewell,
The heel on the finishing blade of grass,
The self-confidence of the falling root,
Needs death, death of the grain, our death,
Death of the old gang; would leave them
In sullen valley where is made no friends,
The old gang to be forgotten in the spring,
The hard bitch and the riding-master,
Stiff underground; deep in clear lake
The lolling bridegroom, beautiful, there.[16]

[15] Stephen Spender, "W. H. Auden and His Poetry," in Monroe K. Spears, ed., *Auden: A Collection of Critical Essays* (Englewood Cliffs, N.J.: Prentice-Hall, 1964), p. 34.
[16] W. H. Auden, *Collected Shorter Poems, 1927–1957* (New York: Random House, 1964), p. 39.

The quotation is necessarily long to illustrate the cumulative effect of the two catalogues, culminating in the mysterious "the lolling bridegroom, beautiful, there."

The same irrationality that joins the objects in the sequence is applied sometimes to items within the catalogue: "the finishing blade of grass," "the self-confidence of the falling root." His similes, frequently, are not similes at all, and things are associated within images that have no common ground: "The winter holds them like the opera," "The poets exploding like bombs," or:

> They carry terror with them like a purse
> And flinch from the horizon like a gun [17]

These images, C. Day Lewis says, "can only by courtesy be called images . . . the idea of a purse makes almost no contribution to the idea of 'They carry terror with them.'" [18] Some images approach surrealist irrationality:

> On a high chair alone
> I sat, my little master, asking why
> The cold and solid object in my hands
> Should be a human hand, one of your hands. [19]

Auden wrote one poem in which he ironically plays with free-association: the speaker, waiting for his friend to come to a rendezvous, is "writing/Down whatever nonsense/ Comes into my head":

> Why association
> Should see fit to set a
> Bull-dog by a trombone

[17] "Poem XXX," *Look, Stranger* (London: Faber and Faber, 1935), p. 63.
[18] *The Poetic Image* (New York: Oxford University Press, 1948), p. 96.
[19] "The Lesson," *Collected Shorter Poems*, p. 214.

On a grassy plain
Littered with old letters,
Leaves me simply guessing,
I suppose it's La Con-
dition Humaine.

As at lantern lectures
Image follows image;
Here comes a steam-roller
  Through an orange-grove,
Driven by a nursemaid
As she sadly mutters:
"Zola, poor old Zola
  Murdered by a stove." [20]

Joseph Warren Beach, applauding the excision of these stanzas from a later version of the poem, thinks that these random images suggest that Auden had recently visited an exhibition of paintings by Dali and seen a current motion picture about Emile Zola.[21] The stanzas, of course, are not to be taken seriously, but the point of quoting them is that they satirize a method that is not far removed from Auden's own. For example:

[O for] these shops to be turned to tulips in a garden bed,
And me with my crutch to thrash each merchant dead
As he pokes from a flower his bald and wicked head—
  Cried the six cripples to the silent statue,
  The six beggared cripples.[22]

or, from "Casino":

[20] Poem I, Part II, *Another Time* (London: Faber and Faber, 1940), p. 68. Reprinted under the title "Heavy Date" in *Collected Shorter Poems*, p. 393, but without these two stanzas.

[21] *The Making of the Auden Canon* (Minneapolis, Minn.: University of Minnesota Press, 1957), p. 265.

[22] *Collected Shorter Poems*, p. 87.

Only the hands are living; to the wheel attracted,
Are moved as deer trek desperately towards a creek
   Through the dust and scrub of the desert, or gently
   As sunflowers turn to light.

And, as night takes up the cries of feverish children,
The cravings of lions in dens, the lovers of dons,
   Gathers them all and remains the night, the
   Great room is full of their prayers.[23]

The freedom that allows Auden to compare the motion of hands toward a roulette wheel to the movement of deer toward a creek, or the casino hall absorbing the gamblers' prayers to the night taking up the cravings of lions in dens, is one, I submit, that he learned from the surrealists. A few examples from André Breton will perhaps clarify the similarity: "le tapis meurt comme les vagues" [24] (the carpet dies like the waves); "les jardins de la provocation pure" [25] (the gardens of pure provocation); "l'orgueil de l'armoire" [26] (the pride of the closet); "je veillais sur . . . ma pensée comme un gardien de nuit dans une immense fabrique" [27] (I watched over my thought like a nightwatchman in an immense factory); "la femme nue/dont les cheveux glissent comme au matin la lumière sur un réverbère qu'on a oublié d'éteindre" [28] (the nude woman/whose hair glides like light in the morning on a lamppost that has not been extinguished).

---

[23] *Ibid.*, p. 97.
[24] André Breton, "Monde," *Poèmes* (Paris: Gallimard, 1948), p. 153.
[25] "Le Puits enchanté," *ibid.*, p. 157.
[26] "Passage à niveau," *ibid.*, p. 201.
[27] "Les Attitudes spectrales," *ibid.*, p. 81.
[28] "Hôtel des étincelles," *ibid.*, p. 83.

Of the major poets of our time, Dylan Thomas was the one most influenced by surrealism. At first glance, his poems appear to have the impenetrable surface of true surrealist creations, and critics were quick to call him a surrealist. Louis MacNeice, for example, wrote in 1938 that Thomas's are good examples of poems "apparently written on surrealist principles. . . . He is like a drunk man speaking wildly but rhythmically, pouring out a series of nonsense images." [29] Certainly, a great many of Thomas's images, especially in his earlier work, bear the surrealist stamp: "the waters of your face," "the worm beneath my nail/ Wearing the quick away," "time like a running grave," "scythe of hairs," "the candle shows its hairs," "bearded apple," "sea-legged deck," "bagpipe-breasted ladies," to cite only a few. These images seem at first to have no point beyond themselves, and much early criticism of Thomas centered upon the idea that these images were indeed impenetrable, that Thomas's poems, like music, are nondiscursive, but that also, like music, they produce an undefinable emotional effect. But the ingenuity of critics soon revealed that Thomas's images are not pure, not unadulterated by prose meaning, but rather, far from being nonsensical, are extraordinarily complex constructs that carry very definite meanings.

In 1935, Thomas himself denied any knowledge of surrealism. His editor, Richard Church, had reacted to the manuscript of 18 Poems by pleading with Thomas to throw off the "pernicious effect" of surrealism on his poetry. In his reply, dated December 9, 1935, Thomas claimed that he could not be influenced by surrealism because, he said, "I have very little idea what surrealism is; until quite recently

---

[29] *Modern Poetry: A Personal Essay* (London: Oxford University Press, 1938), pp. 159–160.

I had never heard of it; I have never, to my knowledge, read even a paragraph of surrealist literature." [30] But this, as Thomas's biographer points out, is something less than the truth: Thomas knew David Gascoyne, whose poems he had surely read; he was a frequent contributor to *New Verse;* and, although he disliked him, he also knew Roger Roughton.[31] As for never having read a paragraph of surrealist literature, this, too, must be disbelieved, for, as Mr. Keidrych Rhys says, Thomas was an avid reader of *transition,* whose back numbers he borrowed.[32] In 1951, in the "Poetic Manifesto" published by the *Texas Quarterly,* Thomas showed that he knew quite well what surrealism was about, but insisted that his own poetic practice had little in common with it—that, whereas the surrealist is satisfied to present the chaos of the unconscious, his purpose was "to make comprehensible and articulate what might emerge from subconscious sources." [33]

It is clear that Thomas benefited from Freud's analyses of dream-imagery and that he constructed his images by a process akin to that by which dream-images are made. He has himself described the process:

I make one image—though "make" is not the word; I let, perhaps, an image be "made" emotionally in me and then apply to it what intellectual and critical forces I possess—let it breed another, let that image contradict the first, make of the third image bred out of the other two together, a fourth contradictory

[30] Letter quoted in Constantine FitzGibbon, *The Life of Dylan Thomas* (Boston: Little, Brown, 1965), pp. 173–174.

[31] Rayner Heppenstall, *My Bit of Dylan Thomas* (London: Privately printed, 1957), n.p. Thomas called Roughton "Roger Ringworm."

[32] Letter to the Editor, London *Times Literary Supplement* (March 26, 1964), p. 255.

[33] Quoted by FitzGibbon, *Dylan Thomas,* p. 328.

image, and let them all, within my imposed formal limits, conflict. Each image holds within it the seed of its own destruction,
and my dialectical method, as I understand it, is a constant
building up and breaking down of the images that came out of
the central seed, which is itself destructive and constructive at
the same time.[34]

What exactly Thomas means by one image "contradicting"
another is not clear. C. Day Lewis suggests that by " 'contradictions' . . . we must understand the bringing together,
in images, of objects that have no natural affinity; or perhaps, it might be more accurate to say, objects that would
not on the face of it, seem to make for consistency of impression." [35] If we accept this suggested interpretation, the
similarity of Thomas's procedure to Pierre Reverdy's famous
definition of the image is at once apparent:

The image is a pure creation of the mind [*esprit*]. . . . The
characteristic of the strong image is that it is born of the spontaneous bringing together of two very distant realities of which
the *mind alone* has seized the connection. . . . If the senses
completely approve of the image, they kill it in the mind.[36]

But Reverdy warned that "two realities without connection
do not come together. They oppose each other, which can
sometimes produce a seductive momentary surprise, but it
is not a formed image." Breton, indirectly commenting on
Reverdy's qualification, accurately describes Thomas's procedure:

[34] Quoted by Henry Treece, *Dylan Thomas* (London: Lindsay
Drummond, 1949), pp. 47–48.

[35] *The Poetic Image*, p. 123.

[36] *Le Gant de crin*, quoted in *L'Art poétique*, ed. by Jacques
Charpier and Pierre Seghers (Paris: Editions Pierre Seghers, 1956),
p. 526.

The mind [*l'esprit*] seizes with a marvelous quickness the slightest similarity that can exist between two objects chosen by chance, and poets know that they can always, without fear of deceiving, say of one that it is like the other. . . . But in reality or in the dream, [desire] must make the raw material go through the same channel: condensation, displacement, substitution, touching-up.[37]

It is clear that among Thomas's images are many that have gone through the process described by Breton and Freud. A simple example is "bearded apple": [38] two distant realities, apple and hair, have, in their context of Eden and serpent, been fused by the force of their sexual connotations. The image also suggests the Bearded Christ, the fruit of the original apple.[39] More complex, "scythe of hairs," [40] has been analyzed by W. Y. Tindall: hairs, again, have sexual connotation, and a "scythe of hairs," then, is an apt image for female and male genitals. But a scythe is also an image for time and death, and Thomas's image, fusing all these elements, and perhaps more, connotes the idea that birth and sexuality are steps to death.[41] The image of the "sea-legged deck," [42] hovering just below visual realization, is a complex play on words and meanings. Based on the phrase "sea-legs," it transfers sea-leggedness from the sailor

[37] Breton, *Les Vases communicants*, 2d ed. (Paris: Gallimard, 1955), pp. 148–149.

[38] "Incarnate Devil," *Collected Poetry of Dylan Thomas* (New York: New Directions, 1953), p. 46. All poems copyright 1946 by New Directions Publishing Corporation.

[39] Thomas's procedures have been analyzed by Lita Hornick, "The Intricate Image" (Unpublished Ph.D. dissertation, Columbia University, 1958).

[40] "When, like a running grave," *Collected Poetry*, p. 21.

[41] William Y. Tindall, *Forces in Modern British Literature* (New York: Vintage Books, 1956), p. 239.

[42] "Ballad of the Long-Legged Bait," *Collected Poetry*, p. 166.

to the deck on which he is standing, and makes the sea under the deck the legs of that deck. And since the sea is a familiar symbol for life, fertility, sexuality—and sexuality, in Thomas's universe, is the beginning of death—the image suggests that the man on the deck, the sailor getting his "sea-legs" on the sexual sea, is on his way to the grave. The image of "the bagpipe-breasted ladies in the deadweed" [43] is more immediately visual and would not be out of place in a Dali painting, but, again, the appearance of gratuity is misleading. The context, full of references to the sea, suggests that the ladies are sirens, luring the sailor to the "deadweed," that is, once again, to sexuality and death.

Lita Hornick suggests that Thomas may have been influenced by the surrealists' use of hair images, a number of which appeared in poems published in *Contemporary Poetry and Prose*.[44] This is, of course, possible, but inconclusive; certainly the association of hair with sex is sufficiently obvious so that Thomas did not need the example of the surrealists. There are, however, two images that suggest closer analogues, if not direct influence. In "L'Air de l'eau" (1934), Breton speaks of the sun "lançant ses derniers feux entre tes jambes" [45] (casting its last rays between your legs), and Thomas, in "On the Marriage of a Virgin" (1941), writes, "this day's sun leapt up the sky out of her thighs." [46] In Thomas's "I, in my intricate image" (1935) appears the phrase "splitting the long eye open," [47] which has its obvious Freudian connotations and which may have been inspired by a painting by Victor Brauner of 1927 that shows the lower half of a human figure with an eye instead of geni-

[43] "Sonnet VI," *Collected Poetry*, p. 83.
[44] "The Intricate Image," pp. 221–222.
[45] Breton, *Poèmes*, p. 148.   [46] *Collected Poetry*, p. 141.
[47] *Ibid.*, p. 42.

tals.[48] Another possible source for the image is the unforgettable scene of an eye being slit by a razor in the Dali-Buñuel film *Un Chien Andalou* (1928). I do not know whether Thomas saw this film, but he certainly could have read the scenario, which was published in the surrealist number of *This Quarter* (1932).

These brief analyses of separate images may give the impression that Thomas's poems, like those of the surrealists, are made of seemingly unrelated images loosely strung together by a process of free-association. Thomas's poems, rather, are made of images that are connected by a rigorous inner logic—a dream-logic perhaps, but a logic nevertheless—and that move centrifugally (the word is C. Day Lewis's) around a center which is itself "a host of images." What prevents these images from flying off, as so often they do in surrealist verse, is, as Day Lewis says, "the great positive intensity" of the experience.[49]

In a few of his short stories, Dylan Thomas gave fuller demonstration of the lesson he had learned from the surrealists. But, again, the same distinction that obtains in his verse must be made for his prose: Thomas deliberately *uses* the surface effects of the surrealists. There is no evidence of automatism in any of his writings, despite their frequently fantastic surface; there is proof, on the contrary, of rigidly controlled artistry. Miss Hornick, who has studied Thomas's work sheets, has shown that many of his fantastic images were achieved by completely rational means, by deliberate application of Freud's observations on the nature of dream-

[48] A reproduction of the painting appeared in *Minotaure*, no. 12–13 (May, 1939), too late, of course, to have inspired Thomas's image. But he could have seen the original, another reproduction, or a description of it.

[49] *The Poetic Image*, p. 128.

images. For example, the work sheets of "Ballad of the Long-Legged Bait" make clear that the fantastic image

> He was blind to the eyes of candles
> In the praying windows of waves [50]

was achieved by displacing the candles, prayers, and windows from the town the mariner leaves behind to the waves around him, in order to create the effect of hallucination.[51]

Hallucination is the key word for those of Thomas's stories that bear the surrealist stamp. These stories, dealing, in one way or another, with delusions, go from the relatively simple to hallucinatory effects of baffling complexity. In the simpler stories Thomas provides a realistic frame for the action, and although the subject of the story may be a paranoid delusion that transforms the world for the protagonist, the reader retains his bearings. But as the stories increase in complexity, the reality which is illusory for the characters in the story begins to disintegrate for the reader also.

The simplest of these hallucinatory stories, told objectively in the third person, is "The Dress," the tale of an escaped madman who had cut off his wife's lips because she smiled at men. The nature of his delusions is made fairly clear when the rising mist that hides him from his pursuers becomes "a mother to him, putting a coat around his shoulders where the shirt was torn. . . . The mist made him warm." Remembering that he had not slept since his escape, he thinks that "if he met sleep, sleep would be a girl. . . . Lie down, she would say, and would give him her dress to lie on, stretching herself out by his side." [52] Breaking into an isolated house,

---

[50] Stanza 7, *Collected Poetry*, p. 167.
[51] Hornick, "The Intricate Image," p. 154.
[52] *Adventures in the Skin Trade* (New York: New Directions, 1955), p. 249.

he finds a girl in a flowered dress sitting in a chair. "Sleep," said the madman. And, kneeling down, he put his bewildered head upon her lap." The madman's obsession is powerful enough to distort the appearances of the real world, but the reader is protected from the delusion by the shield of third-person narration.

"The Mouse and the Woman" is similar to "The Dress" in that Thomas again provides a realistic frame for the story— an insane asylum—within which a madman spins his fantasies. The madman, a writer, out of loneliness and need, writes a woman into life: "And he knew . . . that it was upon the block of paper she was made absolute." The madman, loving the woman made out of his "spinning head," relives the story of Eden—the devil creeps between them, her nakedness suddenly is "not good to look upon" and she goes away. An obscure analogy between the woman and the earth makes the madman "disturb the chronology of the seasons," for with the coming of winter, she must disappear. Thomas, at this point, does a curious thing—the story, so far told in the third person, shifts to the first, and the magician-author addresses the reader: "Consider now the odd effigy of time. . . . Watch me belabour the old fellow. I have stopped his heart." And, as an inexplicable consequence of the momentary stopping of time, "the chaos became less . . . the things of the surrounding world were no longer wrought out of their own substances into the shapes of his thoughts," and the madman ends his adventure by writing on his block of paper, "The woman died." As the story is concluded, the realistic frame of the insane asylum is restored. Thomas, who has taken his reader on a mad spin through a madman's brain, drawn back momentarily to remind us that it was he, like Prospero, who led the dance, finally sets us down again with our feet on the ground.

"The Orchards" increases the complexity. It is the story

of a boy, Marlais, who falls in love with a girl scarecrow in a dream. Obsessed by that dream during his waking hours, the boy walks away from his town to the dream-orchards where he saw his scarecrow lover, and the story ends as dream and reality merge. What is demonstrated in this story is the surrealist doctrine of inner desire imposing itself on external reality. The story is more complex than the two preceding ones because the realistic frame is less secure and melts away progressively as the boy's dream overcomes reality. The matter of the story is familiar—it belongs with the innumerable romantic tales of love conquering the harsh world, or even death. What is not familiar is the manner of this story, the language with which Thomas subtly and gradually transforms an illusion into a reality. For example, early in the story, Marlais, looking out of his window, sees "in a chimney shape . . . his bare, stone boy and the three blind gossips, blowing through their skulls, who hudddled for warmth in all weathers." This is childish fantasy personifying inanimate objects. But later, when under the impulsion of his obsession, Marlais is moving over the roofs of the town on the way to his orchard, "the bare boy's voice through a stone mouth, no longer smoking at this hour, rose up unanswerably: Who walks, mad among us, on the roofs, by my cold, brick-red side. . . . The gossips' voices rose up unanswerably: Who walks by the stone virgins is our virgin Marlais, wind and fire." The childish fantasy has acquired, at least in Marlais's fevered mind, the status of reality. Similarly, in the smaller details of the story, Thomas manipulates realities to achieve surrealist effects: "There was dust in his eyes; there were eyes in the grains of dust ascending from the street." But still, in this story, although reality becomes unsubstantial, Marlais is kept before our eyes by the third-person narrative.

"The Lemon," the last story to be considered, does not

treat the reader so gently. It is, or seems to be—nothing is certain in this story—the dream of a madman, the "I" of the story. The dream is concerned with a scientist who grafts cats' heads on chickens and creates similar monstrosities in a house of horrors inhabited by other people who, like the narrator, seem to be dreaming. The narrator awakens periodically into an awareness of what he calls the "exterior world," as hallucinatory as the "interior world" of the dream, then lapses back into the dream as the mad doctor himself or as one or more of the other characters, shifts back and forth between dream and dream, slides between different planes of reality, none of them real. An attempt to unravel this tangled horror, to chart the levels of the dreams, to differentiate the waking from the dream-world, leaves the reader's head spinning and achieves the end—so precious to the surrealists—of a total, if momentary, "alienation of sensation." This story comes closest, of all English writing influenced by surrealism, to breaking down the distinction between dream and reality; its effect is akin to that produced by Breton and Eluard's *L'Immaculée conception*. But, again, whereas they achieved their results by immersing themselves in automatism, Thomas achieved his by remaining in lucid control of his material and his intentions.

Thomas's handling of the poetic image was to have considerable influence on English writers of his generation. Of these, George Barker was perhaps most affected by Thomas, but, in addition, and partly as a consequence of his method, a whole school of writing developed which called itself the "New Apocalypse."

George Barker may perhaps be characterized as a loosened Thomas, a Thomas without the imaginative intensity that fuses disparate elements into meaningful images. The disparate elements are present in Barker, but they seldom, if ever, fuse. The looseness is in evidence in the following, from the "Dedication" of "Calamiterror," Barker's long poem of the 1930's:

> I see my hand glittering with blood and tears
> Hanging at the bend of my arm like a leech member
> Fatal, inspired to violence, sowing scars [53]

Quasi-surrealist effects are frequent in his verse:

> The falling cliff that like a melting face
> Collapsing through its features, leaves a stare [54]

or,

> My tall dead wives with knives in their breasts
> Gaze at me, I am guilty . . .[55]

The collapse and fragmentation of civilization, the apparent subject of "Calamiterror," is rendered by imitative form, the chaos of the world being mirrored in the chaos of the poem: "I recognized the cosmology of objects/. . . Which contemplated too close make a chaos." [56] The resulting disjointedness bears, on occasion, a superficial resemblance to surrealist imagery:

> The phoenix at his loins prepares its ashes,
> The gasmask womb hanging at his thigh
> Transforms the phoenix ashes into tears,
> The tear leaps to the ground as child.[57]

Identifying himself with the whirling objects of his chaotic world, Barker writes,

---

[53] George Barker, *Collected Poems, 1930–1955* (London: Faber and Faber, 1957), p. 30.
[54] *Ibid.*, p. 31.   [55] *Ibid.*, p. 145.   [56] *Ibid.*, p. 51.
[57] *Ibid.*, p. 38.

I recall how the rosetree sprang out of my breast.
I recall the myriads of birds in the cage of my head,
I recall my third finger the branch of myrtle,
I recall the imprisoned women whirling in my bowels.
I was the figure of the Surrealist Exhibition
With a mass of roses face.[58]

Clearly not a surrealist, Barker has nonetheless learned from the surrealists the freedom and violence of association that characterizes his poems, and perhaps even a kind of half-free-association. He has disapproved of surrealist method in a comment that unwittingly describes his own:

The surrealists [are] myopic. . . . They failed to observe that what was remarkable was neither the sewing machine nor the umbrella nor the dissecting table nor the effect produced by this encounter, but the space in between. If you make the dissecting table big enough and place the sewing machine and umbrella far enough apart, the meeting is no longer dramatic. It looks merely as though a seamstress and an undertaker have left their belongings where they ought not to be.[59]

But this objection did not prevent Barker from painting surrealist word-pictures:

I turn back and see behind me a gallery of figures with the feathered second of their death in their breasts like a mistletoe dart. . . . I see Charles I handling the skull of Cromwell at Igtham Moat, whilst in a room at Whitehall the headless body of Cromwell bends in an attitude of frustration and pity over the head of Charles. . . . On the Italian shore the assassinated shade of Caesar shows its wounds to Mussolini, who in turn reveals the steel vest worn against his body.[60]

[58] *Ibid.*, p. 50.
[59] "The Miracle of Images," *Orpheus*, 2, ed. by John Lehmann (London: John Lehmann, 1949), p. 135.
[60] "A Letter to History," *Folios of New Writing* (Spring, 1940), ed. by John Lehmann (London: Hogarth Press, 1940), p. 153.

Barker's poetics owes something to Alick West's criticism of surrealism and, indirectly, to surrealism itself:

The violent apotheosis of the actual world . . . in which the soldier's sigh runs down in blood down palace walls . . . reveals more concerning the process of poetry than the irrational violation of reality. It reveals that the process of poetry may derive its vitality from those laws which it so flagrantly and so magnificently violates. Thus it is precisely because the soldier's sigh does not run in blood down palace walls that the lines achieve their effect of terror.[61]

However, unlike the surrealist, Barker insists on the tough irreducible fact of "Newtonian reality":

The highest exploitation of the real occurs when through this exploitation the imagination of the poet reveals the conditions of the real. . . . Because I claim that the imagination of the poet illuminates and at best apotheosizes the real or scientific world, and because this illumination or apotheosis performs an analysis of its subject, I claim that the poet suffers an obligation to the real or scientific world.[62]

The surrealists speak of transforming the real world by allowing it to synthesize with the inner world, that is, with desire, with poetry; Barker speaks of poetry apotheosizing the world. The difference is not great.

As World War II approached, it seemed that the surrealist prophecies were being realized. The confusion that had disturbed the preceding generation, Stephen Spender suggests, was becoming a system: "The immense resources of all the governments of the world are now being devoted to

[61] Barker, "Poetry and Reality," *The Criterion,* XVII, no. 66 (October, 1937), 57.
[62] *Ibid.,* pp. 60, 63.

producing surrealist effects. Surrealism has ceased to be fantasy, its 'objects' hurtle around our heads, its operations cause the strangest conjunctions of phenomena in the most unexpected places, its pronouncements fill the newspapers." [63] Accepting the disorder as part of reality, and therefore no longer needing surrealism to point it out, the young poets coming to maturity in the late 1930's attempted a new synthesis. J. F. Hendry, Henry Treece, and G. S. Fraser, in 1938, summarized the situation and proposed a new direction in a brief manifesto which stated, in part:

1. That Man was in need of greater freedom, economic no less than esthetic, from machines and mechanistic thinking.
2. That no existent political system, Left or Right; that no artistic ideology, Surrealism or the political school of Auden, was able to produce that freedom.
3. That the Machine Age had exerted too strong an influence on art, and had prevented the individual development of Man.
4. That Myth, as a personal means of reintegrating the personality, had been neglected and despised.[64]

Claiming as ancestors the Book of Revelation, Shakespeare, Webster, Blake, Kafka, and D. H. Lawrence, among others, the group called itself the "New Apocalypse," received the blessing of Herbert Read, and issued a number of anthologies: *The New Apocalypse* (1939), *The White Horseman* (1941), *The Crown and the Sickle* (1944). Vague enough at the outset, the group's aims became vaguer still; it first dissolved into a movement called "Personalism," and finally into an all-encompassing vagueness under the rubric

[63] "Some Observations on English Poetry between Two Wars," *Transformation 3*, ed. by Stefan Schimanski and Henry Treece (London: Lindsay Drummond, n.d. [1945?]), p. 3.

[64] Quoted by Francis Scarfe, *Auden and After: The Liberation of Poetry, 1930–41* (London: George Routledge & Sons, 1942), p. 155.

of the "New Romanticism." Under its various names, the movement published during the 1940's a confusion of anthologies: the *New Road, Transformation, Orpheus, Voices,* and *Poetry Scotland* annuals; it filled the pages of Tambimuttu's *Poetry (London)* and of John Lehmann's various *New Writing* and *Daylight* periodicals, annuals, and anthologies.

G. S. Fraser, with J. F. Hendry the principle theoretician of the movement in its early phases, claimed for Apocalypse the status of a dialectical development from surrealism. It accepted the positive achievements of surrealism—the realization of man's submerged being; but it rejected the surrealist denial of the right to exercise any control over material offered by the unconscious. Apocalypse insists, Fraser says, "that the intellect and its activity in willed action is part of the living completeness of man." [65] Surrealist art in general, and surrealist poetry in particular, lacks, Fraser says, the massive quality of the total response that "organic" man wants; the surrealist image "tends to be cerebral—'the quarrel of the boiled chicken and the ventriloquist.' To play about with words, with detached impressions, in this way, is to live in a world without organic unity, as meaningless and incoherent as the universe of Hume." [66] "Wholeness," "completeness," "organism" become the touchstones of all Apocalyptic endeavor and the basis for the rejection of surrealism, which claimed freedom for only a part of man, not for the whole man. Man in his freedom is bound neither to objects nor to dreams: "He sees a world of action, one of thought, one of feeling, one of imagination. . . . For him, life . . . is something that moves in all direc-

[65] "Apocalypse in Poetry," *The White Horseman,* ed. by J. F. Hendry and Henry Treece (London: Routledge, 1941), p. 3.
[66] *Ibid.,* p. 14.

tions at once, like man's total consciousness." [67] Apocalyptic writing, then, "is that in which is fused all the elements of experience." [68]

The reluctant model for the Apocalyptics is Dylan Thomas. His poetry, superficially anarchic, demonstrates to their satisfaction the possibilities of fusing the unconscious with the conscious, anarchism with control, personal discovery with myth. "Poetry," Thomas has said, "recording the stripping of the individual darkness, must, inevitably, cast light upon what has been hidden for too long, and, by so doing, make clean the naked exposure." [69] J. F. Hendry believes that the image should show, "as a psycho-analytic symbol, the disease of the poet, and, at the same time, by uncovering it, should cure the disease." [70] Hendry insists that the poet "shall discover and reveal to the world . . . those fundamental, organic myths, which underlie all human endeavor and aspiration, and from the recognition of whose universal application will come a reintegration of the personality with society." [71]

In practice, however, these noble ideals result in weak imitations of Dylan Thomas, of surrealism, or in combinations of both. An example of the first, by Henry Treece:

> The hand that bares the fire-lit blade,
>   It is my own;
> The finger that pulls tight the string
>   Wears my own ring;

[67] Henry Treece, *How I See Apocalypse* (London: Lindsay Drummond, 1946), pp. 74–75.

[68] *Ibid.*, p. 79.

[69] Dylan Thomas, "Replies to an Inquiry," *New Verse*, no. 11 (October, 1934), p. 9.

[70] Quoted by Treece, *How I See Apocalypse*, p. 61.

[71] Quoted by Treece, *ibid.*, p. 62.

The tongue that sings the ancient song
    Tells my own tale;
That moves a mountain in its pride,
    It is my love.[72]

This is little more than a weak echo of Thomas's "The Force That through the Green Fuse Drives the Flower." J. F. Hendry provides an imitation of surrealist texts:

Starred in her shameless atoms she stared through his breast with eyes that held no mirror. Their visions settled on the furniture and on his face, like prisms, or round as the white scales on underwater stones. A strange crab there stirred two claws and shut all things in time between them. Within the pools of the pupils waters in great caverns coiled and uncoiled through the room immensities of evil.[73]

Quoting this passage as an example of good "personalist" writing, Henry Treece claims that it sets out to describe a commonplace phenomenon, a pair of eyes, "in such a way that a dramatic urgency, a new force, is produced. . . . The writer is showing the reader a new world composed of old objects. . . . Hendry is describing a girl's madness seen through her eyes, and the effect of that state on the observer." [74] The debt of this kind of writing both to surrealist explorations of demented states and to Dylan Thomas is obvious.

The favorite device of the Apocalyptic poets is the violent image which attempts to express the fusion of "all the

[72] "The Lost Ones," *Collected Poems* (New York: Alfred A. Knopf, 1946), pp. 88–89.

[73] "The Catacombs of Love," quoted by Henry Treece, "Toward a Personalist Literature," *Transformation 4*, ed. by Stefan Schimanski and Henry Treece (London: Lindsay Drummond, n.d. [1946?]), pp. 217–218.

[74] *Ibid.*, p. 218.

elements of experience," but which, unfortunately, succeeds only in moving in all directions at once. A few examples, chosen almost at random, will suffice to illustrate:

by J. F. Hendry, "The Ship":

> Here is a ship you made
> Out of my breast and sides
> As I lay dead in the yards
> Under the hammers.[75]

by Henry Treece, "The Ballad of the Prince":

> The black old priest whose fingers leap with glee
> Upon the sleeping breast, whose long teeth gnaw
> Red tunnels to the fount-head of the heart,
> To suck the summer-dreams that did no hurt.[76]

by Norman McCaig, "Poem II":

Twelve-fifteen and Rome is burning under the feathers of midnight. An angel curls inside the duster under the table.[77]

by G. S. Fraser, "Reasonings in a Dream":

> Constant and virtuous, whose hope lies deathwards
> Beyond the raven and the hooded snake,
> My lady lies dissected on your tables.[78]

by Norman McCaig, untitled:

> I brought you elephants and volcano tops
> and a eucalyptus tree on a coral island

· · · · ·

[75] A New Romantic Anthology, ed. by Stefan Schimanski and Henry Treece (London: Grey Walls Press, 1949), p. 152.

[76] Collected Poems, p. 118.

[77] New Road, 1944, ed. by Alex Comfort and John Bayliss (London: Grey Walls Press, 1944), p. 141.

[78] Home Town Elegy (London: Editions Poetry London, 1944), p. 28.

I brought you under my arm a fleet of ships
and a complete alp and you went and gardened.
Now heaven fall in a massive trumpet sound
and scuttle your crab head under its angelic saliva.[79]

by Dorian Cooke, "The Priest and the Server":

The priest was changing into a woman. She was more beautiful
than the previous man, her breasts bulging the red chasuble . . .
her green fingers like blades of grass, her voice of the gospel
treading the notes of broken bottles. . . . She breathed a whisper of live eagles in the darkness.[80]

Few writers remained who were not touched by the
breath of the irrational; evidences of it are everywhere. Even
the antisurrealist magazine *Twentieth-Century Verse* could
not avoid it; for example, the short "Poem" by R. B. Fuller:

> In the morning I visited her again, she lay
> O horror! bloodless and the curtains flapping;
> While over the violet sky I thought a bat
> Flew blindly like a bit of black crepe paper.
>
> I would not have believed it, but the second
> Weekday on the emaciated visage
> With two blank eyeholes for the unseeing eyes,
> Rested a little mask of black crepe paper.[81]

Stephen Spender, romantic but rational, availed himself of
the freedom won by surrealism:

> The words of all our time are frozen
> By all our deaths into the winter library
> Where life continually flows into books.[82]

---

[79] *The White Horseman*, p. 78.
[80] *Seven*, no. 3 (Winter, 1938), pp. 3–4.
[81] *Twentieth-Century Verse*, no. 2 (March, 1937), n.p.
[82] *Trial of a Judge* (London: Faber and Faber, 1938), p. 82.

The idea is simple—today's life is tomorrow's history, but the image of a frozen stream in the library flowing into books is a picture by Dali.

Even Louis MacNeice, the least romantic and most rational of the poets of his generation, built his poem "The Springboard" on "two irrational premisses—the dream picture of a naked man standing on a springboard in the middle of the air over London and the irrational assumption that it is his duty to throw himself down from there as a sort of ritual sacrifice. This will be lost on those who have no dream logic." [83]

> He never made the dive—not while I watched.
> High above London, naked in the night
> Perched on a board. I peered through the bars
> Made by his fear and mine but it was more than fright
> That kept him crucified among the budding stars.[84]

Lawrence Durrell, who was not associated with any school or movement and who expressed his opposition to surrealism, nonetheless shows evidence of the new freedom of imagery within his carefully wrought poems:

from "Fangbrand":

> Everywhere night lay spilled,
> Like coolness from spoons [85]

from "A Small Scripture":

[83] Louis MacNeice, "Experiments with Images," *Orpheus, 2,* ed. by John Lehmann (London: John Lehmann, 1949), p. 131.

[84] Louis MacNeice, *Springboard* (New York: Oxford University Press, 1945), p. 45.

[85] From the book *Collected Poems,* by Lawrence Durrell, p. 151. Copyright, ©, 1956, 1960 by Lawrence Durrell. Reprinted by permission of E. P. Dutton & Co., Inc.

> Now when the angler by Bethlehem's water
> Like a sad tree threw down his trance
>
> .   .   .   .   .
>
> A bleeding egg was the pain of testament [86]

from "The Hanged Man":

> The rooks of his two blue eyes eating
> A mineral diet . . .
>> on the dark down there
> Owls with soft scissors cherish him.[87]

Durrell's definition of poetry, although he would deny it, owes a good deal to surrealism:

Poetry by an associative approach transcends its own syntax in order not to describe but to be the cause of apprehension in others:

Transcending logic it invades a realm where unreason reigns, and where the relations between ideas are sympathetic and mysterious—affective—rather than causal, objective, substitutional.

I call this the Heraldic Universe, because in Heraldry the object is used in an emotive and affective sense—statically to body forth or utter: not as a victim of description.

The Heraldic Universe is that territory of experience in which the symbol exists—as opposed to the emblem or badge, which are the children of algebra and substitution.[88]

The influence of surrealism on the English novel is more difficult to assess. Since Kafka became known in England at about the same time as surrealism, the superficial similarities

---

[86] *Ibid.*, p. 75.   [87] *Ibid.*, p. 190.

[88] From *Personal Landscape;* quoted by Derek Stanford, "Lawrence Durrell: An Early View of His Poetry," *The World of Lawrence Durrell,* ed. by Harry T. Moore (Carbondale, Ill.: Southern Illinois University Press, 1962), pp. 39–40.

between the two permitted a blending which resulted in novels having an overall vaguely Kafkaesque intention, but drawing on surrealism for smaller effects. These effects were usually visual and relied heavily on surrealist painting.

Ruthven Todd's *The Lost Traveller*, written in 1936 but not published until 1943, is perhaps a typical example. In the preface to the 1968 reprint, Todd writes, "I have a strong suspicion that the book came to me not in one dream alone, but rather in a series of dreams, spread over a considerable number of months." [89]

If dreams are indeed the source of this book, they are dreams recollected by the waking mind. No attempt is made to produce the immediacy of the dream experience; we have, instead, a situation somewhat analogous to the one Herbert Read recounted in his "Introduction" to *Surrealism*. The opening sentence of the novel gives the game away: "The country where Christopher found himself was certainly very strange." This, clearly removes the narrator from the experience: the recognition of strangeness is that of the awakened dreamer; in the dream itself, nothing is strange.

The pattern of the Quest, common in much writing of the 1930's—in Auden, in Rex Warner's *The Wild Goose Chase*, in Edward Upward's *Journey to the Border*—gives this novel its overall form. The details, however, are borrowed from surrealist paintings. Christopher Aukland, the hero, awakens amid the ruins of a city after a violent explosion: "Broken columns, delicately fluted, lay in the sand, or stood up towards a clean blue sky, flat as a glazed bowl." Christopher leaves this de Chirico scene behind and sets out across a timeless desert by Tanguy over which a motionless sun shines mercilessly from the zenith. Feeling neither tired nor

[89] *The Lost Traveller* (London: Grey Walls Press, 1943). Reprinted by Dover Publications, 1968.

hungry after seemingly endless walking in the sand, Christopher wanders into a Tanguy-Ernst-Dali landscape of cacti,
strange flowers, vultures, lizards, ants, and finally reaches
more familiar ground of recognizable fauna and flora where
time becomes normal once again as the sun sets and night
comes.

After some more dreamlike adventures, Christopher comes
to a city where statues bleed and walls come down at night
around the buildings; where there are two orders of citizens
—normal human beings and faceless workers; where all
defer to "Him," a nameless ruler who, in anticipation of
"Big Brother," does not exist. For having broken unknown
and incomprehensible laws, Christopher is punished by
being sent off in a small boat in quest of the last Great Auk,
a fate prefigured in the first syllable of his surname. Christopher loses his boat in a storm, and is saved from drowning
by some fishermen who beat him into unconsciousness. When
he awakens, he finds himself bound hand and foot in a
corner of the fishermen's hut. One of them approaches him
with a raised stick as Christopher realizes that he himself
has become the Great Auk and remembers the story of the
last Auk which was beaten to death by superstitious fishermen who took the bird for a witch.

It is difficult, indeed impossible, to determine how much
of this novel is a reproduction of genuine dream; for one
thing, it is told coldly and meticulously in the third
person. The very clarity of detail, especially in the beginning of the novel, seems to owe something to the jeweled
precision of Dali's paintings. The silent, empty city with
its enigmatic bleeding statues is certainly an echo of de
Chirico. Some elements are literary echoes, as Todd explains in his "Attempt at a Preface": the egg-smooth faces
of the underlings come from a Japanese fairy tale retold

by Lafcadio Hearn; Omar, the Chancellor, Chief Justice, and embodiment of "Him," owes much to the Bailiff in Wyndham Lewis's *The Childermass;* the death of the last Auk comes from a story he had read.

Todd explained in his preface that during his period of interest in surrealism in the Thirties, dreams were "as logical as anything in life," that he tended "only too often to regard life as if it were an illogical dream," and that the scenes in paintings by Miró, Dali and de Chirico were as real as the life around him. Although Todd admits to the influence of Kafka in another novel of the same period, *Over the Mountain,* he insists that *The Lost Traveller* was "a book which was to enjoy its own validities." Nevertheless, a debt to Kafka is discernible here too: Christopher is accused of crimes he knows nothing about and is subjected to a nightmarish trial; unlike Kafka's K, however, he never acknowledges his guilt. But here the similarity ends: *The Lost Traveller* has none of the symbolic weight of a Kafka novel; it is, in fact, impossible to know what Christopher's strange quest for the Great Auk is intended to mean, if anything. The inevitability of the ending suggested by the hero's surname seems spurious, a mere trick on the author's part, for there is nothing in the hero or the situation to suggest the need for this kind of fulfillment. The form of the Quest seems equally arbitrarily imposed upon the novel, for no reason other than that the author possesses, as he says, "too formal a mind to accept the completely illogical or, at times, formless." What we have, in the end, is essentially an adventure story spiced with some pseudo surrealist imagery and some pseudo significance borrowed from Kafka and quest literature.

The pattern of the quest also informs a more recent example of the genre, Ithell Colquhoun's *Goose of Hermog-*

enes.[90] Described on the dust jacket as an "occult pica-
resque," the novel leans heavily on Grail literature and bor-
rows its external trappings from the Gothic novel and Villiers
de l'Isle-Adam's *Axël.* If authentic dream be one of the
criteria of true surrealist creations, then *Goose* must be
granted a large measure of authenticity, for the whole action
seems one long dream complicated by what appear to be
dreams within the dream. The nameless heroine of the novel
comes to an island owned by her uncle who is a magician
or alchemist in search of a means of conquering death. The
cold distance between narration and action of *The Lost
Traveller* is here dissolved in a first-person narrative which
lends a dreamlike intensity to the action. But the significance
of that action, like that of a dream, remains impenetrable.
There are the usual trappings of the more lurid Gothic
novels: the hidden, all but inaccessible castle; the occult
practitioner; the incomprehensible experiments; the uncom-
municative factotum; sexual possession by ghosts; flagella-
tion; and other assorted horrors. But whether all these
devices, and even the dreams within dreams, succeed in
producing surreality is a question easier to ask than to
answer. That it could not have been written had it not been
for surrealism is abundantly clear, but its very opacity, its
thickness of texture prevent the flash of illumination that is
the sign of the surreal. We are left in the end with one incomprehensible event after another—a succession of trees
that never coalesce into a forest.

The vagueness of the whole subject of surrealism in the
novel is well exemplified by the fact that John Lehmann,
prodded by David Gascoyne, planned a surrealist section
for an issue of his *New Writing,* but, he says, "It all came
to nothing . . . because we failed to get Edward Upward

[90] (London: Peter Owen, 1961).

to contribute *The Railway Accident* and there seemed no other English author sufficiently identified with the movement." [91] Edward Upward was never associated, much less identified, with the movement, except in a very negative way, as we have seen. *The Railway Accident*, even less surreal than his *Journey to the Border*, is one of the "Mortmere" fantasies described by Christopher Isherwood in *Lions and Shadows*. The only link between *The Railway Accident* and surrealism—a very tenuous one—is provided by Isherwood in a foreword to the story: "[The narrator] is just as crazy as the people he describes. Indeed he may be crazier—for we begin to suspect that this entire journey and its sequel may be taking place only in his own imagination. Even his style of narration has the splendor and oddity of madness. . . . And there are strange sly echoes of Proust, Joyce and Henry James which suggest an anarchic mockery of all literary values whatsoever." [92] Brilliant as the story is, it is not surrealist, and Edward Upward rightly refused to let it be published in a surrealist section.

Herbert Read is equally guilty of mislabeling. Entitling his review of *The Amaranthers*, by Jack B. Yeats, "A Surrealist Novel," Read says that "if we had a developed consciousness, a movement such as the Surréaliste movement in France, we should immediately 'place' *The Amaranthers*." [93] No more surrealist than *The Railway Accident*, it is a long, turgid novel that hovers between allegory and farce, and whose point, if it has one, is lost among the

[91] *The Whispering Gallery* (New York: Harcourt, Brace, 1955), p. 251.

[92] Foreword by Christopher Isherwood to Allen Chalmers [Edward Upward], "The Railway Accident," *New Directions*, *11* (New York: New Directions, 1949), p. 85.

[93] *The Spectator*, CLVII, no. 5,640 (July 31, 1936), 211.

numerous, incredibly verbose characters. It has, as Read says, "a particularly Irish kind of waggery" which expresses itself in prose and imagery of this kind:

The dawn came up and it was dreadful looking in shape, colour and engraving, it looked like a time before called "a mess of the long green." Not that such a mess didn't look, and eat well, in its place. But except in a prophetic sense it's a creepy looking dawn.[94]

or:

The dream laid on the bright colours with tranquil strokes. The camel's hair of fancy laid out the oleograph of memory's hanging ornament, flat and high on the wall, held in the crab-like grasp of the Tierra del Fuegonian gold-licked flame (p. 40).

The principal question regarding the surrealist novel is whether such a novel is possible at all. Breton's *Nadja*, often referred to as a surrealist novel, is certainly not a novel in the conventional sense, but the account, presumably factual, of a surrealist personality. It is, rather than a surrealist novel, a novel about surrealism. Julien Gracq's modern Gothic novel, *Au Château d'Argol*, praised by Breton, perhaps comes closer to the spirit of surrealism; it uses its gothic trappings to lead the reader into a world of myth and surreality. It would appear that the only kind of surrealist novel possible is the kind written by Gracq and Colquhoun, that is, the kind that takes off from Breton's later emphasis on myth and the occult. A purely surrealist novel, true counterpart of surrealist poetry, does not seem possible; the rapid succession of surrealist images, effective and cumulative in the narrow span of the poem, would, in a novel, become

[94] Jack B. Yeats, *The Amaranthers* (London: William Heinemann, 1936), p. 6.

diffuse and dull. What does seem possible is a novel that
creates a surrealist effect—that is, that recounts the encounters of "objective chance," with their attendant shocks
of recognition. But these encounters, to produce their effect,
must be *experienced,* believed to be true, or else they will
appear to be, at worst, nothing but wildly contrived coincidences, at best, mystery stories of the Saki variety. The difficulty of defining what constitutes a surrealist novel has led
some to misapply the adjective to works as different as those
of Gertrude Stein and Djuna Barnes.

It may be that the problem of the surrealist novel is, by
definition, insoluble, and that the coupling of that adjective
with that noun represents a contradiction in terms. The
novel, by its very nature, unfolds in time, needs time, postu-
lates the reality of time, even when the object of the novel
is to destroy that reality. Proust's "instants," those momentary conquests of time, need for their realization, the creation of time; hence Proust must take the reader with him
down the long corridors of his memory, must create for the
reader the reality of both that memory and of the present in
order for him to share in the experience of the *instant.* The
very length of Proust's novel, the time needed to read it are
thus an essential element of his purpose: an event recounted
early in the novel becomes part of the reader's memory—to
be recalled many volumes and many hours of reading time
later. The surrealist, on the other hand, by means of his
images and of his "encounters"—which are, essentially, surrealist images projected into another dimension—wants to
short-circuit the long Proustian process. Pierre Reverdy
speaks of the spark produced by the juxtaposition of two
distant realities, and Breton claims that surrealism aspires
to "the sensation of duration abolished in the intoxication

of chance." [95] The liberation provided by surrealism, says Georges Bataille, is the recognition of the value of the instant, the liberation of the instant, and the justification of automatic writing is that it does away with goals, for goals destroy the value, even, in a sense, the very existence of the instant. Breton's morality, says Bataille, is a morality of the instant.[96] "I never make plans," says Breton.[97] With Lautréamont, Gaston Bachelard has observed, "We are in the discontinuity of actions, in the joy of the instants of decision. But these instants . . . are lived in their jerky and rapid succession," in contrast to Bergson's duration which is "completely vegetal," or Kafka's time which, especially in *Metamorphosis*, is slow, running down, "sticky." [98]

The juxtaposition in the novel of disparate situations, to imitate the juxtapositions of the surrealist image, cannot, I think, achieve "the sensation of duration abolished in the intoxication of chance" of which Breton speaks, for these situations must be developed in time, and the reader is, of course, a witness to their development: the resultant effect is merely one of strangeness. In contrast, the illuminating shock produced by the operation of objective chance depends upon an *unconscious* internal process culminating in the encounter with the result of an *unknown* external process. If it were possible to observe both of these processes unfolding themselves in their respective spheres from their origin to their collision, the phenomenon of objective chance

[95] André Breton, *L'Amour fou* (Paris: Gallimard, 1937), p. 38.

[96] "Le Surréalisme et sa différence avec l'existentialisme," *Critique*, no. 2 (July, 1946), p. 109.

[97] "Confession dédaigneuse," quoted by Bataille, "Le Surréalisme," p. 109.

[98] Gaston Bachelard, *Lautréamont*, 2d ed. (Paris: Librairie José Corti, 1956), p. 23.

and especially of its effect would be destroyed, for both chains of events would be seen to be subject to prosaic, deterministic causality. But this, in effect, is precisely what must happen in the novel that attempts to create the shock of objective chance. Perhaps the same objection to the essentially temporal nature of music lies at the root of Breton's indifference to that art.

Unless it attempts the large-scale "mythic" effect or treats surrealist themes in an unsurrealist manner, as do Breton's *Nadja* and the recent *Story of O* by Pauline Réage, the novel must be content with surrealist effects on a small scale— that is, with surrealist images produced for their emotional value. And this, in essence, is what Lawrence Durrell does in *The Black Book*. This novel represents Durrell's attempt to extricate himself from what he calls "the English death." [99] Part of the violence that the book does to English moral proprieties is achieved by parallel outrages on English stylistic niceties. The vehicle is the quasi-surrealist image. A few examples follow:

She is lying there in bed among the apple trees and the frozen lakes, long and cool as a dormitory. The immense gothic monastery between her legs. (p. 28)

The museum clock face is scoured by raindrops: it dies, like a pale face on the stalk of a tower and reminds me of the death of time. (p. 58)

At Catford, where the blind men dance to the violins, while the wind blows their eyelids over them; and their hands are terribly soapy talons! (p. 58)

Death creeps in among the other scents which run laughing from one end of the hotel to the other. (p. 107)

[99] *The Black Book*, Introduction by Gerald Sykes (New York: E. P. Dutton, 1960), p. 7. Originally published in 1937.

On the mantelpiece is a clock. The hands stand to quarter-past-six, and it is striking twelve. By these tokens I know it is exactly ten past ten. (p. 123)

It was the heraldic vision of Miss Smith playing the musical sponge, while to the right of her a sunlit man was pissing a solid stream of gold coins against a wall. Symptomatic of disintegration? And why the hell not? (p. 181)

The long pointed breasts that swung hard against you as the sea birds flew out of her hair. (p. 205)

Shall I pour my hair through my fingers? Shall I tie the grin of the madman around my face like a scarf? (p. 225)

These images, of course, are not in their context for their own sake; they do not communicate themselves as the pure surrealist image does, but rather are the vehicle for the author's particular emotional state—an unsurrealist use of surrealist devices.

Epilogue

~~~~~~~~ The rather paltry showing of organized surrealism in England is perhaps the best justification of the surrealists' excuses for the failure of the movement there. Surrealism, as Herbert Read repeatedly insisted, was merely a special case of something that had always been present and available in the English tradition. Broadly speaking, the English did not need surrealism to do what it had always been possible for them to do. But, as I have tried to show, this view, which is undeniably correct, did tend to dilute, and even debase, the profoundly revolutionary contribution that surrealism could have made. By refusing to recognize in surrealism a doctrine that affects all of man's life, a doctrine that offers a new statement of man's relation to the world, and by insisting that the contribution of surrealism was largely a literary or artistic one, the English deprived themselves of precisely what surrealism had to offer. By insisting that surrealism was really *only* romanticism in a new guise, they missed the point of Breton's calling surrealism the prehensile tale of romanticism.

The failure of surrealism on the level of doctrine, however, did not prevent it from offering to writers and painters a freedom which, although available in the English tradition, had not been enjoyed for some time. By attempting to tap directly the rich sources of inspiration in the unconscious, surrealism gave to writers and painters access to the discoveries of Freud and of depth psychology.

Wallace Stevens, most rational and controlled of poets, recognized the value of the surrealist contribution:

[The surrealists] concentrate their powers in a technique which seems singularly limited but which for all that, exhibits the dynamic influence of the irrational. They are extraordinarily alive and that they make it possible for us to read poetry that seems filled with gaiety and youth, just when we were beginning to despair of gaiety and youth, is immensely to the good. One test of their dynamic quality and, therefore, of their dynamic effect, is that they make other forms seem obsolete. They, in time, will be absorbed, with the result that what is now so concentrated, so inconsequential in the restrictions of a technique, so provincial, will give and take and become part of the process of give and take of which the growth of poetry consists.[1]

[1] "The Irrational Element in Poetry" (1937?), *Opus Posthumous* (New York: Alfred A. Knopf, 1957), p. 228.

Bibliography

PRIMARY SOURCES

Arson: An Ardent Review, no. 1 (March, 1942).

Auden, W. H. *The Collected Shorter Poems, 1927–1957.* New York: Random House, 1964.

——. *Look, Stranger.* London: Faber and Faber, 1935.

Barker, George. *Collected Poems, 1930–1955.* London: Faber and Faber, 1957.

——. "The Hawk and the Dove," *The Criterion,* XIV, no. 54 (October, 1934), 73–77.

——. "The Miracle of Images," *Orpheus,* 2, ed. by John Lehmann. London: John Lehmann, 1949.

——. Poetry and Reality," *The Criterion,* XVII. no. 66 (October, 1937), 54–66.

Bates, Maxwell. Letter to the Editor, *The Listener,* XVI, no. 395 (August 5, 1936), 274.

Beaton, Cecil. "Libyan Diary," *Horizon,* VII, no. 37 (January, 1943), 20–41.

Belgion, Montgomery. "French Chronicle" *The Criterion* XII, no. 46 (October, 1932), 80–90.

——. "Meaning in Art," *The Criterion,* IX, no. 35 (January, 1930), 201–216.

Berners, Lord. "Surrealist Landscape (To Salvador Dali)," *Horizon,* VI, no. 31 (July, 1942), 5–6.

Blunt, Anthony. "Another Superrealist," *The Spectator*, CLVII, no. 5,637 (July 10, 1936), 57.

——. "Early Cubism and Superrealism," *The Spectator*, CLVIII, no. 5,687 (June 25, 1937), 1188.

——. "Post-Cubism," *The Spectator*, CL, no. 5,470 (April 28, 1933), 603–604.

——. "Rationalist and Anti-Rationalist Art," *Left Review*, II, no. 10 (July, 1936), iv–vi.

——. "The 'Realism' Quarrel," *Left Review*, III, no. 3 (April, 1937), 169–171.

——. "Superrealism in London," *The Spectator*, CLVI, no. 5,634 (June 19, 1936), 1126–1127.

Breton, André. *Young Cherry Trees Secured against Hares.* Trans. by Edouard Roditi. London: A. Zwemmer, 1946.

Bronowski, J. "Recollections of Humphrey Jennings," *Twentieth Century*, CLXV, no. 983 (January, 1959), 45–50.

Brunius, J.-B., E. L. T. Mesens, and Roland Penrose. Letter to the Editor, *Horizon*, VIII, no. 46 (October, 1943), recto of back cover.

Buchan (no first name). "Wanted: a Goya," *Poetry and the People*, no. 20 (June, 1940).

Calder-Marshall, Arthur. "New Road, Old Country," *Tribune*, no. 357 (October 29, 1943), 15.

Carrington, Leonora. *Une Chemise de nuit de flanelle.* Trans. from the English by Yves Bonnefoy; foreword by Henri Parisot. Paris: Librairie Les Pas Perdus, 1951.

——. "Down Below," *VVV*, no. 4 (February, 1944), pp. 70–86.

——. *La Maison de la peur.* Preface and illustrations by Max Ernst. Paris: Collection "Un Divertissement," 1938.

——. "The Seventh Horse," *VVV*, no. 2–3 (March, 1943).

——. "Waiting," *VVV*, no. 1 (June, 1942).

Caudwell, Christopher. *Illusion and Reality: A Study of the Sources of Poetry.* London: Macmillan, 1937.

Chalmers, Allan (pseud.). See Edward Upward.

Clifton-Taylor, Alec. Letter to the Editor, *The Listener,* XVI, no. 392 (July 15, 1936), 132.

Coffey, Brian. Review of André Breton, *Position politique du surréalisme* and David Gascoyne, *A Short Survey of Surrealism, The Criterion,* XV, no. 60 (April, 1936), 506–511.

Colquhoun, Ithell. *Goose of Hermogenes.* London: Peter Owen, 1961.

Comfort, Alex. *Art and Social Responsibility: Lectures on the Ideology of Romanticism.* London: Falcon Press, 1946.

——, and John Bayliss, eds. *New Road, 1943.* Billericay, Essex: Grey Walls Press, 1943.

Connolly, Cyril. "Farewell to Surrealism," *World Review* (March, 1952), pp. 30–36.

——. "French and English Cultural Relations," *Horizon,* VII, no. 42 (June, 1943), 373–385.

Contemporary Poetry and Prose, nos. 1–10 (May, 1936–Autumn, 1937).

Cooke, Dorian. "The Priest and the Server," *Seven,* no. 3 (Winter, 1938).

Counterpoint, no. 1 (n.d. [1945?]).

Cullis, Michael. "Recent Verse," *New English Weekly,* IX, no. 14 (July 16, 1936), 276–277.

Daiken, Leslie H. Letter to the Editor, *New English Weekly,* VIII, no. 7 (November 28, 1935), 139.

Davies, Hugh Sykes. "Homer and Vico," *New Verse,* no. 8 (April, 1934), pp. 12–18.

——. "Myth," *Experiment,* no. 5 (February, 1930), n.p.

——. *Petron.* London: J. M. Dent & Sons, 1935.

——. "Sympathies with Surrealism," *New Verse,* no. 20 (April–May, 1936), pp. 15–21.

"Déclaration du groupe surréaliste en Angleterre," *Le Surréalisme en 1947.* Paris: Editions Pierre à Feu, 1947.

del Renzio, Toni. "André Breton a-t-il dit passe," *Horizon,* XV, no. 88 (May, 1947), 297–301.

——. "Can You Change a Shilling?" *View,* series 3, no. 3 (October, 1943), p. 83.

——. *Incendiary Innocence* ("An Arson Pamphlet"). London: privately printed, 1944.

——. Letter to the Editor, *Horizon,* VIII, no. 48 (December, 1943), 433–434.

——. "The Light That Will Cease to Fail," *New Road, 1943,* ed. by Alex Comfort and John Bayliss. Billericay, Essex: Grey Walls Press, 1943, pp. 180–183.

Dint, nos. 1 and 2 (1945).

Durrell, Lawrence. *The Black Book.* Introduction by Gerald Sykes. New York: E. P. Dutton, 1960.

——. *Collected Poems.* New York: E. P. Dutton, 1960.

——. *Zero and Asylum in the Snow.* Rhodes: privately printed, 1946.

Eliot, T. S. *Collected Poems and Plays.* New York: Harcourt, Brace, 1952.

——. *Selected Essays.* New York: Harcourt, Brace, 1932.

Eluard, Paul. *Poetry and Truth, 1942.* Trans. by Roland Penrose and E. L. T. Mesens. London: London Gallery Editions, 1944.

——. *Thorns of Thunder.* Ed. and with an introduction by George Reavey; Preface by Herbert Read; Trans. by Samuel Beckett, Denis Devlin, David Gascoyne, *et al.* London: Europa Press and Stanley Nott, n.d. [1936].

Elvin, R. "A Sceptical Introduction to the Surrealist Exhibition," *Literary Review,* I, no. 5 (July, 1936), 39.

The Enemy, no. 1 (January, 1927); no. 2 (September, 1927).

Enright, D. J. "The Muse in Confusion: An Aspect of Contemporary Verse," *Focus One,* ed. by B. Rajan and Andrew Pearse. London: Dennis Dobson, 1945.

——. "Ruins and Warnings," *Scrutiny,* XI, no. 1 (Spring, 1942), 79–80.

Fairbairn, W. R. D. "Prolegomena to a Psychology of Art," *British Journal of Psychology,* XXVIII, no. 3 (January, 1938), 288–303.

——. "The Ultimate Basis of Aesthetic Experience," *British Journal of Psychology,* XXIX, no. 2 (October, 1938), 167–181.

Fergar, Feyyaz. *Gestes à la mer*. London: Grey Walls Press, 1943.

Flint, F. S. "French Periodicals," *The Criterion*, III, no. 12 (July, 1925), 601–602.

——. "French Periodicals," *New Criterion*, IV, no. 2 (April, 1926), 405–407.

Ford, Charles Henri. *The Garden of Disorder and Other Poems*. Introduction by William Carlos Williams. London: Europa Press, 1938.

Fraser, G. S. "Approaches to Reality," *Seven*, no. 2 (Autumn, 1938), pp. 32–37.

——. *Home Town Elegy*. London: Editions Poetry London, 1944.

Freud, Sigmund. *The Basic Writings of Sigmund Freud*. Trans. and ed. with an introduction by A. A. Brill. New York: Modern Library, 1938.

——. *A General Introduction to Psychoanalysis*. Trans. by Joan Riviere. Garden City, N.Y.: Garden City Publishing, 1943.

——. *New Introductory Lectures on Psycho-Analysis*. Trans. by W. J. H. Sprott. 2d ed. London: Hogarth Press, 1937.

Fulcrum, no. 1 (July, 1944).

Gascoyne, David. *Man's Life Is This Meat*. London: Parton Press, n.d. [1936].

——. "Poetry: Reality," *Literary Review*, I, no. 3 (May, 1936), 6–8.

——. "Premier manifeste anglais du surréalisme," *Cahiers d'Art*, X (1935), 106.

——. Review of Hugh Sykes Davies, *Petron*, *New Verse*, no. 18 (December, 1935), p. 19.

——. *A Short Survey of Surrealism*. London: Cobden-Sandersen, 1935.

Goldring, Douglas. "Salvador Dali at Zwemmer's," *The Studio*, CIX (January, 1935), 36.

Greenberg, Clement. "Surrealist Painting," *Horizon*, XI, no. 61 (January, 1945), 49–56.

Grigson, Geoffrey. "A Letter from England," *Poetry* (Chicago), XLIX, no. 2 (November, 1936), 101–103.

——. *The Crest on the Silver: An Autobiography.* London: Cresset Press, 1950.

——, ed. *The Arts To-Day.* London: John Lane, The Bodley Head, 1935.

Harvey, J. Brian. "Four Poets," *Left Review*, II, no. 10 (July, 1936), 530–531.

Hastings (no first name). Review of Gascoyne, *Man's Life Is This Meat, Left Review*, II, no. 4 (January, 1936), 186–187.

Hayward, John. Letter to the Editor, *New English Weekly*, VIII, no. 7 (November 28, 1935), 139.

Hendry, J. F. "The Apocalyptic Movement in Modern Poetry," *Poetry Scotland 2* (1945), pp. 61–66.

——, ed. *The New Apocalypse: An Anthology of Criticism, Poems, and Stories.* London: Fortune Press, n.d. [1939].

——, and Henry Treece, eds. *The Crown and the Sickle.* Preface by Henry Treece. London: P. S. King & Staples, n.d. [1944].

——. *The White Horseman.* London: Routledge, 1941.

Heppenstall, Rayner. *My Bit of Dylan Thomas.* London: privately printed, 1957.

——. Review of Hugh Sykes Davies, *Petron, The Criterion*, XV, no. 59 (January, 1936), 332–334.

Hinks, Roger. "Art Chronicle: Constructivism," *The Criterion*, XVII, no. 66 (October, 1937), 87–93.

——. "Art Chronicle: Surrealism," *The Criterion*, XVI, no. 62 (October, 1936), 70–75.

Holme, C. Geoffrey. "Surrealism Criticised," *The Studio*, CXII, no. 521 (August, 1936), 55.

Hoog, Armand. "La Chute de la maison noire: Contradictions in French Surrealism," *Transformation 4*, ed. by Henry Treece and Stefan Schimanski. London: Lindsay Drummond, n.d. [1947?].

Humphrey Jennings 1907–1950: A Tribute. London: Published

by the Humphrey Jennings Memorial Fund Committee, n.d. [1960].

Hutt, G. A. "Jolas' Julep," *Left Review,* I, no. 12 (September, 1935), 528.

International Surrealist Bulletin No. 4. London: A. Zwemmer on behalf of the International Surrealist Exhibition, 1936.

Jackson, T. A. "Marxism: Pragmatism: Surrealism—a Comment for Herbert Read," *Left Review,* II, no. 11 (August, 1936), 365–367.

Jacobs, Ivor. "Auden Aftermath," *Horizon,* VIII, no. 46 (October, 1943), 285–288.

Jennings, Humphrey. *Poems.* Introduction by Kathleen Raine. New York: Weekend Press, 1951.

Koestler, Arthur. "Literary Idolatry," *Tribune,* no. 361 (November 26, 1943), pp. 12–13.

Lehmann, John. *I Am My Brother.* New York: Reynal, 1960.

———. *The Whispering Gallery.* New York: Harcourt, Brace, 1955.

———, ed. *Folios of New Writing.* Spring, 1940; Autumn, 1940; Spring, 1941; Autumn, 1941. London: Hogarth Press.

Lewis, C. Day. *The Poetic Image.* New York: Oxford University Press, 1948.

———, ed. *The Mind in Chains: Socialism and the Cultural Revolution.* London: Frederick Muller, 1937.

Lewis, Wyndham. *The Diabolical Principle and the Dithyrambic Spectator.* London: Chatto & Windus, 1931.

———. *Men without Art.* London: Cassell, 1934.

———. *Time and Western Man.* Boston: Beacon Press, 1957.

Lienhardt, R. G. "Freedom and Restraint in Poetry and Criticism," *Focus One,* ed. by B. Rajan and Andrew Pearse, London: Dennis Dobson, 1945.

Lindsay, Jack. *After the 'Thirties: The Novel in Britain and Its Future.* London: Lawrence and Wishart, 1956.

———. *Perspective for Poetry.* London: Fore Publications, 1944.

Lloyd, A. L. "Surrealism and Revolution," *Left Review,* II, no. 16 (January, 1937), 895–898.

MacColl, D. S. "Super- and Sub-Realism," *Nineteenth Century and After,* CXVII, no. 700 (June, 1935), 701–711.

McGreevy, Thomas. "London's Liveliest Show," *The Studio,* CXX (October, 1940), 137.

MacNeice, Louis, "Experiences with Images," *Orpheus,* 2, ed. by John Lehmann. London: John Lehmann, 1949.

——. *Modern Poetry: A Personal Essay.* London: Oxford University Press, 1938.

Madge, Charles. Review of David Gascoyne, *A Short Survey of Surrealism, New Verse,* no. 18 (December, 1935), pp. 20–21.

——. Review of *Petite Anthologie poétique du surréalisme, New Verse,* no. 10 (August, 1934), pp. 13–15.

——. "Surrealism for the English," *New Verse,* no. 6 (December, 1933), pp. 14–18.

Mair, John. "Sense and Abstraction," *Literary Review,* I, no. 1 (March, 1936), 4–5.

March, Richard. "The Swallow's Egg: Notes on Contemporary Art," *Scrutiny,* V, no. 3 (December, 1936), 243–256.

Masson, André. "A Crisis of the Imaginary," *Horizon,* XII, no. 67 (July, 1945), 42–44.

——. "Painting Is a Wager," *Horizon,* VII, no. 39 (March, 1943), 178–183.

Melville, Robert. "Surrealism: An Aspect of Its Influence," *The Listener,* LXVI, no. 1,695 (September 21, 1961), 432–433.

Mesens, E. L. T. *Third Front and Detached Pieces.* Trans. by Roland Penrose and the author. London: London Gallery Editions, 1944.

——, ed. *Message from Nowhere.* London: London Gallery Editions, November, 1944.

——, and J. Brunius. *Idolatry and Confusion.* London: London Gallery Editions, March, 1944.

Mortimer, Raymond. "The Art of Displeasing," *The Listener,* XV, no. 388 (June 17, 1936), 1150–1152.

Nash, Paul. "The Life of the Inanimate Object," *Country Life,* LXXXI (May 1, 1937), 496–497.

———. "The Object," *Architectural Review*, LXXX, no. 480 (November, 1936), 207–208.

———. *Outline: An Autobiography and Other Writings*. Preface by Herbert Read. London: Faber and Faber, 1949.

Newton, Eric. "Nonsense," *The Saturday Book, 1941–42*, ed. by Leonard Russell. London: Hutchinson, 1941.

New Verse, nos. 1–30 (July, 1935–April, 1938).

Nicholson, Norman. "The Image in My Poetry," *Orpheus*, 2, ed. by John Lehmann. London: John Lehmann, 1949.

Nicolson, Benedict. "Decline and Fall," *New Statesman and Nation*, XLII, no. 1,084 (December 15, 1951), 704.

O'Connor, Philip. *Memoirs of a Public Baby*. New York: British Book Center, 1958.

———. "Society Notes," *Twentieth-Century Verse*, no. 15–16 (February, 1939), pp. 151–154.

Onslow-Ford, Gordon. *Towards a New Subject in Painting*. San Francisco: San Francisco Museum of Art, 1948.

Patchen, Kenneth. *The Outlaw of the Lowest Planet*. Selected and with an introduction by David Gascoyne. London: Grey Walls Press, 1946.

Penrose, Roland. *The Road is Wider Than Long: An Image Diary from the Balkans, July–August, 1938*. Photographs by the author. London: London Gallery Editions, n.d. [1939?].

Péret, Benjamin. *A Bunch of Carrots*. Selected and trans. by David Gascoyne and Humphrey Jennings. London: Parton Press, 1936.

———. *Remove Your Hat*. Selected and trans. by David Gascoyne and Humphrey Jennings. London: Parton Press, 1936.

Plomer, William. "Surrealism Today," *New Statesman and Nation*, XIX (June 29, 1940), 794.

Porteus, Hugh Gordon. "Art," *New English Weekly*, IX, no. 12 (July 2, 1936), 235–236.

———. "Art," *New English Weekly*, IX, no. 13 (July 9, 1936), 252–253.

———. "Art: The Higher Dream," *New English Weekly*, VIII, no. 13 (January 9, 1936), 253–254.

———. "Art: Notes on a Vexed Topic," *New English Weekly*, VIII, no. 11 (December 26, 1935), 215.

———. "Art: The Surréaliste Exhibition," *New English Weekly*, IX, no. 10 (June 18, 1936), 193–194.

Quennell, Peter. Review of Tristan Tzara, *De nos oiseaux, The Criterion*, IX, no. 35 (January, 1930), 359–361.

———. "Surrealism and Revolution," *New Statesman and Nation*, VI, no. 131 (n.s.) (August 26, 1933), 237–238.

———. "The Surrealist Exhibition," *New Statesman and Nation*, XI (n.s.) (June 20, 1936), 967–968.

Read, Herbert. "Art and Crisis," *Horizon*, IX, no. 53 (May, 1944), 336–350.

———. "Art and Religion," *The Listener*, XVI, no. 395 (August 5, 1936), 256–258.

———. "Art and the Revolutionary Attitude," *Southern Review*, I, no. 2 (Autumn, 1935), 239–252.

———. *Art and Society*. 2d rev. ed. London: Faber and Faber, 1945.

———. *Art Now*. London: Faber and Faber, 1933.

———. "Art—the Situation Today," *London Mercury*, XXX, no. 180 (October, 1934), 574–575.

———. *A Coat of Many Colours: Occasional Essays*. London: George Routledge & Sons, 1945.

———. *Collected Essays in Literary Criticism*. London: Faber and Faber, 1938.

———. *Contemporary British Art*. Harmondsworth, Middlesex: Penguin Books, 1951.

———. *The Forms of Things Unknown: Essays towards an Aesthetic Philosophy*. New York: Horizon Press, 1960.

———. *In Defense of Shelley and Other Essays*. London: William Heinemann, 1936.

———. "Introduction," *Paul Nash*, "Contemporary British Painters" no. 1. London: Soho Gallery, 1937.

——. Letter to the Editor, *New English Weekly*, VIII, no. 7 (November 28, 1935), 139.

——. Letter to the Editor, *New English Weekly*, IX, no. 14 (July 16, 1936), 280.

——. Letter to the Editor. London *Times Literary Supplement* (January 11, 1936), p. 35.

——. *The Meaning of Art*. Rev. ed. Harmondsworth, Middlesex: Pelican Books, 1949.

——. *The Nature of Literature*. New York: Grove Press, n.d. [1958]. (Reprint of *Collected Essays in Literary Criticism*.)

——. "Originality," *Sewanee Review*, LXI, no. 4 (Autumn, 1953), 533–556.

——. *Paul Nash*. "The Penguin Modern Painters." Harmondsworth, Middlesex: Penguin Books, 1944.

——. *The Philosophy of Modern Art*. London: Faber and Faber, 1952.

——. *Poetry and Anarchism*. London: Faber and Faber, 1938.

——. *The Politics of the Unpolitical*. London: Routledge, 1943.

——. *Reason and Romanticism*. London: Faber and Gwyer, 1926.

——. Review of Dylan Thomas, *The Map of Love, Seven*, no. 6 (Autumn, 1939), pp. 19–20.

——. Review of T. A. Jackson, *Dialectics, Left Review*, II, no. 10 (July, 1936), 518–520.

——. "The Significance of Paul Delvaux," *The Listener*, XIX, no. 493 (June 23, 1938), 1336–1337.

——. "Surrealism—The Dialectic of Art," *Left Review*, II, no. 10 (July, 1936), ii–iii.

——. "A Surrealist Novel," *The Spectator*, CLVII, no. 5,640 (July 31, 1936), 211.

——. "Views and Reviews," *New English Weekly*, VIII, no. 5 (November 14, 1935), 91–92.

——. "Vulgarity and Impudence: Speculations on the Present State of the Arts," *Horizon*, V, no. 28 (April, 1942), 267–276.

———. "What Is Revolutionary Art?" *Five on Revolutionary Art,* ed. by Betty Rea. London: Wishart, 1935.

———, ed. *Surrealism.* London: Faber and Faber, 1936.

———, and Hugh Sykes Davies. "Surrealism—Reply to A. L. Lloyd," *Left Review,* III, no. 1 (February, 1937), 47–48.

Reed, Henry. "The End of an Impulse," *New Writing and Daylight,* ed. by John Lehmann. London: Hogarth Press, Summer, 1943.

Review of André Breton, *What Is Surrealism?* and Paul Eluard, *Thorns of Thunder.* London *Times Literary Supplement,* June 13, 1936.

Review of David Gascoyne, *A Short Survey of Surrealism.* London *Times Literary Supplement,* January 4, 1936.

Roberts, Michael. "Aspects of English Poetry, 1932–1937," *Poetry* (Chicago), XLIX, no. 4 (January, 1937), 210–217.

———. "Notes on English Poets," *Poetry* (Chicago), XXXIX, no. 5 (February, 1932), 271–279.

———. Review of Herbert Read, ed., *Surrealism, The Criterion,* XVI, no. 64 (April, 1937), 551–553.

Roughton, Roger. "The Human House," *Horizon,* IV, no. 19 (July, 1941), 50–57.

———. Letter to the Editor, *The Listener,* XVI, no. 390 (July 1, 1936), 38.

———. "The Sand under the Door," *The Criterion,* XVII, no. 66 (October, 1937), 67–80.

———. "Three Poems," *The Criterion,* XV, no. 60 (April, 1936), 445–457.

———. "Tomorrow Will Be Difficult," *Poetry* (Chicago), XLIX, no. 1 (October, 1936), 19.

Savage, D. S. "The Literary Situation in England," *Sewanee Review,* LIII, no. 4 (Autumn, 1945), 654–658.

———. "London Letter," *Poetry* (Chicago), LI, no. 5 (February, 1938), 277–282.

Scarfe, Francis. *Auden and After: The Liberation of Poetry, 1930–41.* London: George Routledge & Sons, 1942.

———. "Paranoiac Studies," *Kingdom Come,* III, no. 11 (Winter, 1942), 28–31.

———. "The Poetry of Dylan Thomas," *Horizon,* II, no. 11 (November, 1940), 226–239.

Schimanski, Stefan, and Henry Treece, eds. *A New Romantic Anthology.* London: Grey Walls Press, 1949.

Sewter, A. C. Review of Herbert Read, ed., *Surrealism, Burlington Magazine,* LXXI, no. 414 (September, 1937), 150.

Sitwell, Edith. *Aspects of Modern Poetry.* London: Duckworth, 1934.

———. *Collected Poems.* New York: Vanguard Press, 1954.

———. "On My Poetry," *Orpheus, 2,* ed. by John Lehmann. London: John Lehmann, 1949.

———. "Three Eras of Modern Poetry," *Trio: Dissertations on Some Aspects of National Genius* by Osbert, Edith, and Sacheverell Sitwell. London: Macmillan, 1938.

Spender, Stephen. "Lessons of Poetry, 1943," *Horizon,* IX, no. 51 (March, 1944), 207–216.

———. "Modern Poets and Reviewers," *Horizon,* V, no. 30 (June, 1942), 431–438.

———. "Movements and Influences in English Literature, 1927–1952," *Books Abroad,* XXVII, no. 1 (Winter, 1953), 5–32.

———. "Poetry in 1941," *Horizon,* V, no. 26 (February, 1942), 96–111.

———. *Poetry since 1939.* London: Longmans, Green, for the British Council, 1946.

———. "Some Observations on English Poetry between Two Wars," *Transformation, 3,* ed. by Stefan Schimanski and Henry Treece. London: Lindsay Drummond, n.d. [1945?].

———. "The Year's Poetry, 1940," *Horizon,* III, no. 14 (February, 1941), 138–148.

Stanford, Derek. "Compass and Bearings: An Essay on Modern Art and Society," *New Road, 1944,* ed. by Alex Comfort and John Bayliss. London: Grey Walls Press, 1944.

——. "Movements in the Mirror," *Outposts, 11* (Autumn, 1948), pp. 12–14.

——. "Three Directions in French Writing," *New Road, 5,* ed. by Wrey Gardiner. London: Grey Walls Press, 1949.

Stevens, Wallace. "The Irrational Element in Poetry," *Opus Posthumous.* New York: Alfred A. Knopf, 1957.

Surrealist Objects and Poems. Foreword by Herbert Read. London: London Gallery Editions, n.d. [1937].

Swingler, Randall. "What Is the Artist's Job?," *Left Review,* III, no. 15 (April, 1938), 930–932.

Symons, Julian. "The Case of Mr. Madge," *Kingdom Come,* II, no. 3 (Spring, 1941), 73–74.

——. "Of Crisis and Dismay: A Study of Writing in the 'Thirties," *Focus One,* ed. by B. Rajan and Andrew Pearse. London: Dennis Dobson, 1945.

——. *The 'Thirties: A Dream Revolved.* London: Cresset Press, 1960.

Taylor, Simon Watson, ed. *Free Unions.* London: privately printed, 1946.

This Quarter, Vol. V, no. 1 (September, 1932). Surrealist number.

Todd, Ruthven. *The Lost Traveller.* London: Grey Walls Press, 1943. Reprinted, New York: Dover Publications, 1968.

——. Review of Herbert Read, ed., *Surrealism, Literary Review,* I, no. 10 (December, 1936), 32.

——. *Until Now.* London: Fortune Press, n.d.

Transatlantic Review, Vols. I and II (January, 1924–January, 1925).

transition, nos. 1–27 (April 1927–April/May, 1938).

Treece, Henry. *Collected Poems.* New York: Alfred A. Knopf, 1946.

——. "Dylan Thomas and the Surrealists," *Seven,* no. 3 (Winter, 1938), 27–30.

——. *How I See Apocalypse.* London: Lindsay Drummond, 1946.

——. "Literary London," *View,* I, no. 1 (September, 1940), 5.

———. "The New Apocalypse," *Outposts*, 12 (Winter, 1948), pp. 14–17.

———. "A Statement on Poetry To-Day," *Kingdom Come*, III, no. 10 (Spring, 1942), 21–26.

Turnell, Martin. "Surrealism: The Social Background of Contemporary Poetry," *Arena*, I, no. 3 (October–December, 1937), 212–228.

Twitchett, E. G. "Poetry Chronicle," *London Mercury*, XX, no. 116 (June, 1929), 204–205.

Upward, Edward. *Journey to the Border*. London: Hogarth Press, 1938.

[Upward, Edward] Allen Chalmers. "The Railroad Accident," *New Directions, 11*. New York: New Directions, 1949.

Warner, Rex. *The Wild Goose Chase*. New York: Alfred A. Knopf, 1938.

Watt, Alexander. "Salvador Dali," *New Statesman and Nation*, VIII, no. 184 (n.s.) (September 1, 1934), 264–265.

West, Alick. "Surréalisme in Literature," *Left Review*, II, no. 10 (July, 1936), vi–viii.

West, Anthony. "The Precious Myth," *The Mint: A Miscellany of Literature, Art and Criticism*, ed. by Geoffrey Grigson. London: Routledge and Sons, 1946.

Westbrook, Eric. "Fantastic Art in Britain," *The Studio*, CXLII (July, 1951), 1–9.

Woodcock, George. "Elegy for Fur-Covered Horns: Notes on Surrealism in England," *Limbo* (February, 1964), 49–52.

Yeats, Jack B. *The Amaranthers*. London: William Heinemann, 1936.

Z., M. D. [Morton Dauwen Zabel]. "Recent Magazines," *Poetry* (Chicago,) XVIII, no. 6 (September, 1936), 353–355.

SECONDARY SOURCES

Adams, Robert M. *Strains of Discord: Studies in Literary Openness*. Ithaca, N.Y.: Cornell University Press, 1958.

Barr, Alfred H., Jr. *Masters of Modern Art*. New York: Museum of Modern Art, 1954.

Beach, Joseph Warren. *The Making of the Auden Canon.* Minneapolis, Minn.: University of Minnesota Press, 1957.

Berry, Francis. *Herbert Read.* "Writers and Their Work," no. 45. London: Longmans, Green, for the British Council, 1953.

Block, Haskell M. "Surrealism and Modern Poetry: Outline of an Approach," *Journal of Aesthetics and Art Criticism,* XVIII, no. 2 (December, 1959), 174–182.

Brooks, Cleanth. *Modern Poetry and the Tradition.* Chapel Hill, N.C.: University of North Carolina Press, 1939.

Burke, Kenneth. "Surrealism," *New Directions, 1940.* Norfolk, Conn.: New Directions, 1940.

Daiches, David. "Contemporary Poetry in Britain," *Poetry* (Chicago), LXII, no. 3 (June, 1943), 150–164.

Durrell, Lawrence. *Key to Modern Poetry.* Norman, Okla.: University of Oklahoma Press, 1952.

Fishman, Solomon. "Sir Herbert Read: Poetics vs. Criticism," *Journal of Aesthetics and Art Criticism,* XIII, no. 2 (December, 1954), 156–162.

Fraser, G. S. *The Modern Writer and His World.* Harmondsworth, Middlesex: Penguin Books, 1964.

——. *Post-War Trends in English Literature.* Tokyo: Hokuseido Press, n.d.

Gauss, Charles E. "The Theoretical Backgrounds of Surrealism," *Journal of Aesthetics and Art Criticism,* II, no. 8 (Fall, 1943), 37–44.

Gilbert, Stuart. "Five Years of *Transition,*" *Transition,* no. 22 (February, 1933), pp. 138–143.

Glicksberg, Charles I. "The Aesthetics of Surrealism," *T'ien Hsia Monthly,* IX, no. 4 (November, 1939), 364–374.

——. "D. H. Lawrence, the Prophet of Surrealism," *Nineteenth Century and After,* CXLIII (April, 1948), 229–237.

——. "Herbert Read: Reason and Romanticism," *University of Toronto Quarterly,* XVI, no. 1 (October, 1946), 60–67.

——. "Mysticism in Contemporary Poetry," *Antioch Review,* III, no. 2 (Summer, 1943), 235–245.

Hays, H. R. "Surrealist Influence in Contemporary English and

American Poetry," *Poetry* (Chicago), LIV, no. 4 (July, 1939), 202–209.

Hoffman, Frederick J. *Freudianism and the Literary Mind.* Baton Rouge, La.: Louisiana State University Press, 1945.

———. "From Surrealism to 'The Apocalypse': A Development in Twentieth-Century Irrationalism," *ELH: A Journal of English Literary History,* XV, no. 2 (June, 1948), 147–165.

———, et al. *The Little Magazine: A History and a Bibliography.* Princeton, N.J.: Princeton University Press, 1947.

Hornick, Lita. "The Intricate Image." Unpublished Ph.D. dissertation, Columbia University, 1958.

Korg, Jacob. "Modern Art Techniques in *The Waste Land,*" *Journal of Aesthetics and Art Criticism,* XVIII (June, 1960), 456–463.

———. "The Short Stories of Dylan Thomas," *Perspective,* I (Spring, 1948), 184–191.

Lewis, C. Day. *The Poetic Image.* New York: Oxford University Press, 1948.

Matthews, J. H. "Surrealism and England," *Comparative Literature Studies,* I, no. 1 (1964), 55–71.

Mills, Clark. "Aspects of Surrealism," *Voices,* no. 101 (Spring, 1940), pp. 47–51.

Rhodes, S. A. "Candles for Isis," *Sewanee Review,* XLI, no. 3 (July–September, 1933), 293–300.

Starkie, Enid. *From Gautier to Eliot: The Influence of France on English Literature, 1851–1938.* London: Hutchinson, 1960.

Stead, C. K. *The New Poetic: Yeats to Eliot.* New York: Harper Torchbooks, 1964.

Summers, Montague. *The Gothic Quest.* London: Fortune Press, 1938. Reprinted, New York: Russell & Russell, 1964.

Thody, Philip. "Lewis Carroll and the Surrealists," *Twentieth Century,* CLXIII, no. 975 (May, 1958), 427–434.

Tindall, William Y. *Forces in Modern British Literature.* New York: Vintage Books, 1956.

———. *The Literary Symbol.* New York: Columbia University Press, 1955.

——. "The Poetry of Dylan Thomas," *The American Scholar*, XVII, no. 4 (Autumn, 1948), 431–439.

——. *A Reader's Guide to Dylan Thomas*. New York: Noonday Press, 1962.

Treece, Henry. *Dylan Thomas*. London: Lindsay Drummond, 1949.

——, ed. *Herbert Read: An Introduction to His Work by Various Hands*. London: Faber and Faber, 1944.

Tschumi, Raymond. *Thought in Twentieth-Century English Poetry*. London: Routledge and Kegan Paul, 1951.

Walcott, John Cotton. "English and American Surrealists," *Forum*, XCVII, no. 3 (March, 1937), 192–193.

Index

Allott, Kenneth, quot. 99, quot. 187-188

Alvensleben, Baron Werner von, 222

Aragon, Louis, 3, 44, 48, 68, 69, 71, 93, 159, 235, 239, 240, 241-242, 243, 247

Araquistaín, Sonia, 249-250

Arson, 231-233

Artists' International Association (A.I.A.), 148, 216

Auden, W. H., 86, 107-108, 197, 272-276

Automatism, 2-18, 40, 52, 61, 64, 130-131, 214; and dreams, 5-7, 12; and prophecy, 22-23, 205; and spiritism, 20-21

Barker, George, 286-289

Baudelaire, Charles, 174

Beaton, Cecil, quot. 230

Belgion, Montgomery, 82-83

Berners, Lord, quot. 100-101

Blake, William, 83, 127, 257

Blunt, Anthony, 85, 155-157, 216

Brauner, Victor, 22, 41, 250, 281-282

Breton, André, 1-66, 68, 69, 72, 80, 93, 95, 121, 132, 134, 135, 141-143, 146, 165, 169, 170, 173, 176, 184, 186, 192-193, 210, 225, 231, 236, 245, 255-256, 258, 276, 279-280, 303, 304, 306

Bronowski, J., 81, 88

Brunius, Jacques, 227, 230, 238, 239, 246, 247, 250, 252, 258

Buchan, 229

Calas, Nicolas, 79, 232-233, 237, 255

Calder-Marshall, A., 236n, 247

Carrington, Leonora, 237, 248-249

Carroll, Lewis, 28, 60, 107, 127, 257

Caudwell, Christopher, 159, 200-205

Cherkeshi, Sadi, 251

Chirico, Giorgio de, 19, 160, 161, 166, 223, 232, 237

Church, Richard, 277

Coleridge, Samuel Taylor, 83, 97, 122, 129, 190-191, 237, 250, 298, 300

Collage, 37-38, 47-48, 266

Colquhoun, Ithell, 222, 227, 232, 233-234, 237, 246, 300-301, 303

Comfort, Alex, 247

Connolly, Cyril, quot. 36, quot. 65

Contemporary Poetry and Prose, 179, 182-190

Cooke, Dorian, quot. 295

Crevel, René, 68, 69, 81

Criterion, The, 70, 82, 85, 89, 96, 163, 164-165, 182

Dali, Salvador, 31, 32, 33, 34, 35, 42, 63, 81, 84, 101, 129, 133, 136, 138-139, 141, 154, 156, 157, 162, 164-165, 171, 181, 207, 234, 266, 269, 282, 295, 299, 300

Davies, Hugh Sykes, 86, 88-92, 94, 102-107, 119, 121, 134, 140, 144-146, 184, 188-189, 190-192, 193, 194-196, 223, 259
Delvaux, Paul, 166, 181, 223, 250
Dialectics, 12, 14-18, 19, 125
Duchamp, Marcel, 29-31, 32, 47, 58, 82, 166
Durrell, Lawrence, 296-297, 306-307

Eliot, T. S., 67, 191, 213, 253, 264, 265-269
Eluard, Paul, 23, 33, 42, 49, 68, 71, 81, 99, 121, 134, 140, 169, 176, 181, 224, 239, 240, 241-242, 243
Engels, Friedrich, 23, 24
Ernst, Max, 37, 47-48, 81, 129, 141, 166, 171, 234, 237, 250, 299

Fairbairn, W. R. D., 205-210
Fergar, Feyyaz, 230, 246, 250-252, 258
Fédération Internationale de l'Art Révolutionnaire Indépendant (F.I.A.R.I.), 226
Flint, F. S., 70
Ford, Ford Madox, 68, 69
Forster, E. M., quot. 247
Fraser, G. S., 290, 291, 294
Free Unions Libres, 253-255, 259
Freud, Sigmund, 4-7, 12, 13, 15-17, 23, 36, 38-39, 40, 56-57, 58, 59, 62, 114-115, 123, 124, 202, 206, 211, 222, 264, 266, 267, 273, 309
Fuller, R. B., quot. 295

Gascoyne, David, 86-87, 94-96, 98, 119, 133, 134, 136, 140, 162, 167-176, 178, 181, 184, 187, 188, 196, 258, 278, 301
Giacometti, Alberto, 28, 31, 98, 250
Gilbert, Stuart, 79, 247
Gothic novel, 192-193, 212
Gracq, Julien, 303
Grigson, Geoffrey, 97, 152, 271

Hegel, G. W. F., 55-56, 57, 58, 125, 208, 210; see also Dialectics
Hemingway, Ernest, quot. 69
Hendry, J. F., 290, 291, 292, 293, 294

Heppenstall, Rayner, 92
Hinks, Roger, 164-165
Hulme, T. E., 263
Humor, 55-61

Idolatry and Confusion, 239-240
Image, surrealist, 38-50, 52
Imagism, 262-264
Incendiary Innocence, 242-245
International Surrealist Bulletin No. 4, 146-148, 183

Jackson, T. A., 118-119
Jarry, Alfred, 59, 80, 253
Jennings, Humphrey, 88, 135, 136, 140, 168, 177, 178, 179-181, 184, 216, 217, 219, 227, 258, 259
Jolas, Eugene, 71, 72, 75, 77-79, 80, 181
Joyce, James, 28, 67, 70, 74, 78, 86, 264
Jung, Carl G., 24-26, 77, 110

Kafka, Franz, 211, 297-298, 300, 305
Koestler, Arthur, 239

Language, 45-48
Lautréamont, Comte de, 8, 37, 43, 49, 58, 179, 305
Lear, Edward, 107, 127
Left Review, 96, 118, 155, 157-159, 179, 194, 216
Legge, Sheila, see Phantom, the Surrealist
Lehmann, John, 232, 301
Lévy, Eliphas, 54
Lewis, C. Day, 200, quot. 274, quot. 279, 282
Lewis, Matthew Gregory (Monk), 80, 128, 212, 223
Lewis, Wyndham, 72-76, 151, 154
Little Review, 67-68
Lloyd, A. L., 66, 194
London Bulletin, 179, 183, 218-224

McCaig, Norman, quot. 294
McGreevy, Thomas, quot. 229-230
MacNeice, Louis, quot. 277, quot. 296

Maddox, Conroy, 223, 226, 231, 232, 234, 247, quot. 254, 258
Madge, Charles, 97-98, 120, 178
Magritte, René, 160, 166, 172, 181, 234, 250
March, Richard, 163-164
Marx, Karl, and Marxism, 13, 19, 123, 129, 211
Mass-Observation, 177-178
Masson, André, 79, 235, 255
Maturin, Charles, 80, 128, 253
Mednikoff, Reuben, 219, 227, 228
Melville, Robert, 136n, 222-223, 231, 232, 234, 237, 258
Melly, George, 231, quot. 254, 258
Merveilleux, le, 19, 41, 64, 165
Mesens, E. L. T., 68, 134, 187, 218, 223, 224, 227, 230, 233, 234, 235, 238, 239, 240, 244, 245, 246, 247, 250, 251, 258, 259
Message from Nowhere, 246, 259
Miró, Joan, 140, 166, 206, 250, 300
Moore, Henry, 135, 136, 148, 152, 184, 223, 258
Mortimer, Raymond, 160

Nash, Paul, 135, 136, 153, 184, 197-200
New Apocalypse, 235, 286, 290-295
New Road, 1943, 235-238
New Verse, 94, 97-108, 167

Object, surrealist, 28-39, 129-130, 176-177, 181, 195, 197-198
Objective chance, 18-28, 40, 55, 61, 62, 64
Occult, 50-55, 244
O'Connor, Philip, quot. 99, 101, 102
Onslow-Ford, Gordon, 227, 228, 232
Oppenheim, Méret, 36, 136

Pailthorpe, Grace W., 196-197, 219-222, 227, 228
"Paranoia-criticism," 33-34, 42, 57
Paul, Elliot, 72
Penrose, Roland, 134, 153, 184, 216, 217, 218, 224, 238, 246, 258
Péret, Benjamin, 68, 168, 169, 241-242, 258
Phantom, the Surrealist, 137, 181, 188

Plomer, William, 229
Porteus, Hugh Gordon, 154-155, 156
Pound, Ezra, 67, 70, 185, 263, 266
Pre-Raphaelites, 128-129
Priestley, J. B., 131, 152
Proust, Marcel, 304

Quennell, Peter, 83, 162

Radcliffe, Mrs. Ann, 80, 83, 128, 212
Raine, Kathleen, 168, 169, 176, 239
Read, Herbert, 92-93, 94, 107, 108-132, 134, 138, 141, 143-144, 148-149, 151, 152, 155, 158, 170, 182, 184, 186, 190, 193, 194-195, 214-215, 216, 227, 228, 247, 258, 259, 260, 261, 290, 298, 302, 303, 308
Reavey, George, 140, 181, 219
Renzio, Toni del, 231, 232, 233-240, 242-248, 250, 255-256
Reverdy, Pierre, 42-43, 69, 170, 279-280, 304
Rickword, Edgell, 159
Rimbaud, Arthur, 8, 50, 51, 58, 78, 107
Rivera, Diego, 225
Roberts, Michael, 85
Rodker, John, 67, 68
Roughton, Roger, 99-100, 161, 168, 183-186, 187, 189-190, 278
Roussel, Raymond, 47, 58

Sage, Robert, 71
Sitwell, Edith, 269-272
Sitwell, Osbert, 247
Soupault, Philippe, 2, 68
Spender, Stephen, quot. 273, quot. 289-290, 295-296
Stead, C. K., 265-266
Stevens, Wallace, quot. 309
Summers, Montague, 212
"Superrealism," 119, 120-121, 143
"Supreme point," 12-13, 20, 51-52, 64-65, 74
Surrealist group in England, 134-135, 184, 223, 227, 230, 252-253, 256-259
Swift, Jonathan, 59, 80
Swingler, Randall, 216
Synge, J. M., 80

Tanguy, Yves, 166, 171, 172, 173, 234, 237, 298
Taylor, Simon Watson, 230, 246, 253, quot. 254, 255, 258
This Quarter, 80-82, 94, 282
Thomas, Dylan, 138, 189, 277-286, 292, 293
Titus, Edward W., 80
Todd, Ruthven, 135, 137, 138, 178, 179, 181, 297-300
Tomlin, E. W. F., 182
Transatlantic Review, 68-70
transition, 67, 70-80, 213
Treece, Henry, 290, 292, 293, 294
Trevelyan, Julian, 76, 88, 136, 216, 217
Trotsky, Leon, 225
Tyler, Parker, quot. 221

Tzara, Tristan, 58, 68, 69, 81

Upward, Edward, 200, 210-211, 301-302

Vaché, Jacques, 56, 58, 80

Walpole, Horace, 80, 154, 192, 212
Walton, William, 139
Watt, Alexander, 84
West, Alick, 158-159, 216, 289
West, Anthony, quot. 242
Williams, William Carlos, quot. 65-66
Wordsworth, William, 191

Yeats, Jack B., quot. 302-303
Young, Edward, 80, 83, 97

The Surrealist Movement
in England

Designed by R. E. Rosenbaum.
Composed by Vail-Ballou Press, Inc.
in 11 point linotype Caledonia, 3 points leaded,
with display lines in monotype Deepdene.
Printed letterpress from type by Vail-Ballou
on Warren's 1854 Text, 60 pound basis,
with the Cornell University Press watermark.
Bound by Vail-Ballou Press
in Columbia Bayside Linen
and stamped in All Purpose foil.

E3